SCHOLARSHIP, SACRAMENTS AND SERVICE

Historical Studies in Protestant Tradition

Essays in Honor of Bard Thompson

edited by
Daniel B. Clendenin and W. David Buschart

Texts and Studies in Religion
Volume 49

The Edwin Mellen Press
Lewiston/Queenston/Lampeter

Library of Congress Cataloging-in-Publication Data

This book has been registered with the Library of Congress.

This is volume 49 in the continuing series
Texts and Studies in Religion
Volume 49   ISBN 0-88946-838-9
TSR Series   ISBN 0-88946-976-8

A CIP catalog record for this book
is available from the British Library.

The Edwin Mellen Press
Box 450
Lewiston, New York
USA 14092

The Edwin Mellen Press
Box 67
Queenston, Ontario
CANADA, L0S 1L0

The Edwin Mellen Press, Ltd.
Lampeter, Dyfed, Wales
UNITED KINGDOM SA48 7DY

Printed in the United States of America

BARD THOMPSON

1925-1987

ACKNOWLEDGMENTS

The editors would like to thank those who assisted in the preparation and publication of this volume. Scott McDonald and the Graduate School of Drew University, and Richard W. KixMiller provided generous financial support. From Edwin Mellen Press, we thank Herb Richardson, Ruth Richardson and John Rupnow for seeing this book through to completion. Technical assistance in the preparation of the manuscript was given by Ron Baker, Heidi Cochrane, Cecile Collier, Randy Lee, Maureen LeLacheur, and Dan Penning. Last but not least, Bertha D. Thompson provided helpful assistance and encouragement all along the way.

CONTENTS

PART ONE:
THE CHURCH AND MINISTRY

PART TWO:
THE CHURCH AND MODERN THOUGHT

EPILOGUE

CONTRIBUTORS

W. David Buschart serves as Assistant Professor of Systematic Theology at Canadian Theological Seminary, Regina, Saskatchewan.

Daniel B. Clendenin is Assistant Professor of Theology at William Tyndale College in Farmington Hills, Michigan. He is the author of *Theological Method in Jacques Ellul* (University Press of America, 1987), and has served as a guest professor in Africa and Asia.

Kenneth J. Collins serves as Associate Professor in the Department of Philosophy and Religion, Methodist College, Fayetteville, North Carolina.

Charles Courtney is Executive Director of the Society for Values in Higher Education, based on the campus of Georgetown University, Washington, D.C. He is on leave from his duties as Professor of Philosophy of Religion at Drew University, where he has been a member of the faculties of the Theological and Graduate Schools since 1964.

Horton Davies is Putnam Professor Emeritus of the History of Christianity at Princeton University and Visiting Professor of Liturgics at Drew University. Formerly he served as Head of the Joint Department of Church History at Mansfield and Regent's Park Colleges of Oxford University, and founding Professor of Divinity at Rhodes University, Grahamstown, South Africa. He is the author of the five-volume survey *Worship and Theology in England* (Oxford and Princeton, 1961-1975).

Janet Forsythe Fishburn is Associate Professor of Teaching Ministry and American Church History in the Theological and Graduate Schools of Drew University. She authored *The Fatherhood of God and The Victorian Family: The Social Gospel in America* (Fortress, 1981). She is currently working on historical and sociological research of ministry and theological education.

Henry F. French is Professor of Theology at Japan Lutheran Theological Seminary in Tokyo.

Yasuko Morihara Grosjean completed the B.D. and S.T.M. degrees at the Graduate School of Theology at Oberlin, and her Ph.D. at Drew University. She currently serves as Assistant Dean of the Graduate School, Drew Univer-sity.

Howard G. Hageman is President Emeritus of New Brunswick Seminary, New Jersey. He currently serves as Visiting Professor in Liturgical Studies at Drew University, and as President of the Mercersburg Society. He has authored several books and articles on the subject of liturgics in the Reformed tradition.

Charles A. Jones, III is an ordained minister in the Presbyterian Church, USA. He currently serves the Presbyterian Church of Livingston, New Jersey. Before that he served two parishes in Florida. He has done extensive research in the theology of Charles Hodge and the Mercersburg theologians.

Edward LeRoy Long, Jr., held teaching posts at Virginia Polytechnic Institute and Oberlin College before moving to Drew University, from which he retired in 1986 as James W. Pearsall Professor of Christian Ethics and Theology of Culture. Among his many books are the classic *A Survey of Christian Ethics* (Oxford, 1967) and the more recent *A Survey of Recent Christian Ethics* (Oxford, 1982).

Russell E. Richey is Associate Dean for Academic Programs in The Divinity School, Duke University. Prior to that he was on the faculty of the Theological and Graduate Schools of Drew University. Editor of three books, most recently *Rethinking Methodist History* (1985), and many articles, he continues research in institutional aspects of American religion and in Methodist history.

Kenneth E. Rowe is Professor of Church History and Librarian of the Methodist Archives and History Center at Drew University. Since 1976 he has edited *The Methodist Union Catalog*. He is the author of *The Place of Wesley in the Christian Tradition* (Scarecrow, 1980) and *United Methodist Studies: Basic Bibliographies* (1982, 1987).

Bard Thompson served as Dean of the Graduate School of Drew University from 1969 until 1986. Following his retirement as Dean, he continued to serve as Professor of Church History at Drew and was a member of the Center of Theological Inquiry, Princeton, New Jersey. His *Liturgies of the Western Church* (Fortress, 1961) is currently in its twelfth printing, *A Bibliography of Christian Worship* was published posthumously in 1989.

PREFACE

Despite their many differences, Luther and Calvin both accepted the maxim from Cyprian's *Epistles* (73.21) *Extra ecclesiam non sit salus*. In his "Brief Explanation" of the Creed, Luther wrote of the church: "I believe that no one can be saved who is not found in this congregation, holding with it to one faith, word, sacraments, hope and love, and that no Jew, heretic, heathen or sinner can be saved along with it, unless he become reconciled to it, united with it and conformed to it in all things." Hearkening back to Cyprian, in his *Institutes* Calvin likewise wrote of the church as the necessary Mother of all who would believe, the provider of "a wealth of comfort" and the locus in which one could "establish with certainty" their election. Today, and perhaps especially to Protestants, such words sound archaic, imperialistic and oppressive. But the situation in the sixteenth century was hardly different and it would be hard to accuse the reformers of neglecting or ignoring the faults of the church. Indeed, Calvin recognized that at times even the true church "swarmed with many faults."

Thus the Reformation tradition humbly and firmly insists that the reformed church not only reforms but continually stands in need of reform. On the one hand, in both its institutional life and its thought, the church is an historical entity and subject to change, a body which reflects its own space and time. This is the way it should be, for the church is both a pilgrim people which aspires to its heavenly city only from this side of history, and a people which embraces the world because it knows that the world is created and loved by God. As fermenting wine requires wineskins that expand, the church properly seeks to be constantly changed and reformed so as to allow the treasure with which it is entrusted to have its due effect. On the other hand, without ever excusing its faults, the church is a transcendent reality, for as Calvin observed "God is its author." It gratefully cherishes its apostolic inheritance and never imagines that it *ex nihilo*. For this reason the church seeks to preserve the best of its past and seek continuity with that past.

From the relationship between ministry and scholarship to the perennial challenges of religious pluralism, from the preparation of its ministers to the amelioration of the problem of evil, from changes in its liturgy to its understanding of truth, the reformed church continually stands in need of reform. The essays in the present volume both explore and illustrate the reality of change and continuity in the church. In an especially enlightening essay that was one of the last pieces he wrote, Bard Thompson, whose life this volume commemorates, uncovers points of continuity between the Renaissance and Reformation.

DBC
WDB

September 1989

PART ONE:
THE CHURCH AND MINISTRY

MINISTRY AND SCHOLARSHIP
IN THE REFORMED TRADITION

Edward LeRoy Long, Jr.

Early in the Reformation, Protestant ministers
adopted a symbolic change in their liturgical dress.
Zwingli introduced the *Schaube*, or gown of the secular
scholar in 1523. Within a year Luther followed suit by
replacing the monk's cowl which he had been accustomed
to wearing in the pulpit with the attire associated
with persons of learning. Commenting on these changes,
Wilhelm Pauck declared, ". . . the scholar's gown was
the garment of the Protestant minister. It symbolizes
all the changes that were wrought by the Reformation in
the nature and the work of the ministry."[1]

The close relationship between ministry and
scholarship symbolized by this change of dress has
profound implications. While it is misleading to imply
that the Protestant Reformation produced a total and
complete transformation in the nature of ministry from
a situation in which there was little or no learning on
the part of the clergy to one in which there was little
else but learning, there is a profound sense in which
the Reformation brought ministry and scholarship closer

---

[1]Wilhelm Pauck, "Ministry in the Time of the
Continental Reformation," in *The Ministry in Historical
Perspectives*, ed. H. Richard Niebuhr and Daniel Day
Williams (New York: Harper and Row, 1956), 147.

together than they had been before or have been since.

In the Roman Catholic tradition the primary
function of priests had been defined as sacerdotal.
The performing of the sacraments was not seen as
dependent for its effectiveness on the range and scope
of the learning possessed by those in the clerical
office. To be sure, there were many clerics who were
excellent scholars as well, but being a theologian and
being a priest were seen as two functions, not one.
Monastic orders very often encouraged scholarly study,
but they always understood vocation as something
distinct from erudition. Only with the changes brought
about by the Reformation did scholarship as such become
a pivotal function for the exercise of ministry,
essential to its very identity.

Luther launched the Reformation on the basis of
insights gained while engaged in the study of the
Bible. He needed to conceptualize and articulate the
faith in order to overcome the distortions which had
affected it, and he initially sought to share his
insights which he was formulating for this purpose
through scholarly disputation. The activities into
which the subsequent events led him are of secondary
significance in comparison with the convictions about
the nature of grace by faith alone to which he came in
his study, wrote about voluminously, and preached from
the pulpit. We honor Luther more for the understandings born of these scholarly accomplishments than for
any of the roles he played in the events and controversies of his subsequent career. Similarly, there is
ample justification for saying Calvin was, as John T.
McNeill has aptly put it, ". . . a humanist man of
letters who after conversion made the Bible his

literary study."[2] Calvin firmly believed that learning
and study were the means of arriving at and propagating
faith, and strived throughout his entire lifetime to
overcome any kind of religious devotion that bracketed
scholarly endeavors out of the experience of the
believer. His stance became a distinctive strand in
the Reformed tradition. In defining that tradition,
John H. Leith has quite rightfully included, among its
special emphases, a place for "The Life of the Mind as
the Service of God."[3]

One of the enduring legacies given to us by Bard
Thompson is his posthumous work on the Renaissance and
the Reformation. Standing ecclesiastically in the
Reformed tradition he stood in the scholarly world as a
student of the Renaissance as well, which made him an
even better son of the Reformers than those theologians
who deal with the Reformation only as an isolated
theological phenomenon.

The Reformers did not, of course, think of
scholarship as self-legitimizing. To the extent that
they saw scholasticism as a mere curiosity about ideas
and concepts they distrusted it. Their tension with
humanists like Erasmus came at precisely this point.
For Calvin the knowledge of God was central, but not
knowledge for its own sake. The Reformers were no more
sympathetic to scholarship pursued apart from the
concerns of ministry than they were of a ministry
severed from learning.

The Reformed tradition, shaped and inspired by its
founders, has wrestled to keep the connection between

---

[2]John T. McNeill, *The History and Character of
Calvinism* (New York: Oxford University Press, 1954), 203.

[3]John H. Leith, *An Introduction to the Reformed
Tradition: A Way of Being the Christian Community*
(Atlanta: John Knox, 1977).

ministry and scholarship viable and pivotal. It has
struggled against many odds, not always successfully.
Alternative perspectives in theology have arisen to
place the emphases of the ministry on other matters.
Even in Protestant settings, various kinds of anti-
intellectualism have arisen to undercut the significance attached to the use of intellect in both culture
and in church. Ecclesiastical life has sometimes lost
sight of the fundamental premises of the Reformers and
been the victim of pressures that have pushed the
practice of that ministry away from its historical
heritage. Jaroslav Pelikan's cryptic observation
cannot be gainsaid: "The Protestant Reformation was
launched by a cadre of intellectuals, but the latter-
day heirs of the Reformation sometimes seem determined
to do everything they can to live down this past."[4]

Nevertheless, in the Reformed tradition scholarly
achievement has been a principal touchstone for
thinking about the nature and function of ministry, and
it is impossible to discuss the nature of ministry in
the church bodies associated with that tradition without understanding the scholarly model as a foundational
one--perhaps even the foundational one--for religious
leadership.

I

The most consistent embodiment of the Reformed
perspective subsequent to the Continental Reformation
was achieved by the Puritan movement. Despite an
emphasis on the role of the will that could easily have
turned into a repudiation of intellect, the Puritan
tradition was intentional in its concern to cultivate a
learned ministry. In doing this the Puritans in

---

[4]Jaroslav Pelikan, *The Christian Intellectual*
(New York: Harper and Row, 1965), 17.

England formulated a complex position that took into account many developments. On the one hand, they were aware that humanistic learning was on the upswing. Instead of condemning it they matched a learning that was directed toward human ends alone with a learning that made the knowledge of the Word and the service of God paramount. As laypersons became generally better educated, the Puritans saw that the clergy also became better prepared intellectually. While, like the Continental Reformers, the English Puritans were suspicious of a learning that was aimed only at worldly matters, they were even more suspicious of an unlearned enthusiasm for spiritual things such as that sometimes exhibited by radical Christian groups. Puritans welcomed the establishment of universities, and made a major effort to provide their ministers the benefits that came from attending them--primarily with the intention of facilitating an increased competence in the interpretation of the Word through preaching.[5]

In its early years the Puritan movement in the American colonies exhibited in the New World attitudes remarkably similar to those in the Puritan movement in England. In addition to an interest in the cultivation of moral fidelity, it was interested in fostering the development of a learned clergy, since only such a clergy could preach the Word with insight and conviction. It founded universities, such as Harvard and Yale, to supply persons of requisite skill. The preacher in the local setting was often the most highly educated member of the community, and not infrequently contributed to the general as well as the spiritual

---

[5]See John Morgan, *Godly Learning: Puritan Attitudes towards Reason, Learning and Education, 1560-1640* (Cambridge: Cambridge University Press, 1986), especially chapter six.

education of the young. Perry Miller's account of *The New England Mind* turns to the work of preachers for much of its evidence concerning the intellectual development of the period. American Puritans, like their English counterparts, were anxious to embrace intellectual achievements that could "give to reason a larger part than hitherto it had played in the life of the spirit."[6]

The work of Jonathan Edwards was a high point in the unique interaction between scholarship and ministry characteristic of this period. Edwards was a parish preacher. From that base of operations he left a legacy of productive theological writing that has given him a unique role in the religious history of the American people. He stands, alongside Luther and Calvin, as one of the great Protestant figures in whom ministry and scholarship have been combined in a working synthesis of enduring significance.

This working relationship between ministry and scholarship showed a momentum that had selective manifestations through most of the nineteenth century. Just as Harvard and Yale were founded in the early history of the country for the preparation of an educated clergy, so many denominational colleges (or colleges, like Oberlin, founded by evangelical leaders) were created in the nineteenth century for the preparation of Christians who would minister to the growing nation--as clergy or as laity. Higher education was taken to be an essential part of the church's agenda.

II

But something happened to endanger and erode the synthesis of ministry and scholarship characteristic of

---

[6]Perry Miller, *The New England Mind: From Colony to Province* (Cambridge, MA: Harvard University Press, 1953), 418.

these impulses. Unlike Miller, who turned to the
thinking of clergy for material depicting the New
England thought world, no historian of contemporary
American life would be likely to utilize the work of
preachers as primary material for tracing the intellectual contours of the last few decades, or turn to
sermons as the necessary stuff with which to provide an
account of contemporary intellectual history. The
learned ministry has suffered an eclipse in American
church life. This has several roots and has taken
place over a long period of time. Different challenges
to the scholarly model and barriers to its substantive
achievement have occurred in the intervening generations, each doing something to create a gulf between
the functions of ministry and those of scholarship.
Several of the most decisive trends have taken place in
the last half of the twentieth century.

In tracing "The Rise of the Evangelical Conception
of the Ministry in America: 1607-1850,"[7] Professor
Sidney Mead offers several explanations for the
transformations that took place in the functions of
ministry in the American context. Back of much that
happened was the growing role of congregations in most
ecclesial polities. All denominations experienced some
loss of connectionalism. In many groups, this placed
the dynamics for calling, yes even for certifying,
ministry almost entirely in the hands of local congregations. Under the conditions of American life that
developed, first on the frontier and later under an
increasingly crass industrialization, scholarly
accomplishments seemed less crucial than immediate
availability and highly visible zeal. In some denomi-

---

[7]Chapter eight in *The Ministry in Historical
Perspectives*, ed. Niebuhr and Williams.

nations--most of which were in the penumbra rather than
at the center of the Reformed heritage--ordinations
came to be performed on less and less academically
qualified persons, not a few of them without college
and seminary training. Those ready-at-hand were
pressed into service to meet immediate needs. On the
frontier, conditions called for persons who could fight
for law, order, and rectitude. Less and less attention
was paid to the historical forms associated with Old
World Christianity. This led, as Mead points out, to
the lowering of historical sensibilities and also to a
rising biblicism. In industrial areas, where the
influence of the entrepreneur grew dominant, scholarship was deemed equally superfluous. This also gave
plausibility to an assumption that it was possible to
do away with accretions associated with the tradition
and move back to a kind of religious practice presumed
to be that of the New Testament church. In this
process scholarship as well as a sense of historical
practice suffered. Certainly, Jesus had never made the
doctorate a prerequisite for discipleship or ministry!

Moreover, according to Mead, the most prevailing
and prevalent theological development was the rise of
the evangelical spirit. The evangelical model acquired
a new and different set of characteristics on the
frontier from those it had in puritan New England. The
Great Awakening had involved scholarly endeavor; it had
created theological reflection; it had occurred largely
within existing ecclesial structures. Revivalism as
found on the frontier put a premium on individualistic
renewal and intensity of zeal. To be sure, nineteenth-
century revivalism was concerned both about social

reform, as Timothy Smith has argued,[8] and about
learning, as demonstrated by the founding of colleges
such as Oberlin. But to the extent that revivalism
harbored a propensity for placing more attention on the
personal piety of the minister than on scholarly
achievements it eventually did much to undercut the
importance of learning as a qualifying prerequisite for
religious leadership. Scholarly endeavors were
relegated to a secondary place--if honored at all. In
time the wandering evangelist became an accomplice of a
deep seated anti-intellectualism in American life.
Analogously, the entrepreneurial temper made evangelism
into a kind of religious equivalent of quantitative
productivity--reaping conversions for Jesus without
putting a corresponding stress on the quality of understanding needed to be among the saved.

The "saw dust trail" form of revivalism that arose
in a culture offering freedom for any and all forms of
religious activity utilized the emotional and even the
bizarre as it plied its claims. The scholarly element
was difficult to find and learning was deprecated.
This was not a necessary and inevitable feature of an
evangelical perspective in the wider meaning of that
term, but a quality that many expressions of revivalistic evangelism acquired, particularly as found on the
American frontier and under conditions which measured
success by commercial models of productivity.

Admittedly, it is unfair to take untutored
evangelists as representative of the entire Christian
ministry, let alone of Reformed versions of that
ministry. Such evangelists were but a fringe phenomenon. But they illustrate a more widespread tendency

---

[8]Timothy L. Smith, *Revivalism and Social Reform
in Mid Nineteenth-Century America* (New York: Abingdon,
1955).

and they provide the cultured despisers of religion
with convenient examples of all that they distrust and
dislike about the practice of religion. The harangue
of fire and brimstone associated with movable tents or
rented halls, unleashed more with vehemence than
reason, and offered largely without pastoral follow
through, exhibits a particularly flagrant and troublesome form of a divorce between ministry and scholarship, but it is not the only form that the separation
has taken. The severed connection between scholarship
and ministry which has affected most mainline Christianity has been more subtle and less blatantly manifest. It is more difficult to delineate, yet it has
plagued the practice of ministry in American life for
generations, quite possibly because it has not been so
obvious.

III

One pressure working at cross purposes with the
scholarly practice of ministry has been an ever growing
emphasis on the pastoral function as a means of helping
individuals cope with personal difficulties. This has
affected the practice of ministry more pervasively in
the last three decades than any other factor.[9] The
"cure of souls" requires admirable skill and has a long
standing place in the history of the church, but if
made into the main function of ministry it alters the
identifying dynamic. There is important learning
entailed in becoming a good pastor--particularly a good
pastoral counselor--but it is like a learning that
makes a good family doctor in contrast to that which

---

[9]See David S. Schuller, "Identifying Criteria
for Ministry," in *Ministry in America: A Report and
Analysis, Based on an In-Depth Survey of 47 Denomina-
tions in the United States and Canada,* ed. David S.
Schuller, Merton P. Strommen, and Milo L. Brekke (San
Francisco: Harper and Row, 1980), 32.

makes a medical professor or researcher. It is the
kind of learning that finds its culmination in a
practical skill rather than in the forging of concep-
tual understandings. It centers more on the service of
persons than on the transmission of ideas; it utilizes
interactional process more than it probes new ways of
articulating truths. Scholarly acumen is not a *sine
qua non* of the beloved pastor, who can sustain and
succor the members of the flock without necessarily
mastering high intellectual skills or keeping abreast
of the most recent developments in scholarly understanding.

Another subtle pressure that has diminished the
centrality of the scholarly model for ministry has been
the increasing place accorded administrative or
managerial skills as requisites for churchly success.
Ministers increasingly have found themselves engaged in
institutional maintenance, often on a complex and
demanding level. The role of the minister has been
transformed into that of an organizational director,
what H. Richard Niebuhr called the "pastor-director."[10]
Bureaucratic/managerial skills have become increasingly
expected in the practice of ministry, and ministers who
perform such roles with orderly dependability benefit
from the reward systems of ecclesial life much as
executives who do them well advance in the business
world. The pressures for such achievements have come
not only from local congregations who wish their local
parish to thrive statistically, but from those connec-
tional systems in which operational and strategic suc-
cesses are more respected than theological and liturgical continuities. In many ecclesiastical organizations

[10]H. Richard Niebuhr, *The Purpose of the Church
and Its Ministry* (New York: Harper and Brothers, 1956),
48.

the "coin of the realm" has become successful
management rather than scholarly acumen.

IV

But a historical perspective on these matters
requires an account not only of the pressures that have
been operative to separate the ministry from the
scholarly but to separate the scholarly from the
ecclesiastical. Just as the frontier did so much to
alter the nature of religious life in this country,
equally powerful influences have altered the premises
and patterns of higher education. The controversy over
Darwinism and creationism did much to drive a wedge
between the intellectual community and many Christian
groups, although to be sure there were many Christians
that found it both possible and important to develop a
modus vivendi for dealing with the challenges presented
by the new theories of human origins. The biblicism
that became so prevalent in large portions of American
church life, reaching a symbolic apex in the Niagara
Declaration of 1902 but exercising a growing impact
ever since, has made much confessional religion
antithetical to the fundamental temperament of a
scholarship informed by the Enlightenment and anxious
to emulate the methods of modern science. As ecclesiastical bodies resisted the insights of science, or
had to fight battles against groups within their midst
who did, the scholarly world became ever more secular
in order to be considered faithful to its understanding
of truth. The academic enterprise often situated
itself in tension with, if not over and against, the
prevalent perspectives of large parts of the religious
community.

While many clergy have continued to wear the
scholar's gown in the conduct of worship (if they wear
a gown at all), many scholars have been vigorously

seeking to cast off the religious mantle. Much
education has become an autonomous enterprise, neither
needing nor wanting to be identified with confessing
communities. Universities that were originally founded
for the training of a learned clergy have turned their
primary attention elsewhere--to the training of
doctors, lawyers, business executives, and teachers,
increasing numbers of whom are needed by society. The
training of these other professionals has come to be
resourced on higher levels than the training of
clergy--partly, of course, because of the astonishing
increase in the sophistication needed to exercise such
professional roles in a complex society, but also
because many ecclesiastical groups have ceased to
appreciate the importance of the scholarly acumen that
once characterized the ministry. Faculties of divinity, if not allowed to languish altogether, have been
marginalized in many institutions. Moreover, the
battles remembered from the evolution controversy,
coupled with the continuing intensification of biblicism, have driven those in search of intellectual
openness and academic freedom to detach themselves as
much as possible from any ecclesiastical control over
the exercise of their educational role. Many colleges,
originally designating themselves as Christian, have
disassociated themselves from their heritages--in
practice if not in sponsorship. Even divinity schools
that have desired to emphasize intellectual achievement
have found it helpful to declare their freedom from
ecclesiastical control.

In time, reaching its zenith since the Second
World War, a whole new attitude toward the nature of
religious studies has developed--identifying them with
the liberal arts in general rather than with confessing
communities. In places where the study of divinity had

been allowed to languish the study of that subject
matter was frequently reintroduced on new premises
associated with the term religious studies. In other
places studies about religion have been introduced for
the first time as the new premises for the study of
religious phenomena proved congenial to the mind-set of
the academic world. Indeed, some of the most impressive departments of religion in America have been
created in the last three or four decades in state
supported universities where a confessional orientation
would be both inappropriate and illegal. As a result
of these achievements, scholarship in religion has
become a professional activity having its own identity
and integrity, neither seeking nor needing ecclesiastical warrant. This development has not necessarily
prevented particular individuals from exercising two
roles, one scholarly/pedagogical and the other minis-
terial/pastoral, but it has discouraged and even
prevented them from combining them. Their teaching is
one genre of activity; their ministry, another--each
function being exercised in a different way and in a
different place. Increasingly over the past several
decades, many professors of religion have found
satisfaction in the scholarly modality alone and have
neither sought ordination nor thought of themselves as
engaged in ministry. Why buck the public image of
ministry as something at odds with the intellectual when the teaching of religion has become richly
valuable in the scholarly modality alone?

Moreover, the language of theological scholarship
has become increasingly specialized as the scholarly
guild has found itself talking mainly, if not entirely,
to itself. This has made the task of ministers
increasingly difficult. The theological literacy of
the general population, from which the membership of

churches is drawn, has become increasingly impoverished
and the discussion of theological issues increasingly
specialized. The parish minister is caught between
these two pressures, and, overwhelmed, too often
settles for inspirational chit-chat and spiritual
cheerleading.

V

The twin developments that have been described---
the one estranging ministry from scholarship and the
other scholarship from ministry--are also reflected in
changes that have taken place in the meaning of the
term 'professional,' particularly with respect to the
function of the clergy. The term professional when
used in the characterization of ministry has both a
historical usage and a more recent popularity. Whereas
the historical usage involved the scholarly, the more
recent implications have tended to emphasize the
functional.

Charles E. Hambrick-Stowe, writing in *The Encyclopedia of the American Religious Experience*, has
delineated six operative aspects or conceptions of
ministry, of which the last is that of the professional. While his categories include both the priest-
ly/sacerdotal and the revivalist conceptions alluded to
in this discussion, they do not involve a special
category of the scholarly. Rather, the scholarly is
included under the rubric of the professional, of which
the ministers of the Reformed churches are cited as
especially important examples. According to Hambrick-
Stowe,

> Presbyterian, Reformed, and Congregational
> ministers were among the nation's religious
> leaders, a highly educated class, the first to
> consider themselves professionals. They founded
> institutions of higher learning and saw

publication as part of their calling.[11]
In Hambrick-Stowe's account, the professional approach
is closely related to the development of the seminary
as a special institution, something that was at its
peak in the early nineteenth century. Education for
ministry ceased to take place in the university
as-a-whole and became the special province of a
professional school.

In contrast to that earlier meaning of the term,
in which the scholarly dimension is an assumed aspect
of the professional, a recent attempt to interpret
ministry as a profession explicitly declares that the
"image arises out of the *work of the minister*, not *the
thought of the professor*."[12] That sharply drawn contrast, perhaps not intended, does not altogether
deprecate the role of learning, but it does suggest
that it thinks of learning in an operational rather
than a scholarly model. Its author acknowledges the
place that learning has in the professions, but
describes that learning according to the standards of
technical competence. While the professional is an
educated expert, knowledge is embraced by the professional as a means to practice. Reviewing the use of
the term in relevant literature, the analysis in
question provides this definition of what it means to
speak about the minister as a professional:

> The *clergyman* [or clergywoman] studies theology(or
> divinity), practices the profession of the
> ministry, most commonly in and through the church.
> He [or she] is accountable to ecclesiastical

---

[11]Charles E. Hambrick-Stowe, "The Professional
Ministry," in *The Encyclopedia of the American
Religious Experience*, ed. Charles H. Lippy and Peter W.
Williams (New York: Charles Scribner's Sons, 1987), 1572.

[12]James D. Glasse, *Profession: Minister*
(Nashville: Abingdon, 1968), 20.

superiors, professional colleagues, and lay
associates for high standards of practice, and he
[or she] labors for "the increase among men [and
women] of the love of God and neighbor."[13]

As the term "professional"[14] has come to be
applied to the clergyperson the use of the term
"doctor" as applied to the minister has also come to
acquire additional implications. The term "doctor of
the church" is an honorable one in the Reformation
heritage, and it has a complex history. Throughout
most of the sixteenth and seventeenth centuries a
fourfold pattern of ministry was evident in the
Reformed ministry, consisting of pastors, doctors,
elders, and deacons. Pastors preached and administered
the sacraments while doctors engaged in catechetical
instruction or the proprietary supervision of church-
sponsored schools. Both were well trained and subject
to scrutiny as to competence and orthodoxy. In most
situations (sometimes governed explicitly by polity and
other times implicitly by practice) both groups shared
the governance of the church with the elders and
deacons. But the division of labor between pastors and
doctors was not hard and fast. Doctors frequently
shared in the preaching and the administration of the
sacraments. The office of the doctor, however,
suffered a certain ambiguity as to its ministerial
standing, sometimes having parity with the office of
the pastor in matters of liturgy and governance, and at

---

[13]Ibid., 41.

[14]For a discussion of the differentiation
between the term "scholar" and the term "professional"
as applied to the professions-in-general and not merely
to the ministry, see chapter four of Jaroslav Pelikan,
*Scholarship and Survival: Questions on the Idea of
Graduate Education* (Princeton: The Carnegie Foundation
for the Advancement of Teaching, 1983).

other times being clearly differentiated.[15]

In the eighteenth century, American denominations dropped the designation "doctor of the church" and placed those who preached and those who taught under the single rubric "minister." The functional significance of the designation "doctor" was eclipsed and the term came to designate an advanced level of preparation, primarily for teaching. The term also came to be used for honorific purposes in cases where individuals were accorded special recognition by colleges or universities. More recently, with the introduction of the doctor of ministry as a professional degree the term has also come to signify an advanced level of professional preparation for the pastoral role. In light of this complex history the term "doctor" can no longer be used as a simple measure of the extent to which scholarship as such is involved in ministry. Certainly, according to the Reformed heritage, there is nothing inappropriate about obtaining a doctorate as a preparation for ministry, though the creation of a second kind of earned doctorate reflects the development of professionalization more than it does a return to a close connection between scholarship and ministry.

The traditional doctorate has been the Ph.D., which certifies its holder as prepared for a career as a scholar/teacher. In many instances, this degree has provided a special level of sophistication and competence for someone serving in the pastorate. While parishes are sometimes fearful that Ph.D.'s have lost touch with common folk, or (conversely) some Ph.D.'s consider themselves overly trained for doing the

---

[15]See Robert W. Henderson, *The Teaching Office in the Reformed Tradition: A History of the Doctoral Ministry* (Philadelphia: Westminster, 1962).

routine duties of the average parish, the experience of Ph.D.'s in parish leadership positions has not infrequently been one of satisfaction to both themselves and the churches served. Nevertheless, the governing model for this doctorate is a scholarly model, concentrating on the mastery of ideas and preparing a person for a career in the academy.

As noted, the last several years have seen the development of a second doctorate, designed to raise the general competence of those who are in the parish ministry or its equivalent. The D.Min. degree was originally adopted by some institutions as a means of providing seminary students with a longer time for mastering the substance and stance of the scholar/pastor than was possible in the three-year Master of Divinity program. In many cases, however, the D.Min. degree has come to be a professional degree that functions more to certify a serious level of continuing education than to bring about any major transformation in thinking about the nature of ministry. While the regimens by which it can be earned vary, generally it takes those already at work in ministry, brings them together for additional study on schedules and in places compatible with continuing responsibilities in their regular roles, focuses to a large extent on the practice of ministry, and bestows the title "doctor" on those who culminate the course of study by completing a project that demonstrates leadership ability. In most of the programs, the learning done is treated more as a means than as an end. The pursuit of this degree typically enhances the leadership qualifications of those who undertake the course of study needed to obtain it, but generally speaking, its consequences are to make them more professional, not more scholarly.

The contrast between these two degrees is some-

times drawn for invidious purposes. Bracketing those
temptations, let not the deeper significance of the
contrast be lost. The fact that two doctorates have
developed--one for the preparation of scholars and the
other for the continuing education of ministers--is
evidence that the tensions between these two roles are
still with us and do not get eliminated by the rubic of
professionalization or the more widespread use of the
designation "Dr."

One achievement in which Bard Thompson had a
pivotal role as Dean of the Graduate School at Drew
University demonstrates the possibility of having a
doctorate that is equally appropriate in either
framework. The liturgical studies program, which he
was instrumental in creating and sustaining, has
prepared persons equally well for either scholarly or
ministerial roles without a double tracking of the
regimen. In it, concerns appropriate for scholarship
and concerns appropriate for ministry have existed
together more adequately than in most of the programs
of study that are currently followed either in preparation for teaching and scholarship or in preparation for
ministry.

VI

How can ministry and scholarship be brought into a
closer functional partnership than is currently the
case? What are the potential resources for effecting
such a rapprochement in all Christian traditions and
not merely in churches of the Reformed heritage? These
questions will be dealt with first by considering
things that can be done to build up appreciation for
scholarship in the church, not least on the parish
level.

The most obvious suggestion, one that is repeated
with considerable frequency in the literature about the

role of the pastoral ministry, is to provide and
encourage ministers to engage in study and learning
through intentional regimens of serious reading and
through participation in continuing education programs
of depth and rigor. Thomas J. Mullen, noting that "the
role of the pastor as teacher is a sadly neglected one
in Protestantism," indicates that this requires both
the pastor and the parish to be deliberate in assigning
priorities and finding ways of keeping the chores of
institutional maintenance from absorbing all the time
and energy of the minister.[16] He also bluntly declares
what many suspect but are often too restrained to point
out: "The kind of intellectual discipline expected of
[those] entering the ministry usually does not compare
to that expected of [those] entering a field such as
law or medicine."[17]

While the pressure to engage in ongoing scholarly
reflection can come in official ways--as, for instance,
in a requirement that ministers take continuing
education as a condition of remaining in good connec-
tional standing--it would be more significant if it
were to come as an expectation of congregations. They
should expect scholarship from their ministers and
express appreciation when it is provided. They should
be deliberate and intentional in planning the life of
the parish in ways that call for, support, and sustain
the minister's impulse for intellectual achievement.
One of the contributions the teaching of religion as an
academic study in colleges and universities, which is
taking place on a greatly expanded scale and has the
possibility of raising the sophistication of the laity

---

[16]Thomas J. Mullen, *The Renewal of Ministry*
(Nashville: Abingdon, 1963), 94-95.

[17]Ibid., 105.

about matters religious and theological, can make is to
nurture lay persons capable of such expectations.
Joseph Sittler once inveighed against "The Maceration
of the Minister,"[18]--by which he meant the triumph of
operational preoccupations over scholarly understanding. Sittler suggested that the cure for this threat
to the scholarship of the clergy was for parishes to
become more appreciative of the value and importance of
the minister's scholarly endeavors. This is not likely
to come about without deliberate effort, intentional
planning and increased attention to raising the
theological acumen of the entire membership of the
churches.

In the extensive study project on readiness for
ministry conducted by the American Association of
Theological Schools the research data turned up a
distinctive expectation for a learned ministry on the
part of the laity in churches of the Reformed tradition. Reporting on this, the study concluded, "The
ideal of the minister as theologian and thinker lies at
the center of the Presbyterian-Reformed self-image."[19]
Today, the task is to translate that ideal into
parish-wide attitudes and strategies. Speaking of the
current situation in the churches, particularly those
of the Reformed tradition, John H. Leith observes,

> We place our ministers under heavy obligation to
> see that the Word is rightly preached and taught.
> But this function is the responsibility of the
> entire congregation. It is the congregation who
> must see to it that the Word is preached with
> competence and diligence, that teaching takes
> place and pastoral care is exercised.

---

[18]Joseph Sittler, *The Ecology of Faith* (Philadelphia: Muhlenberg, 1961).

[19]Arthur M. Adams, Dean R. Hoge, and Lefferts
A. Loetscher, "Presbyterian-Reformed Family," in
Ministry in America, ed. Schuller, et al., 459.

More than this it is the responsibility of
the congregation, and particularly of the session,
to see that the competence with which the Word is
preached and taught in a particular church is not
surpassed by the competence of the best lawyers,
the best doctors, the best teachers, the best
business leaders in their fields.[20]

Another possible way to build up the place of
scholarship in ministry would be to become more
deliberate in soliciting vocations for the ministry.
In the time when Bard Thompson and his contemporaries
entered theological training, there were notable parish
ministers making significant contributions to theological reflection and biblical scholarship. It was not
unknown for persons engaged in active ministry to write
books consisting, not merely of collected sermons, but
of thoughtful wrestling with major issues in ways that
made them accessible to a general readership. The
works of Harry Emerson Fosdick did this. George
Buttrick exercised major editorial responsibility for
The Interpreter's Bible while serving as the regular
minister of a metropolitan church. While these are
unusual but not unique cases, they provided significant
instances of a ministry in which scholarship played a
distinctive role. They were part of a wider scholarship in ministry. Moreover, they demonstrated a knack
for putting the most profound theological ideas into
clear and vivid language that was understood by
ordinary listeners, and responded to with excitement.
They gave individuals thinking about entering the
ministry models of intellectual excellence, and they
inspired students in seminary to give attention to
scholarly achievements as well as to care about the
practical arts of ministry. The church needs an

---

[20]John H. Leith, "Our Protestant Vocation," in
The Presbyterian Outlook 170:34 (October 10, 1988): 7
and 11.

increasing number of contemporary counterparts.

A third contribution to overcoming the divorce
between scholarship and ministry could involve a
self-conscious resolve on the part of ministers to be
more concerned with the portrayal of the historical
heritage. "Pastors," writes Roland M. Kawano, "need a
vision not so much of where the church is going but of
where it has been."[21] Unfortunately, the church is
affected by, and helps perpetuate, a general neglect of
history in the contemporary scene. Calls for "teaching
the Bible" in Sunday schools are frequently made
without sensing the difficulties of appropriating the
message of scripture apart from historical contexts and
the history of its interpretation. One does not have
to utilize the label "hermeneutics" to do good expos-
itory work on the parish level, but unless a preacher/
pastor knows what is entailed in the interpretation of
materials and writings from the past and is able to
share that knowledge with all who are involved in
Christian education, the mentoring will be superficial.

This discussion of historical stewardship brings
us to the discussion of what can be done by the
scholarly community, most particularly the seminary,
to nudge us toward a renewed synthesis of ministry and
scholarship. Krister Stendahl, as dean of a
university-centered divinity school, has argued forcefully that the "primary constituencies of a divinity
school are communities of faith."[22] That fact must
not, as sometimes happens, be used as an excuse for

---

[21]Roland M. Kawano, "A Model for Learned
Pastors," *The Christian Century* 97:15 (January 23,
1980): 74.

[22]Krister Stendahl, "Rooted in Communities of
Faith: A Reaffirmation of a Learned Ministry," *Theological Education* 13:2 (1977), 62.

focusing cheaply on practical skills, but rather
requires a rigorous foundational grounding in the
subject matter of theology. Hence, Stendahl declares,
"Serious work in scripture and history, theology and
ethics, is never a luxury [for ministers] but a
must."[23] But, such competence as the minister acquires
in the several substantive dimensions of divinity must
be shared and imparted to a community for it to be
effective. In this sense, the knowledge of the
minister must be utilized in a different way than the
learning of a doctor or a lawyer is utilized. It
cannot be merely a resource for rendering services to
others, but must be used as a guide for bringing others
to the appropriation of the insights for themselves and
making them operative in a community of similarly
informed persons.

All of this intensifies the requirement to bolster
the scholarly dimension of seminary curricula. While
it is hard to imagine, there are divinity schools that
do not require a thorough grounding in the full history
of the Christian tradition. There are theological
educators who place more emphasis upon the orginality
of constructs than upon the mastery of the tradition.
It is faddish to deal with new occasions without regard
for the guidance that inheres in a proper understanding
of the ways in which Christians in the past have
responded to analogous circumstances--not always
satisfactorily. In other situations the appeal to
tradition is made a barrier to dealing with new
occasions creatively. It is reactive to utilize the
past as means of discrediting every movement of
creative change. It is the essence of trained and
matured scholarship--and, by inference, of trained and

---

[23]Ibid., 67.

matured ministry--to utilize the fullest possible range
of historical understanding in the work of dealing with
contemporary circumstances.

To be sure, the tradition must be re-understood by
each new generation. Currently, as Blacks and women
increasingly gain a position to do so, they impel a
re-understanding of the tradition. The contribution of
their forerunners will require attention by a scholarly
guild that has sometimes neglected this part of the
heritage. As this happens we shall all become the
richer for it.

Nor does the knowledge of any one single tradition, even that of the community of faith with which a
given church is identified, provide the broadest
possible base for understanding. Think, for instance,
of what Christians can learn about the possibilities of
combining ministry with scholarship by examining the
work and role of the Jewish rabbi. Indeed, the unity
of the scholarly and the ministerial roles has remained
prevalently and significantly present in Jewish
religious leadership patterns. The rabbi and the
Reformed pastor have much in common. They both rely
primarily on the teaching function for the cultivation
of faith. It would benefit a tradition in which that
unity has been eroded to study one in which it has not.

Moreover, it could benefit us to understand the
Confucian tradition, and the Hindu/Buddhist experien-
ces, in trying to think about the relationship between
intellectual understanding and religious commitment.
The traditions have not developed the tensions between
learning and religious fidelity to the extent, or with
the emotive baggage, that has so often proved counter-
productive in the Christian west.

Scholarship moves toward a rapprochement with
ministry whenever it undertakes the nurture of others

and not merely the cultivation of ideas. The scholar
who disdains all caring, who supposes toughness alone
is the touchstone of competence, and who cares so much
for concepts that persons no longer matter, lacks as
much of a wholesome fullness as the most unlearned and
sentimental of ministers. In its distrust of learning
for its own sake the Reformed tradition has also
provided us with a resource for guarding against
intellectual arrogance and that supercilious haughti-
ness that can characterize those who treat learning as
a means of legitimizing pride.

VII

Scholarship and ministry are both at their best
when they are shared beyond the confines of the peer
group. The scholar who hoards knowledge betrays the
most sacred duty of the calling, which is to introduce
as many others as possible to the information, perspectives and understandings that enrich and ennoble human
life. Similarly, the minister who regards spiritual
well-being as something which can be bestowed without
involving the recipient in the effort to grasp its
meaning teeters the border of chicanery. The scholar
succeeds most richly through the creation of a community of understanding; the minister succeeds most
profoundly to the extent ministry becomes a total
congregational achievement.

As against the alternatives, ministry and scholarship are more nearly alike than they are different.
Both are dedicated to improving the condition of
persons rather than attaining material aggrandizements
or mere popularity. Both are committed to the nurtur-
ing of growth rather than the exploiting of resources.
Both are at their best when cherishing freedom and
relying solely upon persuasion for attracting allegiance. Both realize that vision and hope are crucial

dimensions of human existence, and look upward toward
those ideals rather than downward to "bottom lines."
Both affirm the value of truth over falsehood,
integrity over intrigue. Both are potentially
beleaguered in a situation of crass commercialization
and the adjudication of issues by raw and naked power.
Each has more to lose than to gain from the weakening
of the other.

In the Reformation a partnership of scholarship
with ministry proved a powerful means of purifying
religion from the perversions and accretions that
threatened its health and legitimacy. In our own day,
when our very survival is at stake, a common effort
from ministry and scholarship offers the best hope for
saving the human enterprise from its possible self-
destruction.

INCIDENCE OF RENAISSANCE CULTURE
IN EARLY PROTESTANTISM[1]

Bard Thompson

My book, *Renaissance and Reformation*, has the
dialectical virtue of existing and not existing. On
completion it may serve the purposes of college
students and seminarians, both of whom I have taught
over the years. Its very title, however, proves to be
a predicament. How are the two cultures represented by
the words "Renaissance" and "Reformation" to be
interpreted in relationship to each other? Luther's
collision with Erasmus over free will and salvation
(1524-25) was so colossal that decent Protestants ever
since are apt to believe that humanists are an alien
species and that the "Renaissance" and "Reformation"
represent two sides of an impassable chasm in Western
intellectual history. We manage somehow to get around
the fact that Zwingli, Bucer, Melanchthon, and Calvin
were all formed to some appreciable extent by northern
humanism, and that Luther spent nearly twenty pages in
the latter part of *The Bondage of the Will* demanding to
know why Erasmus was not as good a humanist as *he* was.
I find it perfectly plausible to believe that Luther

[1]This is a slightly abbreviated version of a
paper presented at the Center of Theological Inquiry,
Princeton, New Jersey, March 15, 1987. It is published
here with the permission of Mrs. Bertha D. Thompson.

was a humanist--at least to the extent we may be
willing to apply that nomenclature to ourselves. Such
a possibility, at any rate, may be provocation enough
to begin the discourse that follows.

I

In the first half of the sixteenth century, a
change occurred in the cultus of the Western Catholic
Church. In the celebration of Mass, Latin yielded to
vernacular languages. Silent recital gave way to "the
shouted Word." The appeal to the five-sensed individual was curtailed (if you believe Luther) to the
Protestant with uncommonly big ears. Thus, the
esoteric yielded to the modern; empathy, to listening;
a universal language, to particular ones; the objective
(to some degree), to the subjective. The Mass became
the Lord's Supper, its doctrine of sacrifice everywhere
repudiated. The sermon became the *sine qua non* of
Protestant worship. Liturgies were designed to be
expressions of Scriptural warranty, more or less
strictly applied, or to conform to the custom of the
ancient church.

Even more provocative is this: the very Protestant
tradition that expressed so much skepticism over the
nature of human beings thrust upon that very pack of
sinners a stack of communicative responsibilities--
speaking and listening, teaching and learning, reading
and understanding--unheard of in the church since the
Acts of the Apostles. Their Eucharistic piety notwithstanding, the Reformers tilted the Protestant
cultus toward an "intelligent" communication of
religious benefit; and even the more conservative among
them, say, Luther, or Cranmer, depreciated to some
extent the communicative properties of "the image."

How could that have been? The Saxon pachyderm
(Luther) squashed Erasmus the mouse for no other reason

than that the mouse kept saying that human beings were
religiously intelligent and moral. And it was the same
Luther who warned us to stay away from the street-
walker, Fra Hulda--natural reason dolled up as a
purveyor of divine wisdom. The same Luther once tried
to make a congregation believe that while he and his
friends Phil and Nick were having a few beers in a
Wittenberg saloon, the Word and the Holy Ghost were
just outside, smiting the Pope of Rome and the Holy
Roman Emperor all by themselves. And that was how
Wittenberg became the cradle of the Reformation.
Nonsense! There was too much preaching, too much
teaching, too much listening, too much learning in the
Reformation agenda to make Luther's hyperbole credible.
We know, of course, that faith is not born out of human
perspicacity, nor is it in any respect whatsoever the
result of human exertion, whether preacher's or
listener's. But you, Luther, were the one who taught
us that "God does not give the Holy Spirit without the
Word, but through the Word," and that the Word is
communicated by preaching.

How shall we explain such findings? I am like you
are: I enjoy seeing the parade go by--the late medieval
procession on the road to Wittenberg. I delight in
seeing the Ockhamists march, each one doing his very
best. And the Precursors--Wyclif and Hus and the boys
from Mt. Tabor. The mystics led by Meister Eckhart,
looking inward. Nicholas of Lyra and the Exegetes.
Saints and conciliarists and imitators of Christ.
Borgias and della Roveres advancing ponderously under
the weight of the papal tiara. As worthy as those
people may have been, they do not contribute very much
to the matters that press us here. I will therefore
make bold to offer you another agenda, a Renaissance
agenda, yet not without trepidation on my part, because

many of the self-evident truths I will ask you to believe lie either hidden in prestatistical mists or uneasily on my own intellectual bosom. In any event, I cannot offer you causes, but merely coincidences from the culture of the Renaissance which mirror themselves in interesting ways in the affairs of the Protestant Reformation.

II[2]

I will use "printing" to mean a cluster of technological achievements--movable metal type, oil-based ink, a wooden handpress, and paper--associated with a printshop operation in or near Mainz by Johannes Gutenberg in the middle of the fifteenth century.

The appearance of printing a half-century before Luther raises two questions for observers of early Protestant traditions. First, to what extent did printing contribute to the dissemination of Protestant ideas? Second, did printing stimulate Protestant "intellectualism" and accelerate the depreciation of "the image?"

It would be difficult to exaggerate the transformation in communication brought about by printing. Within fifty years of the Gutenberg event, the age of the scribe had given way to that of the printer. "He prints more in one day than could be copied in one year," said an Italian humanist of a German printer who had just set up shop in town.[3] By 1500 there were

---

[2]If this were a documented paper, the notes would indicate a particular indebtedness to Elizabeth L. Eisenstein, *The Printing Revolution in Early Modern Europe* (Cambridge: Cambridge University Press, 1983).

[3]Wrote the French humanist Jacques Peletier:
Ah, one can print in one day
What it would take thirty days to say
And a hundred times longer to write by hand.

presses operating in 260 European towns, from Messi
in Sicily to Stockholm in Scandinavia. Venice alone
supported 150 such establishments, more than any other
city in the world, and hand uttered over 4,000 edi-
tions--twice the output of its rival, Paris. Bookstalls lined the Merceria from the Rialto all the way
to San Marco, enticing passers-by with their publications. There Aldus Manutius printed the classics in
octavo volumes, invigorating the renaissance of
classicism; and there Daniel Bomberg, first important
printer of Hebrew books, accomplished a similar
renaissance of Semitic scholarship. It has been said
that a person born in 1453, when Constantinople fell,
lived by the age of fifty in a world of eight million
printed books--more than all of the scribes of Europe
had managed to copy since Constantine founded the city
(330).

Luther described printing as "God's highest and
extremest act of grace, whereby the business of the
gospel is driven forward." An astonishing statement,
you will agree. Yet, small wonder! Between 1517 and
1520, as the Reformation got underway, he sent thirty
pamphlets and broadsides to the printer; they sold
300,000 copies. (Beatus Rhenanus informed Zwingli that
"sold" was the wrong word; they were *snatched* from
booksellers' hands.) In 1517, for instance, he had
written out some propositions in academic Latin,
inviting debate. "They were meant exclusively for our
academic circle here," he explained to the Pope; "they
were written in such language that the common people
could scarcely understand . . . ." While scholars
avoided the debate in droves, translators and printers
had a heyday with Luther's *Ninety-five Theses*. In
December, 1517, three separate editions were printed
simultaneously in three German towns. Soon they

appeared in bookstalls and at country fairs all the way
into central Europe. The Reformation was the first
cultural phenomenon to be driven by printing--a
circumstance which the Protestants lost no time
attributing to Providence. "As if to offer proof that
God has chosen us to accomplish a special mission,"
wrote Johann Sleidan (1542), "there was invented in our
land a marvelous new and subtle art, the art of
printing."

For Sleidan, printing was an instrument of
religious discernment. It was the printed word which
"opened German eyes. . . . Each man became eager for
knowledge, not without feeling a sense of amazement at
his former blindness." John Foxe, the Puritan con-
troversialist, was also convinced that printing was a
miracle of God for the specific purpose of bringing the
Reformation to consummation. God conducted the
Reformation, said Foxe, not by the sword, but by
"printing, writing, and reading." It was printing, he
said, which helped people distinguish truth from error.
Printing stirred up their "good wits."

Printing allowed intellectual ballast to be given
to such Protestant schemes as the priesthood of all
believers and a lifetime discipleship to the Word of
God. Luther's German New Testament (1522) and two
catechisms (1529)--both of which were of course uttered
by printing presses--were intended to be used at home
to assist believers in their never-ending incursions
into the inexhaustible Word. Calvin arrived in
Strassburg (1538) just in time to witness the introduction of inexpensive printed hymnals, allowing each one
of the common priests to hold one in hand. An instruction in the Geneva Bible admonished all heads of
English households to preach to their families from
said printed Bible, "that from the highest to the

lowest, they may obey the will of God."

Catholics made a less happy accommodation to that
which Cardinal Nicholas of Cusa called "this holy art
risen in Germany." As early as the Fifth Lateran
Council (1512-17), the Latin Church attempted to
regulate less pleasing aspects of printing, prompting
the acerbic Foxe to pronounce "that either the pope
must abolish knowledge and printing, or printing must
at length root him out." Ah well! Foxe wound up on
the Index with other boys who were naughty.

In Victor Hugo's *Notre Dame*,[4] a scholar observes
with apprehension the arrival of the first printed book
to grace his shelves and expresses the fear that "the
printed book will destroy the building," that is, the
cathedral. The spiritual benefits that have been
invested in images and stored in sacred places of
memory will be made obsolete by a new way of com-
municating grace. Was that the portent of printing?
Consider the following evidences: Erasmus in the
Enchiridion, quoting Cato, "If God is mind, in poems is
he revealed; With pure mind, then, you ought to worship
him"; Zwingli's exasperation in *Commentary on True and
False Religion*, "Why, then, do we still delay to tear
our hearts away from ceremonies?"; Calvin's statement
in "Necessity of Reforming the Church," "God is now
pleased to instruct his Church in a different manner";
the title page of John Foxe's *Acts and Monuments*
(1563), showing two congregations at worship--Catholics
telling their beads, Protestants with books on their
laps; Luther's wry observation that iconoclasts who
tear pictures off walls revere them in books.

To attribute such force to printing, of course, is
never likely to be verifiable. Besides, there is in

---

[4]Eisenstein, *Printing Revolution*, 34.

the Protestant soul a Eucharistic piety (especially in
Calvin, I think) and a respect for liturgical tradition
(especially in Luther, Calvin, and Cranmer) that belie
easy assumptions about the end of the image.

III

In the *Schulordnung* of Mecklenberg (1552),
Melanchthon declared that "reading is the beginning of
Christian doctrine." Exactly! Not much of the
Protestant program would have worked very well without
literacy--neither access to the Scriptures, nor
proficiency in them; neither the receipt of religious
instruction, nor the use of catechisms, psalters,
prayerbooks, and homilies; neither the priesthood of
all believers, nor lifelong discipleship in the
inexhaustible Word--not even much comprehension of
preaching, at least of Calvin's.

Yet literacy was not an indelible characteristic
of Western society. At the beginning of the Middle
Ages, at the disintegration of the Roman Empire,
illiteracy was common among layfolk; and the advance of
feudalism left obsolete even those commercial functions
that had once been performed by literate people. The
decline in the number of learned people also coincided
with the transalpine expansion of Christianity and the
conversion of those rightly or wrongly described as
barbarians, shrinking the educated constituency of
Christianity even more. As the chief civilizing agency
in the West, the church found itself with a virtual
monopoly on learning. As a consequence, the word
clericus came to mean *litteratus*, a lettered or learned
man, who could read, understand, compose, make verse in
Latin, while *laicus* came to mean *illiteratus*. "Are
laymen illiterate?" was a tautology: "layperson" and
"untaught" were synonyms. (The Protestant idea of a
"common priesthood" was, by comparison, extraordinary.)

It was the first of the medieval popes, Gregory the
Great (590-604), who referred to "images as the books
of the uneducated"--a statement which no one ever since
seems to have forgotten. The patriarchal figures of
Western monasticism were among the prominent educators
of the age. Reading and writing, school and library,
the copying of books and preservation of manuscripts
were part and parcel of communal monasticism.

Medieval history could be written, I suppose,
around successive gains in literacy, with chapters on
successive benefactions--the universities, scholasticism, revival of the professions (each with a body of
literature), the stimulation of trade in the wake of
the crusades, the evolution of a new mercantile class,
the rise of towns and guilds, Renaissance humanism,
printing, and eventually what Spengler called a
Buchund-Lesen Kultur. As time passed, medieval
literacy came to mean minimal ability to read and
write, perhaps only to sign one's name. By 1300,
Latin, on which literacy had been based and by which it
had been judged, began to be displaced by vernacular
languages. By 1450, London tradesmen were "litterati"
in the minimalist sense, as were German artisans, and
as Florentine merchants had been for a long time.

It has been suggested that while advances in
literacy in the later Middle Ages were of advantage to
a few precious souls (merchants, clergy, students,
lawyers), and while the Renaissance addressed its
riches to courtiers, printing may have been the opening
to an unlimited reading public and the Reformation may
have been the first great enterprise to seize such an
opportunity. If that is the case, we can understand
why printing called the vernacular into being as a
universal principle (Luther notwithstanding). As early
as 1520, Ulrich von Hutten said the obvious: it made no

sense to use a means of mass dissemination in order to publish things in a language exclusive to scholars and priests.

In the early Tudor Renaissance, Thomas More lamented the fact that "not more than three-fifths of the English people could read"--which means, of course, that well over half could read as the English Reformation began. In More's *Utopia* every child was taught to read; every adult was expected to cultivate the mind. More's adversary, William Tyndale, assumed universal literacy when he wrote, by way of commending his English New Testament, "I wish that the farmer might sing parts [of the Scriptures] at his plow, and the weaver at his shuttle, and that the traveler might beguile the weariness of his way with their narration." Even more expansive was Thomas Becon's prescription: "*all* Christian peoples" should read the Holy Scriptures "in the English tongue." Such exuberance is only partially justified by statistical evidence.[5]

Carlo Cippola, an observer of the development of literacy in the West, has reached the following conclusions: in the towns of culturally advanced areas, well over half of the population of Western Europe was

---

[5]England: Studies of the diocese of Norwich, 1580-1700, show patterns of illiteracy, resistant to steady improvement. While the clergy, professional people, and teachers enjoyed the full benefits of literacy, and while the gentry was almost entirely literate, only forty-five percent of yeomen were able to read and write in 1580, sixty-two percent, by 1590. The degree of literacy among tradesmen and craftsmen varied considerably according to what they did--from ninety-four percent literacy among grocers, to fifty-five percent literacy among blacksmiths, to three percent literacy among roof thatchers. Substantial illiteracy existed among rural and urban workers, as well as among women, only ten percent of whom could read. More than half of the Christians of Norwich were apparently illiterate.

literate by the end of the sixteenth century; in the
rural areas, where peasant populations and local
dialects persisted, less than half. What statistical
and historical evidence we have supports such conclusions.[6]

Of more importance is how the Protestant establishment meant to exploit the possibility of literacy.
In the Galatians commentary (1535), Luther left no

---

[6]France: In rural France, literacy remained low
throughout the sixteenth century--less than three
percent of agricultural workers, less than ten percent
of better-off peasants were literate. Rural Protestantism was confined to great noble houses or to specific
districts, e.g., the Cevenol, where rural artisans
committed themselves to Calvinism. In Lyon, on the
other hand, in the 1550,s, there were thirty-eight
teachers of reading, one for every 400 children under
twenty. The literacy rate exceeded fifty percent among
apothecaries, surgeons, printers, painters, musicians,
taverners, and metal workers; it stood at fifty percent
for some artisans; at less than fifty percent for
others. City-dwellers were more likely to speak French
than country people and therefore had more access to
the contents of a printed book. In 1560, an octavo New
Testament cost a printer's journeyman a half-day's
wages.
    Germany: Gerald Strauss, an authority on
literacy in the German Reformation, believes that
"reading and writing were more widespread among the
common folk of early modern Europe than has been
thought." In Electoral Saxony, village schools were
common by 1570, although some may have been poorly
staffed or inadequately funded. A Visitation of the
Upper Palatinate in 1579-80 indicated that three-
quarters of the *flechen* and villages had schools. The
Saxon school ordinance of 1580 bade the sexton to
assume the duties of teacher in the smallest and
poorest villages, so that "children of working people
[*arbeitender leute Kinder*] . . . receive instruction in
prayers, catechism, writing, and reading." Authorities
of the Mechlenburg school system declared (on the basis
of I Timothy 4:13): "Paul has intentionally put reading
first." Ortholph Fuchssperger explained in the preface
to his *Art of Reading* (1542), one of many self-help
books available, "Most of us depend on books for what
we need to learn about our duties toward God and our
fellowmen."

doubt about Protestant intentions: "With great zeal and
diligence, we inculcate, urge, and emphasize the
teaching of the faith by speaking, reading and
writing." When asked how he would treat an illiterate
constituent, Calvin replied (*Institutes* I.xi.5), Pope
Gregory being in the back of his mind, not by giving
the constituent an image, but by teaching him to read.
"Images [cannot] stand in place of books." True
teaching is given by God in other ways—by "hearing,"
by "reading," by "publishing," by "explaining," by
"participation in" the Word of God. (Calvin's words,
every one.) Even in Calvin's assertion that "reason is
proper to our nature" and in the discussion of common
grace that follows (*Institutes* II.ii.17-21), there is a
basis offered for intellectual life or for the mastery
of a trade, each of which evoke literacy.

IV

Those who could read at the start of the Middle
Ages could not do so with our facility. They belonged
to an antique world of oral scribal culture in which
communication generally occurred by dictation and group
reading from manuscript books. Although Cicero,
Quintilian, and Jerome, among other ancient authors,
recommended the physical act of writing, many Greek and
Roman writers, including Fathers of the Church (Augustine, for example), composed by dictation to scribes,
sometimes in rhythmical prose, intending their work to
be read aloud, by scholars in a classroom or monks in
community; and even when it was read by a solitary
reader, it was often read with gestures of the mouth
and tongue, in what might pass today as juvenile
muttering. Lacking punctuation, word separation, and a
differentiation between upper-case and lower-case, a
typical Roman book was not well suited for private
reading by sight. On the contrary, the coordination of

eye and tongue was an essential activity of reading.

Somewhat like a piece of music, a written text became fully intelligible, persuasive, powerful, only when it was sounded, either to one's self or to others. John Cassian distinguished between meditation and reading: if the former was silent, the latter was not. St. Benedict warned monks who wanted to read after the noon repast not to disturb others--an admonition that assumes the habit of reading aloud. Isidore of Seville, recognizing that boisterous reading interfered with comprehension, advised lip-restraint and tongue-restraint. In the *Confessions*, Augustine noticed a peculiar thing about Ambrose--he made a habit of reading with his lips sealed. As late as the twelfth century, illuminations and woodcuts show authors dictating their work to scribes, even as God whispered the Holy Scriptures to prophets and evangelists. St. Bernard (1091-1153), for example, is believed to have composed by dictation. People were shown reading in groups. Carrels did more than shelter people from drafty libraries; they enabled their occupants to mutter or to dictate.

Evidences of an oral culture were apparent in medieval England, where, for example, laws were typically promulgated by a crier. Twelfth-century English charters were addressed to "all those seeing and hearing these letters" and closed with a fetching *valete*, "goodbye." Writing to Innocent III in 1200, the Archbishop of Canterbury, Hubert Walter, argued that "oral witness deserves more credence than written evidence." In his *Metalogicon*, John of Salisbury (d. 1180) attempted (among other things) to distinguish between "voice" (*vox*) and "thing" (*res*), and between the spoken and written word. When he asserted that "letters indicate voices" and that "letters speak

voicelessly the utterances of the absent," he seemed to
acknowledge the priority of oral communication. Even
in contemporary English, "I have not heard from him"
means "no word, no letter."

In the *Gutenberg Galaxy* (1962), Marshall McLuhan
interpreted the Middle Ages as a continuation of the
oral scribal culture which extended from classical
antiquity to Johannes Gutenberg. McLuhan believed that
printing was of crucial importance to Western civilization because it was the responsible agent for the shift
from an oral to a print culture, from oral reading to
silent reading. A fair number of scholars have
supported the McLuhan thesis--that oral communication
persisted throughout the Middle Ages until the invention of printing, which must therefore be characterized
as the harbinger of the modern world. In 1982,
however, Paul Saenger, curator of rare books in the
Newberry Library, demonstrated that certain habits of
silent reading--word-separation, for example--developed
during the Middle Ages and that McLuhan had exaggerated
the absoluteness of an oral culture throughout the
Middle Ages and therefore the singular importance of
printing to the introduction of silent reading. Yet,
by showing that the habits of silent reading predated
Gutenberg, Saenger did not succeed in diminishing the
power of printing toward an all-pervasive shift from
oral reading to silent reading, and did not want to.

Progress toward silent reading seems to have begun
as early as the eighth century and to have proceeded
through the Middle Ages, accelerated by the intellectual demands of scholasticism and the universities, and
was brought to conclusion by the new technologies
associated with printing. Silent reading meant swift
reading. It also meant independent reading; it must
have "encouraged" the reader to a certain extent,

putting curiosity under his personal control, perhaps allowing his skepticism to flourish or his mystical propensities to find expression. Silent reading was also of inestimable value to the author; it allowed a scholar, for example, to compare texts, to build his case on precedents, to engage in complex and systematic thought.

The Jerome of Medieval illuminations was either a scribe taking divine dictation or an author dictating to secretaries. In 1450, just at the advent of printing, Antonello da Messina painted "St. Jerome in His Study." Jerome is alone. His lips are sealed. Around him is an array of books and documents, suggesting that he may be checking sources and copying precedents. Jerome had become a silent reader and a modern scholar. In the fourteenth century, Nicholas of Lyra (1270-1340) addressed himself purposefully to "the reader," while Jean Gerson (1363-1429) and Gerhard Groote (1340-84) both recommended visual memory from a book or manuscript as an advantage over the spoken word. In 1289, a reference collection was begun at Merton College, Oxford, as libraries became places where scholars gathered to read, write, and study in silence. If silent reading was blamed as a stimulus to heresy, it was also seen as a new means of spiritual life. A new form of devotional literature appeared in the fourteenth and fifteenth centuries--the Imitation of Christ is an example--composed for silent reading, with prayer and meditation. Intimacy with God could now come through silent reading and the mystical excursions that went with it. Some authors of such literature went so far as to depreciate preaching as a spiritual exercise of comparable worth.

Silent reading, while it contributed handsomely to Protestant intellectualism and to the investiture of

Protestant layfolk, leads straight into a quandary.
What shall we do with the Protestant sermon? While the
Renaissance moved away from oral communication, the
Reformers declared that the Word, to be fully powerful,
must be sounded. By insisting that the virtuous Word
is a spoken Word, the Reformers bucked the trend of
Renaissance social history, leading their constituents
back to a more ancient habit, a more classical,
patristical, biblical habit.

Where did the Protestant sermon come from? From
the history of preaching, I suppose. Hughes Oliphant
Old's latest book, on the history of preaching, is very
persuasive of that possibility; and the fact that
Luther preached 170 sermons in Wittenberg in 1514 must
mean that a continuity of preaching existed. Does that
imply, however, that Savonarola's "Penitenza," preached
in Florence in the 1490's was of a piece with Cranmer's
"Homily of Salvation" preached fifty years later in
Tudor England? Is the origin of Protestant preaching
to be found in Renaissance orations? Preposterous. Or
in Johann Ulrich Surgant's humanistic attempt to give
sermonic expression to the "renascent Word" (Basel,
1502)? Possible.

Is not the Protestant sermon, although an integral
part of the history of preaching, to be explained by
three ideas typical of the Renaissance and Reformation
periods: first, that, as Luther said, the gospel is
sermon, story, tale of salvation; second, that the
Christian church has its basis in its sources; third,
that simplicity travels with those who search for
pristine forms. (Protestants honored the Bible, of
course, because it was God's Word or because God's Word
was in it, not because it resembled Vitruvius' ten
books *On Architecture*. Yet a society accustomed to the
validity of sources found the Bible all the more

infinitely attractive.)

Even if my ideas about the basis of Protestant preaching do not catch your fancy, it is clear, is it not, that printed books and silent reading did not suppress oral culture but intensified it? It gave Protestants something fresh to talk about. It offered Protestants a new way to relate religious expression to authorities old and new.

V

In Santa Croce, the Franciscan church in Florence where many great Italians are enshrined, one finds the remains of Leonardo Bruni (1370-1444), chancellor of the republic and humanist. On his grave the Florentines inscribed, "History is in mourning . . ." What they wept over, however, was not so much Bruni himself as the ancient world, that golden age of civilization, in which the standards of Western civilization were stored, to whose investigation Bruni had devoted his life. "The Renaissance stood weeping at its grave," wrote the eminent art historian Erwin Panofsky, "and tried to resurrect *its* soul." Huizinga described this Renaissance emotion as *heimweh*, homesickness for the ancient past. It was a homesickness directed toward classicism in all of its manifestations. O, to see a rebirth of art, a revival of Ciceronian Latin, a more perfect poetry, the architecture of Vitruvius, the well ordered society of Cato or Scipio, the restoration of primitive Christianity!

Fundamental to the historical perspective of the Renaissance was a firm sense of *historical distance* separating the Renaissance from antiquity. As the eye to the object, as the scientist to his specimens . . . so too, the remains of antiquity lay ready for inspection by the new "sciences" of archaeology, history, philology, and languages. Medieval renaissance had

come and gone--important renaissance such as that of
Charlemagne in the ninth century, that of Otto the
Great in the tenth, that of the cathedral schools in
the twelfth which led to a formidable revival of
classicism. But none of those had quite the sense of
discontinuity with the ancient world--the fact of its
death and the probability of its resurrection--as that
which distinguished the Renaissance of 1300-1600.

That historical perspective had the following
effects for humanists and Reformers alike. First, it
directed them *ad fontes*, to archetypes, to ancient
models and texts. When one hears timid Cranmer invoke
"God's word and the ancient authors," one hears an
appeal to classicism as resolute as any made by
Petrarca, father of Renaissance humanism. "The good
ancient style" (*buona maniera antiqua*), used by
Leonardo da Vinci to describe the aspirations of
Renaissance artists, applied also to Calvin's Geneva
where things were reconceived "according to the custom
of the ancient church." *Rinascita*, employed by Vasari
to explain the significance of Giotto, was an operating
principle for Christian humanists and Protestant
Reformers. "Why," asked Jacques Lefevre, "may we not
aspire to see our age restored to the likeness of the
primitive church?" John Foxe was careful to notice
that the Church of England, so far from being "the
beginning of any new church of our own," was "the
renewing of the ancient church of Christ."

Second, it stimulated an unprecedented passion for
collecting, examining and criticizing antique books and
manuscripts, including, of course, the Bible and the
Fathers. Far and away the most prodigious of the
manuscript collectors was a papal agent, Poggio
Bracciolini (1380-1459), who rummaged through the
cathedrals and abbeys of Europe, like a hog routing for

truffles, searching for classical remains. Armed with
the pope's excommunication against all who might be
tight-fisted, and lightly encumbered by scruples,
Poggio was a conspicuous success. Back to Rome he
came, laden with precious manuscripts, including a
complete text of Quintilian's *On the Education of an
Orator*, discovered in a Swiss convent. Lorenzo Valla
(1407-57), a textual critic, accused the papacy of
"supine ignorance" for trading on the *Donation of
Constantine* throughout the Middle Ages, yet he was the
pope's secretary and one of the intellectual heroes of
the age. (Both worked for the first Renaissance pope,
Nicholas V.) What is the difference between Poggio and
Lorenzo, on the one hand, and, say, Colet and Luther on
the other? John Colet, excited by Italian humanism,
began to unravel the meaning of Paul, from Paul, at
Oxford as early as 1496. Luther began the Reformation,
not by posting theses on indulgences, but by staging a
curriculum-reform at Wittenberg on behalf of Biblical
languages and exegesis, at the expense of Aristotle and
the Schools. He "has brought it about," wrote an
astonished Bucer (1518), "that at Wittenberg the
ordinary textbooks have all been abolished, while the
Greeks and Jerome, Augustine and Paul are publicly
taught." Although suckled by the Schools with scarcely
a taint of humanism, Luther advanced in the belief that
it would likely be the humanists with their linguistic
and critical sophistication who could provide him the
means of disclosing the Gospel.

Third, it created an incentive to study languages
which were perceived to be the keys for unlocking the
treasures of the ancient world. When the distinguished
Greek scholar, Manuel Chrysolarus, was appointed to the
faculty of letters in Florence (1387), Leonardo Bruni
immediately signed up to study Greek, in the prospect

of being able to read the ancients in their language.
"Wilt thou neglect this opportunity," he asked himself,
"so divinely offered?" Bruni was not the only one who
thought that God was involved in the Greek explosion.
Both Lefevre and Luther retailed a story making the
rounds that God himself had caused the fall of Constantinople (1453) so that Greek scholars would flood the
West. How portentous indeed were the following
episodes in the history of Greek: instruction in Greek
is authorized at Oxford (1312); the Aldine Press
publishes Marsilio Ficino's complete text of Plato
(1477); Erasmus' Greek New Testament is published
(1516); Johann Lang begins to tutor Luther in Greek
(1516?); Melanchthon is appointed to the Wittenberg
faculty (1518); Calvin, a legal student, risks health
to study Greek from Melchior Wolmar (1528ff.);
Guillaume Bude's *Commentaries on the Greek Language* is
published in Paris (1529).

No one was more loquacious on the subject of
languages than Martin Luther. "The languages," he said
(1524), "are the sheath in which this sword of the
Spirit [the Gospel] is contained; they are the casket
in which we carry this jewel; they are the vessel in
which we hold this wine; they are the larder in which
this food is stored." Just as the languages enabled
Protestants to reclaim the Gospel, so neglect of the
languages by Protestants will cause them to lose it
again: ". . . we shall not long preserve the Gospel
without the languages."

Fourth, it afforded both Renaissance and Reformation certain theorems about history, which, however
prejudicial they were toward the Middle Ages and Latin
Christianity, proved useful. The history of Western
civilization may be written thus: after a period of
high culture, of which the word *classicus* ("of first

order") is eloquent and the description, "golden age,"
is apt, an interval of decadence set in, separating
Renaissance and Reformation from antiquity. Hence,
historical distance. "Renaissance" and "Reformation"--
words which make no particular sense without being hung
onto that sort of historical structure--mean to effect
a new golden age by returning to the classics of the
old.

The when and why of the fall of Western culture
are of no immediate concern to us here. The dates
range all of the way from the baptism of Constantine
(312?), to the sack of Rome by Alaric (410), to the
onset of the high Middle Ages; and the reasons include
moral lassitude (Alberti), the loss of *virtu* (Machia-
velli: the will to rule), to the arrival of "antichrist
. . . with his papists which feigned a new and false
doctrine contrary to God's word and the true catholic
doctrine" (Cranmer).

Petrarca, as much as any other, popularized the
imagery of night (as in "dark ages") to describe the
age of apostasy or intervention. "Barbarism" was also
much in vogue. "O Barbarism," exclaimed Ulrich von
Hutten, "take a rope and prepare for thy extinction."
Such a sophisticate as Guillaume Bude described the
Middle Ages as a thousand years of civilization "buried
in barbarian mud."

Historical distance also produced a fresh sense of
anachronism. Just as Lorenzo Valla knew that "satrap"
would not have been used in a document genuine to the
fourth century and cited that fact in his demolition of
the *Donation of Constantine*, so Zwingli impugned the
pristine character of the Mass canon by pointing to its
barbarisms.

Equally exuberant was the language used to
describe the new golden age. "I could almost wish to

be young again," wrote Erasmus to Capito (1516), "for
no other reason than this, that I anticipate the near
approach of a golden age." "What a century!" exclaimed
von Hutten. "What genius! It is sheer joy to be
alive. . . . Learning flourishes, men are spiritually
quickened. . . ." The quattrocento painters Andrea
Mantegna and Benozzo Gozzoli both decorated their
landscapes with orange trees in full fruit: the
Renaissance was the springtime of history! Luther made
the point that the new age also brought a new sense of
the reliable. "Since the languages have been restored," he said (1524), "we have the Gospel quite as
purely as the apostles had it . . . . It is altogether
attained to its original purity, far beyond what it was
[even] in the days of St. Jerome or St. Augustine."

No piece of early Protestant literature, I think,
is more expressive of the Renaissance historiography
than Calvin's *Reply to Sadoleto* (1539). Calvin will
simply not be told by the eminent prince of the church
that he (Calvin) has destroyed the unity and integrity
of the holy catholic church because he thought lightly
of 1500 years of pontifical history. The *Reply* is
based on the premises (1) that it is Rome which has
swerved from the true Christianity of the Bible and the
Fathers, (2) that it is the Reformed church which is
struggling to reestablish the church on the basis of
ancient sources, and (3) that the whole urgency of the
Protestant enterprise is ecumenism. "Our agreement
with antiquity is far closer than yours; . . . all we
have attempted to do has been to renew the ancient form
of the church." The Protestant program, no less than
the Erasmian program or the Petrarcan program, is to
bring civilization "back to the source" and "restore it
to its original purity." The Protestant purpose is an
ecumenical purpose--"that religion be revived and that

the churches, scattered and dispersed by discord, might be gathered together in true unity."

VI

It is not likely that we will ever understand the Renaissance fascination with libraries until we stop treating "the sources" as if they were grocery lists. The sources were "springs" from which the living waters of intellectual life came. Therefore libraries, in which the sources were contained, were regenerative places, the CTI's of the Renaissance, where scholars gathered to renew themselves in matters of the mind and spirit.

In 1490, the eminent Venetian printer and humanist, Aldus Manutius, wrote:

> I have resolved to devote my life to the cause of scholarship. In place of a life of ease, I have chosen an anxious and toilsome career. Cato compared human existence to iron. When nothing is done with it, it rusts. It is only through constant activity that polish is secured.

Thus, at least thirty years before Luther, scholars were using the language of the *inexhaustible Word*--that which elicits our *lifelong discipleship*. At the heart of such an arduous undertaking was the Renaissance library and the Renaissance book tradition. As Jean Gerson said, while oral discourse is ephemeral, the book is of permanent, inherent, enduring value, something to be exploited endlessly for new ideas and for criticism. Libraries, where books were collected, where scholars, teachers and learners of all sorts gathered to search the riches of books, were among the true sites of "renaissance" and "reformation." The quattrocento Platonists, Marsilio Ficino and Giovanni Pico della Mirandola, attended the Medici library in Florence, just as Luther and Melanchthon later worked at the university library in Wittenberg.

In the Middle Ages, libraries were maintained chiefly by monastic communities--an achievement to which the universities and friars eventually contributed. But the Renaissance library was a new creation, borne of a new spirit which J. A. Symonds described as "the age of passionate desire." It was born, in other words, of the determination to recover as much as possible of classical antiquity through the gathering, preserving, and eventually printing of its literary remains. Of such enterprise, the careers of Poggio Bracciolini and Pope Nicholas V are particularly illustrative. Feverish collecting led to the establishment of new libraries--not in monasteries any longer, seldom in cathedrals, but at the courts of Renaissance princes and in the bookrooms of Renaissance scholars. Petrarca reveled in his own working library, just as Cicero, his intellectual hero, had done before him. Boccaccio willed his collection (200 volumes) to his confessor. Among the first princes to make libraries were the d'Este of Ferrara, the Gonzaga of Mantua, and that ardent bibliophile of Urbino, Federigo da Montefeltro. To the Medici of Florence, however, we owe a singular achievement--the first *civic* library in the West since Roman times (San Marco, 1441). The second such library was given to Venice in 1468 by Cardinal Bessarion. "For public benefit" read the deed of endowment by which 482 manuscripts in Greek, 264 in Latin, were conveyed to the Venetian Republic. Overshadowing all other benefactors of this sort was Pope Nicholas V (1447-55). As a young humanist, he had written the definitive bibliographic canon by which most of the great collectors built their libraries. As pope (first of the Renaissance line), he founded the Vatican library--a *civic* library which housed 4,000 volumes prior to the sack of Rome (1527).

His trust in the Vulgate having been shaken by
Lorenzo Valla's *Annotations* (which Erasmus had published in 1505), Luther elected to enter the very text
of the Scriptures, using the original languages, and
found himself dependent on the lexicons, commentaries,
and critical editions prepared by Christian humanists
and held in the Wittenberg library: Reuchlin's *Rudimen-
ta Linguae Hebraicae* (1506), which contained a lexicon
and a grammar; Lefevre's *Psalterium Quintuplex* (1509),
a critical text and commentary of the Psalms; Lefevre's
Epistolae Pauli Apostoli (1512), a text and commentary
of the Pauline epistles; Reuchlin's *Septem Psalmi
Poenitentiales* (1512); the New Testament in Greek; and
Melanchthon's *Greek Grammar* (1518). Luther's resources
were all *printed books*. They came from the publishing
emporiums of Paris, Basel, and the towns of Germany.
They contained standard, more-or-less reliable texts,
free at least from the foibles of scribes. They were
as accessible in Cambridge, Einsiedeln, Strassburg, or
Geneva, as they were in Wittenberg; and it is a fair
guess that they were used in all of those places of
scholarly inquiry.

VII

In *On My Own Ignorance and That of Many Others*
(1337), Petrarca came to the unhappy conclusion that
ignorance increases in proportion to knowledge. The
more we know, the more we stand in terror of what we do
not know. There is, therefore, no salvation in
knowledge. It is better to admit being ignorant while
claiming some quarter on virtue, which Petrarca did.

The humanists who followed him did not subscribe
to Petrarca's pessimism. Impressed by the rationality
and educability of human beings, they employed the word
humanitas to refer not to nondescript "humanity," but
to humanity raised to a higher power through education.

Humanitas meant, in other words, that "full humanity,"
which can only be attained through study and reflection. In *Genealogy of the Gods*, Giovanni Boccaccio
(1313-75) said that while "nature produces man,
learning then forms him anew." Our "dignity" (to use a
word in which most humanists delighted) is not so much
a natural endowment as it is a product of that sort of
learning that makes us truly human. Such "forming
anew" of which Boccaccio spoke is the function of a
humanizing curriculum, appropriately called "the
humanities," including grammar, rhetoric, poetry,
history, and philosophy. Certified as "ancient," it
was thought likely to elicit the full potential of
human beings, ethically and intellectually. Pietro
Paolo Vergerio (1370-1444), a Renaissance educational
theorist, also called such a curriculum "liberal,"
worthy of "free" men, because by developing their
highest gifts of body and mind, it diverts and delivers
them from ignoble things and "ennobles" them.

The outcome of education was citizenship, broadly
defined. (Only contemplative humanists such as Ficiono
and Pico would have dissented from that.) Learning,
said Boccaccio, "turns natural man into civil man,
remarkable for morals, knowledge, and virtue." The
Florentine humanist, Giannozzo Manetti (1396-1459), had
a simple prospectus for life: "to understand and to
act." It was a prescription widely admired. Between
1400 and 1600, princes and magistrates, Reformers and
Jesuits, merchants and teachers were all persuaded that
a combination of broad-gauged learning and active
participation in society was good for both public and
personal life. At the same time, there came a chorus
of complaints, starting with Petrarca and reaching
crescendo in Pico, Erasmus, and Colet, that the "cold,
barren intellectuality" of scholasticism had neither

the right agenda nor the right clientele to make better people.

In a letter of 1524 "to the Burgomasters and Councilmen of all cities in Germany," Luther urged the magistrates to make haste to establish systems of public education, using church revenues heretofore directed to pious endowments. He proposed a curriculum based on classical precedent, Roman in particular. It would include ancient languages, history, the other liberal arts, and instruction in Scripture. It would utilize the talents of humanists with whom "God has so richly blessed us" and it would deliver Germans from "our former misery and the darkness in which we sat."

Luther offered the magistrates four advantages to such a system: (1) It would provide good citizens, relieving Germany of rule by "clods and boors"; (2) it would afford everyone access to the Scriptures and, for some, proficiency in the Scriptures, especially through the use of languages; (3) it would be of commercial advantage to Germany; and (4) deliver Germans from a widely perceived cultural backwardness. Luther also proposed that the larger cities maintain public libraries, their collections to include the classics, the liberal arts, and materials necessary for sophisticated study of the Bible.

The literature of Luther's age abounds with similar appeals. In his *Enchiridion* (1503), Erasmus advocated education in the liberal arts as preparation for entering the Scriptures. "To break in on [the Scriptures] with unwashed hands and feet," he said, "is almost a sacrilege." Melanchthon's school plan for Saxony, enacted in 1528, is thought to be the first system of public education in actual operation since Roman times; it followed by a year the Saxon Visitation, in which public education was encouraged as a

benefit to "both church and state." The Sturms of
Strassburg brought literacy and liberal studies to bear
on a burgeoning reformation; Jacob Sturm founded a
system of primary Latin schools in the city; John
Sturm, a *gymnasium* conceived in the best traditions of
Renaissance humanism. In the *Draft Ordinances* of 1541,
Calvin proposed the establishment of a college in
Geneva to offer instruction in "the languages and
humanities"; education of that sort would enable
Genevans to enter deeply into Christian learning and
would prepare young people "for the ministry as well as
for civil government." In *de Regno Christi*, Martin
Bucer advised King Edward VI to establish public
schools throughout England as part of a scheme to
reconstitute the realm as a "Christian commonwealth."

While the Reformers may have rejected the salvific
properties assigned to education by the humanists,
including the freedom of the will which much of their
theory assumed, they did not disavow Boccaccio's "civil
man," i.e., the idea, as old as Cicero, that a proper
outcome of education is citizenship. Nor did they
disdain the Renaissance conviction that grammar,
languages, and the liberal arts afforded people a means
of engaging themselves more and more deeply in things
that mattered most--the Scriptures, the fathers,
catechisms, books of worship and prayers, and sermons
themselves.

Epilogue: Luther and the Eel

In 1523, Luther explained to Eoban Hess that just
as John the Baptist had been the herald of Jesus, the
Renaissance had been the harbinger of the Reformation.
So saying, he drew the two periods together, yet
distinguished them: a predecessor is not the thing
itself. In the following year, however, the *entente*
was severely tested. Erasmus, under pressure from

friends, attacked Luther in *De Libero Arbitrio*.
Responding in 1525, Luther said to Erasmus in *De Servo
Arbitrio*: ". . . Your book struck me as so cheap and
paltry that I felt profoundly sorry for you, defiling
as you did your very elegant and ingenious style with
such trash."

The relationship between Erasmus and Luther had
been in decline for some time. What were the causes of
the dissolution?

Part of the difficulty was a matter of style. If
Erasmus had been summoned to the Diet of Worms, he
might have said, "Here I equivocate!" His was a
humanist's mentality: succor peace and avoid tumult at
all cost. Frederick the Wise once said of Erasmus:
"You never know where you are with him." The simple
Christianity of the Bible and the Old Fathers admitted
as few sharp corners as possible. Even Luther's saw-
toothed thinking (for example: *simul justus et pec-
cator*) irritated Erasmus, whose thought, polished by
the gentle waters of reason, was pebble-smooth.
(Luther called it "contrived.")

In his attempt to restore the simple religion of
Christ to its essential characteristics, Erasmus used
satire against its superfluities. Luther construed
Erasmus' satire as irreverence. It may be one thing to
laugh at Julius II or poke fun at the shrine of St.
Thomas of Canterbury, but another to ascribe the
"invention" of the Trinity to theologians' desire to
create "a pretty number."

From Lorenzo Valla, Erasmus acquired the supreme
importance of the grammatical and philological context
of Scripture. That principle he gave to the Reformation, alongside a critical Greek edition of the New
Testament (1516), and an insistence that the Bible be
open to the generality of men and women. Who could

possibly overestimate the importance of such a gift!
Yet Luther grew more and more impatient of Erasmus'
hesitation, or inability, to get beyond the philological point. The religious idea persistently escaped
him. As Harbison has taught us, it is unlikely that he
could ever have caught the drift of Romans 1:17, the
text from which Luther's illumination came. So Luther
began to interpret his disagreement with Erasmus as
that between Jerome, who had five languages, and
Augustine, whose linguistic ability was limited to one
but who had a decent doctrine of sin and grace.
Eventually he bade Erasmus stand aside, declaring that
he had done all he could with his grammar and was fit
for little else. "He damaged the gospel," said Luther,
"in proportion as he advanced grammar."

Luther suspected that Erasmus' "philosophy of
Christ" simply ran out into moralism. In the earlier
work, *Enchiridion* (1503), where Christ is described as
"example," "ruler," "pattern," Erasmus said that there
"is nothing easier than to take upon yourself the
prospect of perfect life . . ." Even in his diatribe
against Luther of 1524, Erasmus, in his anxiety to
avoid contention, had evaded the very question that
mattered most to Luther--how far the human will
extends, how far the grace of God extends. Those who
know nothing of that question, said Luther, know
nothing of Christianity either.

PENNYSYLVANIA "AWAKENINGS," SACRAMENTAL SEASONS, AND MINISTRY

Janet Forsythe Fishburn

I

The Presbyterian Church, U.S.A., celebrated a
200th anniversary in 1988, remembering the meeting of
the 1st General Assembly in Philadelphia in 1788. The
1st General Assembly consisted of four Synods: Philadelphia, New Jersey and New York, Virginia and the
Synod of the Carolinas. Although leaders who drafted
the Constitution of the new denomination included
educated urban men like John Witherspoon, most of the
congregations were more like missionary outposts on the
frontiers of Pennsylvania, New Jersey, Virginia and the
Carolinas. In the young frontier denomination of 420
congregations, almost half were without pastors. It
was not unusual for one pastor to serve several
congregations.

In histories of early congregations on the
Pennsylvania frontier like Paxtang, Derry, Carlisle,
Donegal and Neshaminy the church buildings are described as one-story rectangular log meeting-houses
with the pulpit on the long side. Members often sat on
logs although a chair was provided for the pastor.
Along with poverty and rustic simplicity, there was a
general lack of decorum in worship. The preface to a
proposed Directory for Worship written in 1788

describes the situation:

> Persons going out and in, during divine service,
> is an odious practice. . . . There are some things
> amiss, while the Minister is preaching, which
> should be corrected. None ought to stand up; much
> less to turn their back upon the Minister; to
> place themselves in sluggish or careless postures;
> or to indulge to sleep, whispering or laughing...[1]

The log meeting-house was typical of most congregations in the new denomination, but some churches
were more prosperous. By 1773, for example, there were
four Presbyterian churches in the seaport city of
Philadelphia, yet these more formal city churches were
an exception in the geographical regions included in
the first four Synods.

In 1750 the congregation of the 2nd Presbyterian
Church in Philadelphia moved into a handsome two-story
brick "church" with a steeple at 3rd and Arch Streets.
This was the second building to house the congregation,
the first having been called "The Old Academy." The
latter served as an academy for poor children but also
as a place for the Methodist evangelist George Whitefield (1714-1770) to preach when he came to Philadelphia. The "Old Academy" was sold in 1748, by which
time Whitefield's last preaching tours to America had
become less frequent.

The interior of the second building had the
formality of a colonial Episcopalian Church with a
center aisle and chandelier. The architect preserved
the meeting-house feature of placing the pulpit on the
long side of the rectangle. Doors did not face the
pulpit as they did in the log meeting-houses. Instead,
the pastor at Second Church, Philadelphia, looked down
the center aisle from a pulpit that directly faced the

---

[1]A Minister of the Presbyterian Church [C. W.
Baird], *Eutaxia, or The Presbyterian Liturgies:
Historical Sketches* (New York: M. W. Dodd, 1855), 97-98.

governor's pew. The building, which included pews in
the gallery for slaves, is a marked contrast to the log
"meeting-houses" found on the frontier.[2] Members
variously described their new edifice as a "church" and
as a "meeting-house." It was really a combination of a
church in the Anglican tradition with a meeting-house
from the Scotch-Irish Presbyterian tradition.

Gilbert Tennent (1703-1764) served as pastor of
the Second Presbyterian Church in Philadelphia from
1743 to 1763. He was the oldest son of William Tennent
(1673-1746), the sole teacher in a frontier academy, or
Log-college, at Neshaminy where he provided a theological education for candidates for ordination. The
pastoral career of Gilbert Tennent took him from
intense involvement with George Whitefield and the
Pennsylvania "awakenings" of 1739 to an entirely
different setting for ministry in 1743. The Second
Presbyterian Church in Philadelphia was a very long way
socially from the "log-house" at Neshaminy where
Whitefield had been entertained by the Tennent family
in 1739.[3]

In 1788 there were some city churches like Gilbert
Tennent's congregation. There were also a few well-
established congregations in prosperous farming towns
like the First Presbyterian Church in Carlisle,
Pennsylvania where an architect-designed stone meeting-
house was erected around 1758. The stone meeting-house
represented a new kind of permanence after years of

---

[2]Conway P. Wing, *A History of the First
Presbyterian Church of Carlisle, Pennsylvania* (Carlisle: Valley Sentinel Office, 1877), 88-91.

[3]E. R. Beadle, *The Old and the New, 1743-1876:
The Second Presbyterian Church of Philadelphia: Its
Beginning and Increase* (Philadelphia: The Ladies
Association, 1876), 28.

conflict over the significance of the "awakenings" on the Pennsylvania frontier. According to a history of the congregation, the first settlers in Carlisle were mostly Scotch-Irish from Ulster, with a few Scots. They arrived between 1729 and 1740, periods of heavy emigration. The earliest record of a pastor is the 1739 installation sermon preached for Samuel Thompson by New Side pastor Alexander Craighead, then the pastor at Derry (now Hershey). Craighead used Ezekiel 33:6 as his text, warning that "if the watchman" fails to "blow the trumpet . . . if he sees the sword coming . . ." "he is taken away . . ." Thompson, an Old Side protester against the "awakenings," was eased out at Carlisle as a "graceless minister" by New Side forces ten years later! In spite of Old Side-New Side politics of the 1740's, the congregation kept growing, in part "because of emigration."[4] By 1758 there were "two houses of worship" in Carlisle, one Old Light and one New Light. First Church continued to prosper and subsequently provided leadership for the new denomination. The General Assembly met at "the Meeting House on the square" in Carlisle in 1792, 1795 and 1796. In 1796, the pastor of this well "established" congregation was elected Moderator of the General Assembly.[5]

Most of the congregations in the new denomination of 1788 were more like the early log meeting-houses in Pennsylvania. Presbyteries struggled to provide even minimal clergy services to meeting-house congregations dotting the countryside going west over the Appalachian Mountains and south down into the Shenandoah Valley.

---

[4]Allan D. Thompson, *The Meeting House on the Square*, 2d ed. (Shippensburg, 1984), 43.

[5]Wing, *History of the First Presbyterian Church*, 1-91.

Despite a geographically dispersed membership Philadelphia was an obvious choice for the meeting of the first General Assembly. It was within easy proximity of the geographical region where Presbyterian congregations had grown rapidly during the "awakenings" of 1739-1745. It had been the port of entry for continuing waves of Scotch-Irish emigrants from Ulster, the region of a settlement of Presbyterian Scots in Ireland. While it is difficult to estimate the Presbyterian population in Pennsylvania during the 18th century, there were at least three major emigrations of Presbyterians from northern Ireland. The first came in 1717 after rent policies made it difficult for poverty-stricken Presbyterian "dissenters" to find housing. One source estimates that from 1729 to 1750, between 6,000 and 12,000 Scotch-Irish came to America from Ulster each year.[6]

The first Presbytery is said to have been a "meeting of ministers" called by Francis Mackemie in Philadelphia in 1706. Presbyterians had not found New York hospitable. Mackemie was jailed in Long Island for preaching without a license in 1707. William Tennent farmed for about eight years in Bedford and East Chester, New York, before moving to the Philadelphia area in 1726. Apparently Tennent served congregations but was unable to make a living in this part of New York, fifty miles from New Haven.

In New Jersey one of the earliest Presbyterian meeting-houses was erected in Freehold. This congregation, eventually served by two sons of William Tennent, erected a building in 1705. Five natives of Scotland founded the congregation, then called and ordained a

---

[6]George Norcross, *The Centennial Memorial of the Presbytery of Carlisle* (Harrisburg: n.p., 1889), vol 1.

pastor in 1706. Conflicts over pastors from New
England and the location of the meeting-house continued
until 1730 when Walter Ker, an elder with Scottish
Covenanter roots, travelled to Neshaminy to recruit
John Tennent, third son of William Tennent.[7] When John
Tennent died in 1732, Freehold called William Tennent,
Jr., the second son of William Tennent, to be their
pastor.

William Tennent, his four sons who became pastors
and other "graduates" of the "Log-college" played a
major role in early Presbyterian history in Pennsylvania and New Jersey. They were leaders in early
Presbyteries and Synods; and above all, they were
evangelical preachers who saw the "awakenings" as an
act of God's grace, an outpouring of the Holy Spirit in
America. However, by 1788, the conflicts of Old
Side-New Side Presbyterians during the 1740's and 50's
belonged to an earlier period of Presbyterian history
in America.

Presbyterians in the United States tend to think
of themselves as Scottish in denominational ethnic
origin. In part this impression comes from the
prominent role played by John Witherspoon (1723-1794)
during the formation of the new nation, and later, of
the new denomination. He may have written a preface to
the Constitution of the Presbyterian Church in America.
Called from Edinburgh to serve as President of the
College of New Jersey, an institution chartered in 1747
for the purpose of educating pastors, Witherspoon did
not come to America until 1768. He belonged to the
first generation of leaders of the new denomination.

---

[7]Ned Landsman, "Revivalism and Nativism in the
Middle Colonies: The Great Awakening and the Scots
Community in East Jersey," *American Quarterly* 34
(1982): 155-56.

But his spirituality and temperament should not be
considered typical of the membership of the new
denomination.

                               II

     Although Scotland was the "mother-church" of the
settlers who came to Pennsylvania from Ulster, the
settlement of Ulster by Scottish Presbyterians began in
the early seventeenth century. Their identity as
Presbyterians had been forged in political circumstances different from those of the "mother-church" in
Scotland. That identity included a resentment against
the power and privilege of "the Churchmen," Anglican
priests of the religious establishment in England and
Ireland. Resentment against English political and
ecclesiastical power in Ireland smoldered for a hundred
years before the "Scotch-Irish"--also called "Ulster
Scots"--came to America from northern Ireland. Not all
of the emigrants who came to America from 1717 on had
lived in Ulster for a hundred years. But there was a
specifically Irish Presbyterian identity in William
Tennent who had been born and ordained in the Irish
Synod of Ulster.

     It is fairly well known that Witherspoon was
cajoled into leaving Edinburgh to come to America in
1768. For the most part, very few Scottish pastors had
any reason to leave Scotland. The Scottish Presbyterian Church had lived through two disestablishments
during the 17th century, times when Presbyterian
pastors were unemployed because Episcopal priests, the
Episcopal liturgy they despised, and kneeling at
communion were legally re-established. But the
Presbyterian Church had been the offically established
religion in Scotland since 1690. American Presbyterian
congregations continued to send to Ireland for pastors
up to the end of the 18th century. Fewer of them sent

to Scotland for pastors because so many congregations
included a majority of members who had emigrated from
Ireland.

The claim that the majority of Presbyterian clergy
in the 18th century were born in the colonies, "were of
English or Irish descent or migrated from Ireland,"
means that most of the pastoral leadership was not
coming from Scotland.[8] When the denomination was
formed in 1788 only the Synod of the Carolinas consisted primarily of Scottish settlers. North Carolina
was settled by migrations of Highlanders eager to
acquire land. The only American Presbytery known to
send to Scotland for ministers regularly was Charleston, South Carolina. In 1738, two-thirds of the
Presbyterian ministers in America had been educated
either at the University of Glasgow or at Yale.[9] The
others had studied at the University of Edinburgh or at
the Log-college founded by William Tennent at Neshaminy
in 1726.

Factual information about the membership of the
Philadelphia Synod of the early years is obscure and
sometimes contradictory. It seems that more members of
the Synod were educated at the University of Glasgow
before the influx of the first Scotch-Irish in 1717.
Mackemie, who came to America in 1681 as a missionary
from Ireland, had studied at the University of Glasgow.
One source reports that twelve of twenty-five pastors

---

[8]William A. Brock, *Scotus Americanus*, (Edinburgh: Edinburgh University Press, 1982), 101. There
was no formal Synod of Philadelphia until the late
1730's. Sometimes writers refer to "the Synod" when
they mean the Presbytery of Philadelphia. The lines
were not clearly drawn.

[9]Ibid.

in the Synod in 1709 had been educated at Glasgow.[10]
By 1716, the ethnic origins of 25 members of the Synod
were mixed. Membership included seven pastors from New
England, three from Wales, eight from Scotland and
seven from Ireland.[11] These figures are from the
period just before the beginning of the Scotch-Irish
migrations of 1717, before William Tennent became a
member of the Synod of Philadelphia in 1718, before
Tennent established the Log-college at Neshaminy in
1726, and before a Synod "Adopting Act" was needed in
1729 to resolve a conflict concerning what it meant to
"subscribe" to the Westminster documents.

III

Before the influx of Scotch-Irish into Pennsylvania and New Jersey in the 1730's there was already
concern about the ordination and discipline of clergy.
Leadership by "Log-college men" trained by Tennent and
an increase in clergy coming from Ireland further
complicated issues. In 1734 Gilbert Tennent asked the
Synod to recommend additional examination of candidates
for ministry and that persons participating in the
Lord's Supper be able to testify to "a work of sanctifying grace in their hearts."[12] His request reveals a
concern that all persons celebrating the sacrament do
so "worthily." The practice of examining persons, or
of self-examination, prior to reception of the
sacrament was known to Scottish and Scotch-Irish

---

[10]Ibid., 99.

[11]Leonard J. Trinterud, *The Forming of an
American Tradition: A Reexamination of Colonial
Presbyterianism* (Philadelphia: Westminster, 1949), 35.

[12]Guy Soulliard Klett, *Presbyterians in
Colonial Pennsylvania* (Philadelphia: University of
Pennsylvania Press, 1937), 142.

Presbyterians as "fencing the tables."[13]

Disagreements over the "awakenings" and preparation for ordination continued to accumulate until the
Synod voted to evict members of the Tennent-led New
Light Party in 1741. Historians often ascribe the
"turning of the tide" against the Tennents to the
revival preaching of George Whitefield and the "awakenings" of 1739[14]. The arrival of Whitefield in 1739 did
include a preaching tour that took him to Philadelphia,
Freehold and Neshaminy, but John Tennent had already
"reaped a harvest" at Freehold in 1730 which continued
there during the pastorate of his brother William.[15]
The Adopting Act of 1729 was qualified in 1736 due to
concern about "revivals" that year. After 1736
subscription to the Westminster documents in the Synod
of Philadelphia was no longer "discretionary"; it was
now considered binding.

A "revival" reported to have attracted 3,000
people to hear Whitefield at Neshaminy in 1739 was no
accidental gathering. The Tennent "harvests" were
conversions that occurred during celebrations of the
Scottish sacramental season. In Scotland these were
semi-annual festivals held by eight or nine congregations in a region for the purpose of celebrating the
Lord's Supper and for spiritual renewal. They were
usually held just before and just after the harvest.

John Tennent reaped his first harvest at Freehold

---

[13]George B. Burnet, *The Holy Communion in the
Reformed Church of Scotland* (Edinburgh: Oliver and
Boyd, 1960), 258-61.

[14]Sydney E. Ahlstrom, *A Religious History of
the American People* (New Haven: Yale University Press,
1972), 269-72. Ahlstrom follows the Trinterud interpretation of colonial Presbyterian history.

[15]Landsman, "Revivalism and Nativism," 156-57.

in April or May of 1730, four or five weeks after his
arrival there. His ability to draw together a con-
flicted congregation in so short a time reveals that he
and his Scottish Convenanter parishioners had a
powerful common bond. The Tennents from the Synod of
Ulster followed sacramental practices similar to those
of the Covenanters. Both viewed the field communion--a
part of the Scottish sacramental season--as an evangelistic medium.

By 1736 the evangelistic preaching of the Tennents
and other Log-college men was sufficiently disturbing
to members of the Synod that the ordination examination
questions asked of twenty-five year old Charles
Tennent, the youngest Tennent son, seem unusually
pointed. Synod members had always thought of William
Tennent as a non-conforming dissenter from Ireland; men
like him who remained in Ireland were accused of an
Arian heresy and formed their own New Light Presbytery
in Antrim in 1726. During his years of ministry in
northern Ireland before emigrating to America in 1718
Tennent had lived in Antrim and in Derry. It was in
Derry that field communions had flourished during the
first two decades of the eighteenth century.

The questions asked of Charles Tennent suggest
that he, too, was suspected of not believing in the
divinity of Christ. He was assigned an exegesis in
which he was to discuss (1) whether Christ was the only
savior of the world and (2) whether the babies of
believers should be baptized.[16]

The Tennents, it seemed, were more concerned with
converting "almost Christian" adults than they were in

---

[16]Thomas C. Pears, Jr. and Guy S. Klett, *A
Documentary History of William Tennent and the Log
College* (n.p.: Presbyterian Historical Society, 1940),
92-94.

the baptism of infants. In the 1730's members of
William Tennent's congregation at Neshaminy had
complained of irregularities in his baptism of "children."

Differences between the two Sides about practices
related to the sacramental season, preaching style and
baptism had erupted long before Whitefield's tour in
1739. Conflicts over methods of ministry were most
dramatic between the pastors of Scotch-Irish origins.
But the startling force of positive response to the
"revival" preaching of Whitefield was the occasion of a
clear joining of sides in 1740-41.

A sermon preached at Nottingham, Pennsylvania, by
Gilbert Tennent in 1740 amounted to a public accusation
that those who "protested" the "awakenings" were
unconverted ministers. He meant men like John Thompson
at Carlisle and John Elder of Paxtang. Elder came to
Pennsylvania from Scotland by way of Ireland. With his
family, he had moved to Antrim the year of the heresy
accusations and formation of the New Light Presbytery
there in 1726. Thompson was a native of Ireland who
was ordained and installed in four small congregations
including Carlisle in 1739. Tennent, who viewed their
opposition as evidence that they conducted "a graceless
ministry," felt strongly that the Synod was deliber-
ately persecuting his family and his father's students.

William Tennent and his three sons--Gilbert,
William, Jr. and Charles--withdrew from the Synod in
1741, accused of being "anti-Presbyterian non-conform-
ists" guilty of schism. Among other things it was said
that they did not consider Synod rules binding, only
advisory. Criticisms of their practices included
activities related to licensing and ordination of
candidates for ministry, engaging in itinerant preaching which had been outlawed, condemning ministers and

people in other congregations as "graceless" and
asserting that "the call of God does not consist in
regular ordination and being set apart to that work."[17]
For the most part they were guilty as charged, especially Gilbert.

The Tennents and a coalition of New Light men
stimulated by Whitefield's success formed their own
Conjunct Presbytery of New Brunswick and New London-
derry in 1741. In 1740 Gilbert Tennent had gone on a
preaching tour to Boston. After accepting the call to
become pastor of Second Church, Philadelphia in 1743 he
admitted that while "itinerating" in New England he had
conducted himself in the style of Whitefield. For a
time, he had engaged in "spontaneous" preaching and had
dressed in the less formal "Methodist" style with no
wig and no preaching gown.

In 1745 the Conjunct Presbytery joined the New
York Synod where they made common cause with third
generation New Englan Puritans who had a New Light
non-conformist spirit similar to their own. The New
Side was branded "New Light" as an epithet by the Old
Side; to the Old Side "New Light" suggested the Arian
heresy of the Antrim New Light party. The American
"New Lights" had a theology more like that of New
England Puritans than the theology of their Old Light
brethren from Ireland.

The New Side in America attributed regeneration to
the power of the Holy Spirit to illumine Scripture,
especially as that affected preaching.[18] Both "New
Light" groups, the Scotch-Irish and the English

---

[17]Ibid., 156.

[18]John Blair, "Observations on Regeneration,"
in *Tennent Sermon Book*, 1855, Speer Library Collection,
Princeton Theological Seminary, Princeton, NJ, 190.

Puritans, had a deep concern for regeneration. Both
believed that a work of God's grace in the heart should
lead to a life in which "works of the Spirit," or
sanctification, were discernible. Both groups believed
that persons who had been regenerated should be able to
testify to "a work of sanctifying grace in their
hearts." This was the issue Gilbert Tennent had raised
with the Synod in 1734 with which the Old Side disagreed.

The two groups that united to become the New York
Synod in 1745 agreed that the revivals were not "of the
devil, but of God." By this time, Gilbert Tennent had
repented of his own excess, especially in condemning
Old Side pastors as "graceless." The two New Light
groups each belonged to a "dissenting" minority since
both had interpreted the revivals as a challenge to the
complacency of an Old Side within judicatories where
other members shared their ethnic origins.

In spite of those differences, the New Light Synod
supported the activities of the Synod of Philadelphia
in seeking the charter granted to the College of New
Jersey in 1746. In an apparent gesture of broad
reconciliation of all parties to the Synod schism,
Gilbert Tennent went to London, Glasgow, the Scottish
General Assembly at Edinburgh, the General Synod in
Ulster and to the separated New Light Presbytery in
Antrim seeking financial support for the new College in
1753. That year he was elected the first Moderator of
the newly united Synod of Philadelphia and New York.

IV

By the time of the Synod schism during the
"awakening" in 1740, more pastors were coming from
Ireland. Even so, Scotch-Irish pastors did not
accompany the emigration of congregations as had been
the case in New England Puritan migrations. There were

many more Irish Presbyterian laity in the middle
colonies than there were pastors coming from Ireland.
Much of the opposition to the Tennents came from Old
Light pastors in Donegal Presbytery like Samuel
Thompson of Carlisle and John Elder of Paxtang. The
Donegal Presbytery consisted almost entirely of pastors
from Ireland, many of whom had been educated in
Scotland and ordained in Ireland. Records indicate
that of eleven pastors who served the Scotch-Irish
congregations at Paxtang, Derry and Carlisle--all near
Harrisburg--between 1730-1750, two were licensed in
Scotland, five were ordained in Ireland, three were
licensed and/or ordained in this country, while John
Roan was born in Ireland and educated at Neshaminy.[19]
Most if not all ordained pastors coming to America from
Ireland had been educated in Scotland because the Irish
Synod had never established its own center for theological education. The Irish Synod of Ulster sent
delegates to the Scottish General Assembly. It might
seem from these indications that the education and
ordination of pastors to serve in Ireland followed the
Reformed pattern of ordaining a theologically educated
candidate for ministry in the calling congregation. But
there were times when practices were irregular because
of distance from Scotland and internal Irish politics
affecting Presbyterians in the Synod of Ulster.

In his *History of the Presbyterian Church in
Ireland* published in 1867, James Reid says that before
"the Restoration" in 1689 there had been underground
academies for the training of pastors in Ireland. Like
other clandestine practices of Presbyterian religion in
Ireland in that period, the academies met in "meeting-

---

[19]Hubertis M. Cummings, *Scots Breed and
Susquehanna* (Pittsburgh: University of Pittsburgh
Press, 1964), 45.

houses." According to Reid, "they began to celebrate
the sacrament in their public assemblies . . . new
ministers were ordained by stealth in private houses,
and even two philosophy schools . . . were established
. . . for the education of intending ministers."[20] He
goes on to observe that the "conventicles"--clandestine
practices associated with the meeting-houses--flourish-
ed in Ireland between 1660 and 1690 but continued to
thrive after 1690 in spite of the restoration of a
Protestant to the throne of England. He reports that
there were many more "nonconformists"--meaning Presby-
terians--than Anglicans in Ulster and that the
Presbyterian churches continued to grow despite
persecution. In fact, in 1692 an observer reported
that ". . . the Presbyterian meetings are crowded with
thousands covering all the fields."[21] Between 1690 and
1711 thirty-two new meeting-houses were erected in
Ulster; between 1711 and 1720, seventeen more were
added.

In May of 1694 a Presbyterian minister responded
to an Anglican Bishop's complaints about Presbyterian
laxity, especially in their celebrations of the Lord's
Supper; at the same time he reiterated a historic list
of Presbyterian complaints against the Episcopal forms
of the established church, including "prelatical
government . . . a prescribed liturgy, with its
kneeling at the Lord's Supper, and the sign of the
cross in baptism."[22]

Presbyterians from England, Scotland and Ireland

---

[20]James Seaton Reid, *History of the Presbyterian Church in Ireland* (Belfast: William Mullen,
1867), 1:411.

[21]Ibid., 412.

[22]Ibid., 433.

had a common and almost irrational dislike of "prelatical government and a prescribed liturgy" that led in
time to the English Puritan Revolution and the subsequent writing of the Westminster documents in 1643.
But the Covenanter Scots from the Highlands--the
location of the most anti-establishment part of the
Scottish Presbyterian Church--had a spirituality more
like that of the Irish of the pre-restoration period
when "conventicles" flourished. The "field communions,"
known as sacramental seasons in Scotland, began as a
Covenanter protest against the Articles of Perth of
1617. The document was written by the King and
approved by a General Assembly packed with loyalist
delegates. Both the circumstances and the content of
the Articles galvanized the Covenanter spirit. The
first Article was most offensive to them; it rein-
stituted kneeling at communion.[23]

Kneeling at communion stood for everything the
Scottish Presbyterians associated with evil in the
Roman and Anglican Churches. Accounts of Presbyterian
communion services in America unfailingly ascribe "a
great solemnity" to the occasion. The solemnity
described has a history going back to the events of
1619 and the origins of the Scottish sacramental
occasion. Though Presbyterians in both Scotland and
Ireland disagreed over the frequency and form of
communion, those who carried the spirit of the Covenanters were more likely to sanction field communions and
to harbor anti-establishment sentiments about church
government.

---

[23]Bard Thompson, *Liturgies of the Western
Church* (Cleveland: William Collins, 1962), 346.

V

In the American setting, especially in Pennsylvania where the Scotch-Irish were so numerous, there
was no established church. Pastors who were Old Side
in America came from a moderate tradition in Scotland
and Ireland in which feelings about "episcopacy" were
less fierce. However, those who were "New Light"
evangelical protestors did not leave behind their
emotional attachment to a spirituality forged in the
experience of the Scottish sacramental season or their
history as non-conforming "dissenters." It was this
history and this spirituality that led William Tennent
and his "Log-college" men to see the "awakenings" in
Pennsylvania as an "outpouring of God's spirit."

In theory, all Scottish Presbyterians subscribed
to the doctrine of election found in the Westminster
Confession. In practice, when Presbyterianism became
the state church in Scotland, all citizens were
baptized into the Church as infants. At its best, the
sacramental season had encouraged evangelical preaching
intended to renew and test the commitments of Christians whose faith grew stale once Presbyterian religion
was established. The sacramental season was a time of
religious excitement accompanied by serious self-
examination on the part of participating laity and
clergy.

> This long history of sacramental revivals bespoke
> the power of the communion season to renew
> Presbyterian communities, to invigorate flagging
> saints and to transform flagrant sinners. Over
> the years the sacramental occasion had come to
> embody an evangelical synthesis of conversionist
> preaching and eucharistic practices. In the
> sacramental occasion the salvation of sinners was
> coupled with the confirmation of saints as
> complementary processes in the revivification of a
> community . . . . These sacramental revivals were
> never aimed simply at the unconverted; they were

for the whole community, churched and unchurched, sinners and saved.[24]

Once established, Presbyterian religion in Scotland became perfunctory in observance of both preaching and the sacraments. The Scotch-Irish who were "Old Lights" on the Pennsylvania frontier had the attitudes of the established "moderate" wing of the Scottish church. Some of them were censored by their Presbyteries in America for their failure to examine their members prior to the administration of the sacrament. That is, they were not "fencing the tables."

It was difficult to maintain traditional practices in the early years on the frontier, but the issues ran deeper than that. There were complaints sent by American Presbyteries to Irish Presbyteries concerning the caliber of clergy who emigrated. A fairly high proportion of those who came from Ireland were intensely orthodox in conviction concerning subscription to the Westminster Confession, but nearly devoid of vital piety. For that reason, historian Leonard Trinterud concluded that anyone who was a "New Light" from Ireland like William Tennant was highly unusual.[25] The most unusual aspect about Tennent was the importance he attached to spiritual self-discipline as compared to the importance attached to church law and polity by the Old Lights from Ireland. For whatever reasons,

---

[24]Leigh Eric Schmidt, *Scottish Communions and American Revivals: Evangelical Ritual, Sacramental Piety and Popular Festivity From the Reformation Through the Mid-Nineteenth Century* (Ph.D. diss., Princeton University, 1987), 87. This first full-length study of the importance of the sacramental season to religion in America was published by Princeton University Press in 1989.

[25]Trinterud, *Forming of an American Tradition*, 36 and 37.

Tennent came to America with an inclusive sacramental
piety more like that of the Covenanters from Scotland
than the exclusive communions of the New England
Puritans. During the early years in New England,
Puritans from England fenced the tables so severely
that at least half the congregation left before the
service of the Holy Supper.

At times the annual sacramental seasons in
Scotland and Ireland had been the focal celebrations of
the church year; but they also were as much folk custom
as a time for spiritual renewal, especially in Scotland. The festival had always been more popular in the
areas where it was most important to distinguish
Scottish Presbyterian culture from English Episcopalian
culture, namely in the northwest and in the border
regions.[26] For Scots without the intense anti-
episcopacy commitments of the Covenanters the festivals
reinforced national identity.

Presbyterians from Scotland and Ireland who became
Old Side in America partook of the laxity of the
established church in Scotland. The Old and New
"sides" of the debate--in Scotland, in Ireland and in
America--brought to the early eighteenth-century
revivals of religion a different interpretation of the
"awakenings," and a different understanding of ministry
and the role of pastors in the Christian tradition.
For New Side pastors like the Tennents, continuity in
the Church depended on the spiritual vitality and
discipline of all of the elect. According to Gilbert
Tennent, "the danger of an unconverted ministry" was
that members of God's elect would not recognize their
spiritual status because the dull doctrinal preaching
of "Pharisee-teachers" seemed to confirm the spiritual

---

[26]Landsman, "Revivalism and Nativism," 155.

complacency of their flock.[27]

The Tennents did not disdain the importance of theological education, a learned ministry or the need for discipline in the church, but they did consider all such "works of men's [sic] hands" secondary to the necessity of "a work of God's grace" in the heart. For people who took the doctrine of election seriously, all works of ministry were secondary to the activity of God's grace, especially as revealed through Scripture, as the source of right belief and right practice of ministry in the church.

When the tables were fenced in Scotland the terms of excommunication were abridgments of moral and civil law. There was no American equivalent to the connection between civil law and excommunication. When New Side evangelicals fenced the tables at a field communion in Pennsylvania, they bid their hearers to examine their hearts and, if need be, disqualify themselves from the table. Yet when Gilbert Tennent preached the "unsearchable riches of Christ" it was a sacramental sermon so reassuring about the power of God's grace that it is unlikely that many "sinners" disqualified themselves.[28]

VI

A letter in the Hutcheson collection in Glasgow

---

[27]H. Shelton Smith, Robert T. Handy, and Lefferts A. Loetscher, *American Christianity* (New York: Charles Scribner's Sons, 1960), 1:326.

[28]Gilbert Tennent, "The Unsearchable Riches of Christ," August 1739, Speer Library Collection, Princeton Theological Seminary, Princeton, NJ. Tennent preached two sermons under this title in August, 1739. In the first he describes sanctification as impossible without God's grace and "the duty and privilege of gospel ministers to preach the unsearchable riches of Christ." In the second, surely a fencing sermon, Tennent preaches "the duty of self-examination."

indicates that in 1746 a Presbytery in Pennsylvania
wrote to Francis Hutcheson, then professor of Moral
Philosophy at Glasgow, asking for "proper ministers and
books." The writer was Old Light Francis Alison. He
complained that the preaching of Whitefield encouraged
a contempt for books, and lamented the present "wretched contention."[29]

The "wretched contention" was the Old Side-New
Side dispute over issues provoked by the preaching
tours of George Whitefield. Historians have disagreed
as to the primary area of conflict. Some have said it
was Tennents's Log-college and theological education,
others that it was polity issues and the power of the
Presbytery, and still others that the dispute was
primarily a theological dispute over how to interpret
the "awakenings."[30] Recent historical reconstruction
places much more emphasis on ethnic origins. Each
aspect of the dispute appears in some form in the
minutes of Presbyteries and the Synod at the time. But
no single interpretation of the differences does
justice to the range of issues apparent in existing
written records.

The standard work on Presbyterian history in the
United States is *The Forming of an American Tradition:*

---

[29]*Brock, Scotus Americanus,* 100.

[30]Archibald Alexander, in *The Log College*
(Princeton: J. T. Robinson, 1845), said that the
"awakenings" were not the issue but that pastors from
Ireland were not reliable and of a different spirit
than the New England party. Richard Webster (*A History
of the Presbyterian Church in America, From Its Origin
until the Year 1760, with Biographical Sketches of Its
Early Ministers* [Philadelphia: Wilson, 1856]) said that
the primary conflict was the interpretation of the
"awakenings." Guy Soulliard Klett (*Presbyterians in
Colonial Pennsylvania* [Philadelphia: University of
Pennsylvania Press, 1937]) says the schism was about
principles, practices and methods and not doctrine.

A Reexamination of Colonial Presbyterianism, first
published in 1949. Historian Leonard Trinterud gives
primary consideration to the role played by the
Tennents and the Log-college in creating a balance of
polity and theology that "saved the doctrine and ethics
of the church" during the controversy over subscription
to the Westminster documents in 1729.[31] In Trinterud's
accounting of events, the Tennents brought together
divergent views of the Subscriptionists and a non-
subscriptionist New England group led by Jonathan
Dickinson. This led, in time, to a new theological
synthesis. According to this narrative of the events
leading to schism and reunion in the Synod, Whitefield
appeared as if from out of nowhere, changed everything
and harvested the labors of William Tennent.

According to the Trinterud scenario the genius of
American Presbyterians was forged in the union of the
Log-College Presbytery and New York Presbytery in 1745
to form the Synod of New York. New Brunswick Pres-
bytery--also called the Log-College Presbytery because
of the dominance of leadership there by the Tennents-
-was expelled from the Philadelphia Synod in 1740.
This "genius" consists of the marriage of an English
Puritan piety found in William Tennent and his students
to a piety similar to that of the second and third
generation New England Puritans who were members of the
New York Presbytery.

In William Tennent, that very unusual man from
Ulster, Trinterud saw evidence of a piety like that of
the New England Puritans. On these grounds he concluded that New York Synod represented the best outcome
of the "Great Awakening" in New England and the Middle

---

[31]Trinterud, *Forming of an American Tradition*,
75.

Colonies. Because of a consistent use of Presbyterian
"discipline and order," the Synod of New York was able
to combat excess through better supervision of clergy
and congregations, honest and "sincere" discipline of
clergy by unsurpassed missionary zeal, patient and
thorough doctrinal exposition.[32]

In the synthesis described by Trinterud the New
Siders prevail and emerge as leaders of the new
denomination in 1788. According to him, they were as
"orthodox" as the Old Side but included practical piety
in their "orthodoxy." He writes that in drafting their
own Constitution the Americans included "a weak
Directory of Worship discouraging the use of forms, the
Westminster Confession and the Catechisms with minor
changes." The theological position of Witherspoon in
articulating this new "practical but orthodox piety" is
described as aligned with the New Side but cool to New
England "New Divinity."

By 1788 "New Divinity" meant the "New England
theology" of Jonathan Edwards (1703-1758) then being
rewritten by men who had been trained in Edwards' home
before matriculating at Yale. The theology of Edwards'
students, eschewed by Witherspoon, included an emphasis
on divine sovereignty and predestination, and an
insistence on regeneration of clergy. The New England
theology to which Witherspoon was "cool" was the
position of the Tennent New Light party that formed the
Synod in 1745. The Trinterud account fails to explain
the connection between a New Light victory of 1745 that
makes them leaders of the denomination in 1788 and a
decidedly Old Light position in the attitudes of
Witherspoon who shared neither their history nor their
spirituality.

---

[32]Ibid., 120-23.

VII

In fact, those who emerged as the leaders of the
new denomination in 1788 were men who were educators
like Witherspoon or pastors of a prestigious and
established church like Dr. Davidson at Carlisle. This
congregation, the site of three General Assembly
meetings in the 1790's, had been served by New Sider
George Duffield from 1759 to 1772.[33] In 1785 the Old
Side and New Side congregations that had split in 1758
came together again under the ministry of Dr. Davidson.
A man known for enthusiastic patriotism, Davidson was
elected moderator of the General Assembly in 1796.
Between 1785 and 1812 Dr. Davidson received 330 new
members by "profession of faith."[34]

There is no clearer sign that a new era had dawned
than the information that members were joining on
"profession of faith." Once the revivals peaked in
1745 pastors could not afford the luxury of examining
members for evidence of sanctification preparatory to
participation in the Lord's Supper. Gilbert Tennent
had relaxed his own practice of examining for a "work
of grace in the heart" in his Philadelphia congregation
by 1745. He required only that participants understand
the principle of regeneration. As Tennent became a
member of the informal church establishment, he too
began to practice a less spiritually rigorous standard
for communicant members.

The leaders of the new denomination were not
typical of the 420 congregations, most of which were
not growing, prosperous city or town churches. The
Directory included in the Constitution of the new

---

[33]Wing, *History of the First Presbyterian
Church*, 105.

[34]Thompson, *Meeting House*, 43.

church was drafted by the Rev. Drs. John Rodgers and
MacWhorter, and the Rev. Messrs. Alexander Miller and
James Wilson. "The whole appeared in 1787, in the
shape of a pamphlet of one hundred and forty-five
pages; of which, the copy we have consulted is,
perhaps, the only one extant."[35] Contrary to
Trinterud's impression that a "weak American Directory"
was adopted as part of the new Constitution, C. W.
Baird, a nineteenth-century pastor, says that the
Directory was voted down.

That means that the Constitution of the new Church
consisted of the Westminster Confession, Catechism and
Directory, with minor changes made regarding only civil
government and magistrates. The sacramental season and
field communions of Scotland and Ireland were not
mentioned in the Westminster Directory which recommended only "due preparation . . . that all may come
better prepared to the heavenly feast."[36]

A pastoral letter circulated with the American
Directory in the Synod of the Carolinas suggests why
that Directory was voted down. The authors of the
pastoral letter use great tact in recommending that
recipients give careful and prayerful attention to the
recommendation of "the Westminster Directory and ours"
that "the Lord's Supper be administered with more
frequency, and fewer public exercises." They point out
that

> your mistake arises from comparing the churches in
> Scotland and Ireland with the churches in America,
> without comparing their different circumstances;
> and the clergy in those countries complain that
> the multiplicity of exercises destroys the
> frequent administration there, notwithstanding the

---

[35][Baird], *Eutaxia*, 229.

[36]Thompson, *Liturgies of the Western Church*, 368.

number of administrators.[37]

The argument advanced by writers of the American Directory in supporting the Westminster Directory on this subject was the impracticality of the Scottish sacramental season. "In some parts of Scotland" this included "three sermons on a fasting day: two action-sermons, a thanksgiving sermon on the evening, and two on Monday. But is all this necessary to the right administration of the ordinance?"[38]

In its place they recommended that the American Presbyterian Church do what had never been standard practice in Scotland and Ireland--follow the directions of the Westminster Directory concerning the administration of the sacrament. That included "a preparatory sermon some time in the preceding week, and one on the morning of the day on which the ordinance is to be administered." Presumably, the preparatory sermon included the fencing of the table and the distribution of communion tokens to all who qualified to partake.

From the apologetic tone of the pastoral letter it is obvious that the writers did not expect their Scottish Covenanter constituency to be impressed with the recommendation concerning communion practices. The more urbane writers of the Directory failed to account for the power of an identity associated with the sacramental season by Covenanters in the Carolinas and by a large Scotch-Irish constituency in Pennsylvania.

Baird reveals another reason for the failure of the American Directory. It contained samples of

---

[37]Pastoral Letter to the Synod of the Carolinas, ca. 1789, Library of the University of North Carolina, Chapel Hill, NC. I am indebted to David Caliri for transcribing the copy of the letter that I am citing.

[38]Ibid.

prayers rather than the "recipe" formula of the
Westminster Directory, "specimens of what these
services ought to be, rather than descriptions of the
mode of making them."[39] That alone could account for a
negative response from Scotch-Irish and Scottish
settlers and their descendents who continued to
populate small log meeting-houses on the frontiers of
Pennsylvania, Ohio, Virginia and the Carolinas. They
had a long memory. As long as the meeting-house was
the "church" in those areas, the sacramental season
continued. As the people gathered year in and year out
they remembered their identity, their own historic
Presbyterian celebration of the sacrament. In so doing
they continued to be "dissenters" who knew that
Presbyterians were not Episcopalians and did not
worship like Episcopalians.

It seems likely that the sacramental season
continued in all but urban areas through the end of the
eighteenth century. A history of the churches of
western Pennsylvania published in 1854 indicates that
the practice "is now, to a great extent, discontinued."
Even then the tone of the observation was defensive, as
members of the more moderate Old Side had always been
defensive about their concern with the excesses of the
sacramental season. Smith writes:

> The practice of distributing tokens to com-
> municants on Saturday or Sabbath morning, previous
> to the communion service, universally prevailed,
> and was, no doubt, introduced into this country
> from Scotland and the north of Ireland. When at
> our early sacraments, so large a proportion of
> intending communicants were from surrounding
> churches, it seemed a highly proper custom . . . .
> We are familiar with all that has been alleged in
> its defence. We are aware of the circumstances
> which seemed to render it necessary in early

---

[39][Baird], *Eutaxia*, Chapter XIII, "The Directory of Worship Revised."

times. But even then, the evils, at least the
embarrassing inconveniences, sometimes resulting
from it, might well have raised the question
whether they did not outweigh any good that was
secured.[40]

The Presbyterian Church in America gradually
became informally established. Just as Old Side
pastors from Ireland had been lax in their practices
like Anglican clergy in the established Church in
Ireland, their counterparts in America began to follow
the practices of an established Church. They baptized
anyone who requested baptism. Members joined on
"profession of faith." They did not expect the
sacramental season to be an awakening. But, until that
time when the sacramental season was truly impractical,
Presbyterians in America could count on regular times
of spiritual renewal each year. As the practices of
the sacramental season died out, Presbyterians in
America began to follow the observance of the Lord's
Supper recommended in the Westminster Directory. In so
doing they became more orthodox than their ancestors
who came from Scotland and Ireland, for "the Scots
never followed the Directory anyway."[41]

---

[40]Joseph Smith, *Old Redstone, or Historical
Sketches of Western Presbyterianism, its Early Minis-
ters, its Perilous Times, and its First Records*
(Philadelphia: Lippincott, Grambo, 1854), 160.

[41]Comment made by Bard Thompson in a conversation about this research. I am deeply indebted to him
for encouraging me in the early stages of this research.

DREW THEOLOGICAL SEMINARY
AND AMERICAN METHODISM:
SOME HISTORICAL REFLECTIONS

Russell E. Richey

If one reads the national paper for the Methodist
Episcopal Church, the *Christian Advocate* (New York),
for the years prior to unification in 1939, one cannot
but be struck with the prominence of Drew Theological
Seminary in the life of Methodism. Methodism's paper
kept Drew in the limelight and cast Drew as the
national seminary. To find such pretension at Drew and
in Drew's histories is, perhaps, not that surprising,
for all the Methodist seminaries strove for eminence.
But the *Christian Adovcate* (New York) claimed as much
for Drew as Drew did for itself. Some Drew story
appeared about every other week.[1] The *Advocate*
reported regularly on the opening and closing of
school, special lectures, the annual inspection and
report of a special multi-conference visiting committee, actions of the Board of Trustees, itinerations and

---

[1]For easy confirmation of this, see the
cardfile of references to Drew carefully assembled by
Drew's archivist, Rae Jones. To illustrate, in 1867
there were 12 references; in 1872, 10; in 1877, 8; in
1882, 17; in 1887, 27; in 1892, 25; in 1897, 20; in
1902, 28; in 1907, 22; in 1912, 22; in 1917, 35; in
1922, 20; in 1927, 41; and in 1932, 35. Thanks are due
to Jones and also the staff of the Archives Center for
assistance in the research for this essay.

publications of Drew faculty, the financial needs of
the school, and its several largely unsuccessful
campaigns. Special celebrations like the 50th anniversary warranted a cover story, with Drew pictures on the
cover and reminiscences from a representative of each
decade of Drew students.[2] Ten years later the paper
modestly reported that over the years Drew had trained
11 bishops, 8 seminary presidents, 55 college presidents, 240 district superintendents, 45 editors of
church publications, 26 presidents of preparatory
schools, 13 seminary deans, 60 school principals, 302
professors or teachers, 249 missionaries and 2509 MEC
pastors, plus 417 pastors of other denominations.[3]
Such triumphalism, which we are happy to report was
uncommon, illustrated both Drew's aspirations and the
receptivity of the *Christian Advocate* to them. We
cannot follow that collusion in detail, but we can look
briefly at a few individuals who illustrate Drew's
place in the life of Methodism.

I will not consider at length why no school, not
Drew or any other United Methodist seminary, claims the
prominence once accorded Drew. That would require
another study altogether, but several factors would
bear investigation. First, the 1939 unification had
quite ironic results. Although it re-established a
national church, it did so by regionalizing the whole.
Seminaries became jurisdictional turf. Second, the
waning of the New York *Christian Advocate* cost Drew
dearly. Its editors had enjoyed a close relationship

[2] *Christian Advocate* [New York] (October 25,
1917): 1007, 1112-13.

[3] *Christian Advocate* [New York] (November 3,
1927): 1333. Compare the tabulation made from 1869 to
1942 in *The Teachers of Drew, 1867-1942*, ed. James R.
Joy (Madison: Drew University, 1942), 35.

with the school. James M. Buckley, editor from 1880 to
1912, retired to the Drew faculty. James R. Joy, editor
from 1915 to 1936, served continuously on the board of
trustees and drew upon his familiarity with Drew to
edit a volume entitled *The Teachers of Drew, 1867-
1942.*[4] Not surprisingly, these long-term editors gave
Drew special attention. Third, Drew went through a
period in the middle decades of this century during
which it sought distance from the Church. That period
and policy ended with what is commonly known there as
the Crisis, at which point the school was virtually
dismantled. As Drew once again reclaims a national
mission, we need to turn to its earlier history for a
proper understanding. At any rate, I focus on Drew's
public image as one way of illustrating what Drew has
wanted to be.

I

Even before its establishment, Drew, in a sense,
had a place in the life of the Church, for its founding
culminated a national debate on theological education.
Should Methodist preachers educate themselves while in
saddle or should they avail themselves of a formal
theological education akin to that offered clergy of
other denominations? Two who spoke for an educated

---

[4]In his prefatory editorial note, Joy observed,
"Though a layman, and neither an alumnus nor a teacher
of Drew, he has known with varying degrees of intimacy
five of the six presidents of the Seminary--all except
the first. He has been acquainted with a majority of
the professors, several of whom have admitted him to
their inner circle of friends. Most of the pastors of
the church of which he has been a member for half a
century have had their training here. Moreover, he has
had such familiarity with the affairs and personnel of
the institution as is afforded by membership for 27
years in the Board of Trustees. To have been selected
to edit this Commemorative Volume was a surprise to
him, though not unwelcome." See *The Teachers of Drew*,
xii-xiii.

ministry later shaped theological education at Drew.
One was James Strong, who would be professor of
exegetical theology from 1868 to 1894. Editor (with
Drew's first president John McClintock) of the multi-
volume *Cyclopedia of Biblical, Theological, and
Ecclesiastical Literature*, compiler of an *Exhaustive
Concordance of the Bible*, and author of numerous other
exegetical works, Strong precipitated an epistolary
debate in the columns of the *Christian Advocate* with an
article in 1853 prophetically entitled "A Central
Theological Seminary."[5]

Two years later Randolph S. Foster echoed Strong's
call for an educated ministry. In a sermon before the
New York East Conference, Foster defended two propositions: (1) The Church needs a thoroughly-educated and
liberally informed ministry; and (2) Methodism needs a
more spiritual and consecrated ministry. In his
concluding section, Foster endeavored to hold these two
together:

> Vain were learning without spirituality and
> consecration . . . . We want prophets of the
> closet as well as the study. . . . We must have
> it: culture and zeal, light and heat, mind and
> heart! Blended they will give us power with men
> and power with God, and we shall prevail.
> Deprived of them, we shall sink down, down, down
> in weakness and imbecility, until not a historic
> vestige will be left of a people who might have
> been great for God in the earth.

However, the stress of his remarks fell on education.
He said of Methodism:

> That an educated and informed people will require
> a better educated and informed ministry, we hold
> to be axiomatic. A teacher must be competent for

---

[5]*Christian Advocate* [New York] (December 22,
1853): 201. The article occupied the lead column and
extended over half the first (folio) page. See
discussion in John T. Cunningham, *University in the
Forest* (n.p.: Afton, 1972), 20-22.

his work, or he will not, *he ought not* to be
heard. He will first be commiserated, then
endured, finally despised. Even really unimpor-
tant defects, if glaring and inexcusable, must
excite disgust and aversion. The same people
begotten by his ministry, and nourished in their
infancy, should they become superior in breadth of
information and aesthetic culture, will no longer
listen to him except by sufferance. Why should
they? Will a man sit as learner at the feet of a
child? Will he, *can he* become the docile listener
at the lips of one he knows to be his inferior?
Whose ignorance shames, and whose inabilities
offend him? Will he, especially when, without
serious compromise of feeling or principle, he can
supply himself and family with the instruction and
entertainment which they crave, but which their
teacher cannot furnish? The supposition is
preposterous.[6]

Soon after Drew's opening, Foster joined the faculty as
professor of systematic theology. He came to that
position from a succession of eminent pulpits in Ohio
and New York and with prior educational experience as
president of Northwestern University. On McClintock's
death, Foster succeeded as president, but he gave Drew
only three years of leadership. Like his successor,
John Fletcher Hurst, and more recently President Fred
Garrigus Holloway and Dean James M. Ault, Foster
stepped from Drew to the episcopacy.

These champions of an educated ministry brought
Drew into being and made Drew a national pulpit.
Before, during and after Drew careers, they helped to
define the needs of the church.

II

Some persons brought a national audience to Drew.
Others stepped from Drew onto a national stage. One
such person was Henry G. Appenzeller. Just over a

---

[6]Randolph S. Foster, *A Treatise on the Need of
the M. E. Church with Respect to Her Ministry* (New
York: Carlton & Phillips, 1855), 13, 27-28, 54, 55,
59-60.

hundred years ago, Appenzeller completed his
ministerial studies at Drew and left to inaugurate
Methodist missions to Korea. The community appreciat-
ing the significance of his endeavor accompanied him to
the train station en masse. A year later, the Drew
student body registered its continuing interest by
asking Appenzeller for a report. At that juncture a
toehold seemed a lot. He reported that he had opened
his school with one student and now had 28 Koreans and
3 Japanese, and that he served a congregation composed
entirely of "the foreign Christans living here" which
met in his house.[7] Fifteen years later the small
toeholds had yielded significant educational, medical
and evangelistic enterprises. In early 1901 Appenzeller addressed the Philadelphia Preachers' Meeting in
an effort to gain financial support for the developing
work. This speech will support much of our prejudice
about missions. The flag and the cross, the gun boat
and the ark, military presence and Christian presence
landed together. Appenzeller did not apologize for
that collaboration, and yet his remarks do not evince a
conquering spirit but rather deep affection and respect
for Korea and things Korean. He described Korean
society, industry, politics, culture, religion, flora,
and geography with the clear intention of gaining the
high regard of the Philadelphia preachers for that
distant society. We illustrate that with his remarks
about the importance of poetry to Koreans:

> The Korean is a child of nature and loves her
> ways. He loves poetry and in the spring time,
> when in other countries a young man's thoughts

---

[7]Henry Appenzeller to H. L. Jacobs, November
19, 1886, Appenzeller papers (11/324, 11-19-86).
(Courtesy of Daniel Davies, who completed a disserta-
tion on Appenzeller and is currently at work on a
larger study of Appenzeller.)

turn lightly to love, the Korean youth with paper,
brush and inkstone seeks some cool sequestered
vale and there, under the inspiration of the
bursting bud and opening flower, gives expression
to the finer sentiments of the soul.

Throughout this speech, sometimes explicitly, more
often implicitly, Appenzeller depicted missions as a
hermeneutic--interpreting Korea for Americans, interpreting Western culture to Koreans, and in the context
of these two exchanges attempting to interpret Scripture. He said:

We went there to convert the people but we had not
gone very far when we found we had to convert the
language as well. There were no scriptures in the
vernacular we could use; no tracts we could
distribute. In fact we found few Koreans sufficiently well acquainted with their own tongue to
be acceptable as personal teachers. As, however,
the wise teacher starts from the known and leads
to the unknown so we took what we had to secure
what we wanted. We have been at this for fifteen
years and are still pursuing. Medical work was
begun by treating the first sick man who came
along and school was opened by teaching the first
Korean who applied.[8]

That spirit and that concern to mediate between the two
cultures gave Appenzeller, and through him, Drew, a
place in the founding of Korean Protestantism.

III

In this study I am not concerned to assess the
impact of Drew on its denomination, although that would
be a far more instructive approach. Rather, I have
focused on Drew's visibility. Had we taken the former
tack, we would certainly want to give considerable
attention to Drew's role in the shaping of Methodist

---

[8]Papers of Henry G. Appenzeller, Union Theological Seminary, #155, Reel 3, "Korea: The Field, Our
Work and Our Opportunity" (pp. 6 and 21). Paper read
by Appenzeller before the Philadelphia Preachers'
Meeting January 21, 1901, and published by request of
that body. We have not found the published version of
this text.

theology. Persons with no Drew connection have
recognized it as substantial. Robert E. Chiles charts
three major shifts in Wesleyan theology, from Wesley to
Watson, from Watson to Miley, and from Miley to
Knudson.[9] The middle, transitional figure, John Miley,
taught systematics at Drew from 1873 until his death in
1895. Thomas Langford cuts a wider swath through the
theological thicket and among the two dozen American
figures included, discusses the following Drew theologians: John Miley, Olin Curtis, John Alfred Faulkner,
Edwin Lewis, Carl Michalson and Thomas C. Oden.[10]

We gain some sense of Drew's on-going national
theological role by focusing on one moment, when
theological controversy swept Drew into national
exposure. Methodism's fundamentalism-modernism episode
seemed, for a time, to be a family affair. The
principals, Drew grads all, were Harold Paul Sloan of
the New Jersey Conference, his student days' contemporary at Drew, Edwin Lewis, and Lewis' elder colleague
in theology, John Alfred Faulkner. Faulkner's public
role was largly passive. By his beliefs, publications
and statements, he exemplified fidelity to the Wesleyan
heritage. Sloan played the accuser. A delegate to the
1920 General Conference (and to successive general
conferences until his election in 1936 to the editor-
ship of the *Christian Advocate*), Sloan led a campaign
to rid Methodism of modernism. His effort focused
initially on the Course of Study, but over the years
generalized to other vehicles of Methodist perfidy. In

---

[9]Robert E. Chiles, *Theological Transition in
American Methodism: 1790-1935* (New York: Abingdon, 1965).

[10]Thomas A. Langford, *Practical Divinity:
Theology in the Wesleyan Tradition* (Nashville: Abing-
don, 1983). Faulkner is discussed under "An Intruding
Voice" and Lewis under "A Manifesto."

1922 Lewis published an article in the *Methodist
Quarterly Review* on "The Problem of the Person of
Christ." Sloan engineered its condemnation by the
Methodist Episcopal Preachers' Meeting of Philadelphia,
which by formal resolution, published in the *Christian
Advocate*, regretted the teaching, protested its
publication in a Methodist journal and implored the
Seminary administration that "the objectionable
teaching . . . not be repeated in the classroom as a
part of the instruction given to our theological
students."[11] In the mid-20's Sloan participated in the
founding of the Methodist League for Faith and Life of
which he became president. He edited and wrote
extensively for its journal, initially entitled *The
Call to the Colors*, and later *The Essentialist*. By
this point Lewis' book, *Jesus Christ and the Human
Quest*, had appeared. Sloan increasingly turned his
guns toward this volume. In the letter announcing the
new organization and addressed to "Fellow Methodists,
Believers in the common Christianity of the centuries,"
Sloan alerted the church to the unitarian infection in
"the educational institutions of Methodism." Under the
bold heading "And Now Some Facts if You Have the
Courage to Face Them," Sloan began:

> Professor Lewis of Drew is denying the incarnation
> in any real sense. He reduces Jesus to an
> extraordinary human being, who by moral decisions
> and with supernatural help achieved progressively
> and at death completely a full divine point of
> view. Dr. Lewis denies personal pre-existence to
> Jesus, and says that the Incarnation by the
> instantaneous transfer of a separate divine
> self-consciousness to human conditions is philo-
> sophically impossible. . . . Professor Rall of
> Garrett is teaching that Jesus made mistakes even

---

[11]*Christian Advocate* [New York] (March 15,
1923): 336. The issue also carried a letter by Lewis
to the Preachers' Meeting defending his beliefs.

with respect to His religious message and expectations. . . . Both of these men deal haltingly with the Virgin Birth. . . . Both of these men exclude the propitiatory significance of the cross of Christ.[12]

In May and November 1927, the Methodist League formally addressed the Board of Bishops, calling its "attention specifically to the defiance of the law and order of the Church now going on in the Department of Systematic Thelogy at Drew Theological Seminary." The League continued:

We are objecting to the teaching of Professor Edwin Lewis of Drew Theological Seminary as contravening both the second and twentieth of our Articles. . . . We would say, in conclusion, that, as its chief spiritual leaders, the Church has a right to expect you to handle energetically this most serious situation.[13]

Although it got no satisfaction from the bishops, the League kept up its attack on Lewis. He was the recurrent target in the six volumes of *The Essentialist*.[14] The heat proved sufficient that the senior

---

[12]Drew University Archives, Drew University, Madison, NJ. Also reproduced in *The Call to the Colors* (June 1926).

[13]*The Essentialist* 3 (November 1927): 166. The journal also reprinted the bishops' terse response which acknowledged the receipt of the League's letter and the bishops' instruction to its secretary to reply saying: "The Bishops are relieved from the duty of investigating and reporting upon charges of erroneous teachings in our Theological Seminaries" (p. 167).

[14]For other attacks on Lewis see following volumes of *The Essentialist*: vol. 2 (February 1927), 193; vol. 3 (July-August 1927), 89-90 and 97; (September 1927), 115-16; (November 1927), 165 and 166-69; (December 1927), 187-89 and 171-94; (January 1928), 224-29; (February 1928), 24-52 and 252-55; vol. 4 (April May, 1928), 3-5, 8-10, 27-28 and 30; vol. 5 (June-July 1929), 56-60; (March 1930), 225 and 248; vol. 6 (May 1930), 34-43. Frederick A. Norwood (*The Story of American Methodism* [Nashville: Abingdon,

class felt impelled to express its appreciation,
confidence and endorsement for Lewis' precept and
example.[15] The League mounted a major campaign against
modernism for the 1928 General Conference. While it
reiterated the charges against Lewis, it surrounded
them with other instances of Methodist infidelity. A
similar diffusion followed that effort and consequent
reassessment. The outcome was the merger of the
League's journal with the *Bible Champion* to form
Christian Faith and Life, an interdenominational
conservative venture. Sloan, who became editor-
in-chief of the new venture, could no longer concentrate on Methodist heresy, and the attacks on Lewis
abated.

But the saga's real end came in 1934 when Lewis
published his own repudiation of modernism, *Christan
Manifesto*. Among the many letters of appreciation
Lewis received was one penned by Harold Paul Sloan, who
wrote:

> I have been thinking of our past relations, or
> mis-relations. I have been thinking with that
> humility with which the Christian man must so
> often, perhaps always, think. I am wondering if in
> your heart there is still any misunderstanding
> between us? What you have affirmed in your
> "manifesto" is what I have striven to hold. What
> you have described as Modernism is what I have
> seen it. Whatever differences in the detail of our
> faith may still exist they do not lie between us
> in my heart or bearing. I honor you as a chosen
> instrument of Christ, and again and again thank

1974], 383) perhaps understandably feels more keenly
the attacks on Garrett's Harris Franklin Rall. William
J. McCutcheon ("American Methodist Thought and Theology, 1919-60," in *The History of American Methodism*,
ed. Emory Stevens Bucke, 3 vols. [New York: Abingdon,
1964], 3:272) concurs with the judgment made here that
Rall and Lewis "bore the main brunt" of Sloan's charges.

[15]Edwin Lewis Papers, 1928 file, Drew University Archives, Drew University, Madison, NJ.

Him for you and your splendid ministry. . . . I
am to be at Drew on the 13th of November, and will
hope at that time to hear you in your class
room.[16]

Early the next year Sloan published a review of Lewis'
book in *Christian Faith and Life*. He began:

Here is a significant book indeed. It is a book
that marks the end of an epoch and the beginning
of an epoch. As with the writings of the Reformation, so here again there is a consciousness of
turning back to the New Testament. There was in
the first century a spring of truth that is
abidingly creative. Professor Lewis is conscious
of this value, and in *A Christian Manifesto* he
lifts it up into new emphasis; yet he measures it
by all the canons of truth that are current in
this modern world.[17]

As Sloan indicated with this olive branch, a tumultous
epoch in Drew's theological leadership of Methodism
came to a close. And as Sloan rightly foresaw, Lewis
played his part in the beginning of another theological
epoch. He would exercise considerable influence as
Drew's actor in the Neo-orthodox drama.

IV

Not all sectors of Drew's national audience had
easy access to the columns of the *Christian Advocate*.
One such audience was the Black membership of the
Methodist Episcopal Church. Drew had apparently always
welcomed Black students. Two finished with the class
of 1889.[18] However, the person who added a warm
embrace to the open door was a white professor of rural

---

[16]Edwin Lewis Papers, 1934 file, Drew University Archives, Madison, NJ. This letter was one of two
with the same date, probably sent under the same cover,
one typed, the other hand-written. The correspondence
between Lewis and Sloan was quite extensive.

[17]Harold Paul Sloan, "*A Christian Manifesto*
Appreciated," *Christian Faith and Life* 41 (January
1935): 76-78.

[18]Cunningham, *University in the Forest*, 118.

sociology who taught at Drew from 1930 to the eve of
the civil rights movement. Ralph A. Felton was a
hands-on student of the rural church. A small sampling
of his writings gives us the flavor of his concern:
The Home of the Rural Pastor, 1948; *The Church and the
Land*, 1947; *Cooperative Churches*, 1947; *The Salary of
Rural Pastors*, 1946; *The Church Farm*, 1946; *A Hundred
Games for Rural Communities*, 1947. He scattered
articles over journals dedicated to rural life. When
Dean Clarence Tucker Craig wrote in 1952 to ask him for
a list, Felton replied, "In regard to periodicals I
will say that I have not kept any record of these that
I have written over past years. . . . About the best
that I can do is to give you those which I have written
since July 1, 1950."[19]

His passion for rural church development which
dated from seminary days and informed his whole career
took him to Cuba, Mexico, Korea and Japan as visiting
professor or consultant. From 1936 to 1938 he was
loaned to Nanking Union Theological Seminary in China.

But perhaps his most enduring contribution was
made to the leadership development of the Black
churches of the rural South. Publications toward the
end of his career signal that concern--*These My
Brethren: A Study of 570 Negro Churches* (1950) and *Go
Down Moses: A Study of Successful Negro Pastors* (1951).
An even better indicator is the fact that Harry V.
Richardson, then president of Gammon and author of the
standard history of Black Methodism, was asked to write

---

[19]Ralph A. Felton to Clarence Tucker Craig,
Felton file, Drew University Archives. The *Festschrift*
issue of *The Drew Gateway* (22 [Summer 1952]) contains,
therefore, only a partial list of Felton's writings and
suppresses one on Felton's manuscript list that I
rather liked, *The Church Bus*.

the biographical tribute on Felton's retirement.[20]
Richardson, who dedicated his first book to Felton,
said:

> In 1943 the writer went to Drew to study under
> Ralph A. Felton. I was interested in the rural
> church among Negroes, especially the church among
> the disadvantaged Negro masses in the agricultural
> South. I found Dr. Felton as much interested as I
> was, and as anxious to find some way of making the
> church an effective means of life improvement for
> its people.

Concluding that training rural Black pastors was the
key, they obtained foundation support for such a
training program. Richardson continued:

> Professor Felton's part in the program is almost
> incredible. Within two years over twenty young
> Negro men and women had been located, trained,
> inspired and put to work. All were trained at
> Drew. Most of them completed the work for their
> master's degrees. As rapidly as rural church
> departments could be opened in the selected
> schools, Dr. Felton had leaders ready to fill
> them. Eventually fourteen of these departments
> were established in seminaries or colleges in nine
> of the Southern states and two northern ones. All
> were directed by Felton-trained people.[21]

By 1952 Richardson could report the existence of a
literature, a network of demonstration projects, an
on-going program of extension classes and the training
of over 9,000 Black pastors. "In all of this," he
indicated, "Ralph A. Felton has had a large hand."[22]

This tradition of concern for Black leadership
continued, but in very different form, under George D.

---

[20]Harry V. Richardson, "A Teacher and a
Prophet," *The Drew Gateway* 22 (Summer 1952): 131-36.
Dark Glory (New York: Home Missions Council of North
America, 1947) was dedicated to Felton; *Dark Salvation*
(Garden City. N.Y.: Anchor, 1976) is Richardson's study
of Black Methodism.

[21]Richardson, "Teacher and Prophet," 133-34.

[22]Ibid., 134.

Kelsey. Kelsey, the first Black member of the faculty, sought to move Drew beyond paternalism. He did so by dedicating himself thoroughly to the highest standards of scholarship and teaching. His major work, *Racism and the Christian Understanding of Man*, exemplifies that style of leadership for the Black community, one as essential to the period of civil rights and integration as Felton's had been to an earlier stage of race relations. It should be no surprise that many of the current Black Methodist leaders--bishops and executives most obviously--have a Drew connection, a living testimony to the public leadership provided by Drew to the Black church.

Afterword

The Christian Advocate appropriately devoted attention to a Drew that devoted itself to important Methodist causes. Theological education, missions, theology, and Black leadership were four campaigns in which Drew played a significant role. These vignettes suggest, I think, the prominence of Drew in national Methodist life. A study of 'prominence' like this one, however, is only the beginning of a larger endeavor which needs historical attention. We need to push beneath prominence and public relations to examine the place of Drew, and indeed all the seminaries in the life of Methodism.[23] That is a chapter of American

---

[23]A very fine start on that project is Gerald O. McCulloh's *Ministerial Education in the American Methodist Movement* (Nashville: United Methodist Board of Higher Education and Ministry, 1980). Parts I and III attend to the place of seminaries in the life of the denomination. Part II examines individual theological schools and includes a useful but brief chapter on Drew (pp. 138-43). Another beginning, *Pilgrimage of Faith: A Centennial History of Wesley Theological Seminary*, 1882-1932 by Douglas R. Chandler, ed. C. C. Goen (Cabin John, MD: Seven Locks, 1984) effectively

church history that is only beginning to be written.
Yet it is surely one that should be written. We need
studies done from various angles that look at the
interaction between seminary and its larger environment. In such studies, the Bard Thompsons, who shaped
institutional cultures, built the structures by which
the church transmits the faith, and trained those who
will train others, will surely be the focus of attention.

---

portrays Wesley Seminary in relation to the Methodist
Protestant tradition. For estimations of seminaries
against the larger expanse of American religion, see
Robert Handy, *A History of Union Theological Seminary*
(New York: Columbia University Press, 1987) and George
M. Marsden, *Reforming Fundamentalism: Fuller Seminary
and The New Evangelicalism* (Grand Rapids: William B.
Eerdmans, 1987).

LITURGICAL REFORM IN NINETEENTH-CENTURY ENGLISH CONGREGATIONALISM

Horton Davies

We are accustomed to regard the nineteenth as the
"stolid" English century, in which the monarchy, the
empire, the architecture and the furniture are solid,
safe, dependable and unexciting. "Respectable" is the
epithet we unhesitatingly apply to it and to the men
who march resolutely across the stage, their sober
faces made squarer by side-whiskers, and the prolific
women who recline, as far as the horse-hair bristles
and their bustles permit, on the sofas of the century.
It was a stiff, rigid-backed, whale-boned, chin-up,
aspidistra age. Such at least it seems from the
vertiginous viewpoint of the present "aspirin age."

In fact, however, it was an age of revolution in
politics, science, art, and theology. *In Memoriam*, *Das
Kapital*, and *The Origin of Species* are all Victorian
explosions in the world of thought. Even the quiet
country parishes of the Established Church reverberated
to the passionate pleas of the Evangelicals as they
hammered at the sides of their pulpits, when they were
not being summoned by the Tractarians as the Anglican
Church militant. In the realm of biblical theology
there were major earthquakes, as first the literal
inerrancy of the Scriptures was assailed by higher
criticism, and afterwards the cast-iron theology of the

divine decrees was fragmented by the new liberalism and
Christian socialism. "Change and decay in all around I
see," seems to us a twentieth-century theme, but these
are Victorian words to describe a Victorian experience.
At the outset we may do well to remember that religion
and worship were disturbing, controversial topics in
the nineteenth century. So much so, that in 1856 it
was decided to postpone the annual meeting of the
Assembly of the Congregational Union of England and
Wales, so deep were the passions aroused by the
attackers and defenders of an inoffensive hymn-book
issued by Thomas Toke Lynch in 1855 under the title,
The Rivulet, Hymns for Heart and Voice.[1] Our concern,
then, is with the revolution or reformation that took
place in the public worship of nineteenth-century
English Congregationalism. For the purpose of this
study we shall limit our interest to prayers, praises,
architecture, and the Lord's Supper.

I

The revolution in worship can be most clearly seen
in the attitude towards prayers. At the start of the
century they were regarded at the best as an irksome
necessity, at the worst as a preliminary that could be
dispensed with. In 1770 Benjamin Wallin deplores the
fact that for many worshipers the "first and chief
prayer, with the previous psalmody, is like what is
vulgarly called the saints bell, which rings the people
into church."[2] A similar indictment is made thirty-two
years later by the anonymous authors of the remarkable
document that heralds the dawn of a new Nonconformist

---

[1]Albert Peel, *These Hundred Years, 1831-1931*
(London: Congregational Union, 1931), 221-22.

[2]Benjamin Wallin, *Gospel Requisites to Acceptable Prayer* (London, 1770), 22.

worship:

> And in most of our congregations, it is customary
> for great numbers to absent themselves till after
> the worship is begun, and not a few till the chief
> prayers are nearly ended. Many seem to think that
> if they are in time to hear the text, they are
> early enough.[3]

On the other hand, even when the congregation
arrived in good time, this was no guarantee that its
demeanor would be reverent. In his farewell to his
congregation, one minister spoke out his mind on the
subject of diffuse prayers and distracted congregations:

> It is mostly found, that if a person stands very
> long in prayer, he either gets to preaching, or he
> uses a great deal of repetition, and travels his
> ground several times over. This leads to discon-
> tent and inattention in the hearers. To add to the
> trial of the mind so circumstanced, I have
> remarked where I have been, some turning a
> hymn-book about; others handling the snuff-box
> about; and another taking up the poker and falling
> to knocking the fire about.[4]

Extemporary prayers were to suffer from abuses
worse than prolixity and propaganda. We read of a
certain Samuel Brewer of the Stepney Congregational
Meeting who frequented the quaysides with a rolling
gait. So intimate and comprehensive was his knowledge
of the coming and going of ships in the nearby docks
that he turned his intercessory prayer into a marine
time-table. Bogue and Bennett relate the story with
zest in their history:

> When a merchant ship was going to sail, he
> specified the captain, the mate, the carpenter,

---

[3]*A New Directory for Nonconformist Churches*
(London, 1812), 56-57.

[4]*The Pulpit, A Biographical and Literary
Account of Eminent Popular Preachers, Interspersed with
Occasional Clerical Criticism by Onesimus* (London,
1809), 2:367.

the boatswain, and all the sailors with great
affection; and, it is said, that impressed with a
belief of the benefit of his prayers, they
frequently brought him home, as a token of
gratitude, something of the produce of the country
to which they went.[5]

We may visualize the vestry at Stepney, looking like a

harvest festival of the British empire, piled high with

pomegranates and apples as proofs of his prevailing

prayers, and the Sabbath silence broken by the chatter-

ing of budgerigars and the squawking of green parrots.

Lest all eccentricities in free prayer be attrib-

uted to a quirk in Congregationalism, I beg leave to

cite an example of how not to pray *ex tempore* which an

Anglican reporter attributes to an Anabaptist layman.

This prayer (or parody) goes thus:

O Lord, a Brother of ours, and Servant of Thine,
being sick and weak, desires the prayers of us thy
Faithful Servants; Lord, if thou knowest him not,
his Name is John Mason; and Father, if thou
knowest not where he lives, behold, O Lord, he
lives right over-against the cocky in Pockthorpe;
and behold, Lord, he is a Lame Man, and walks with
one Crutch, and he is a Cobbler by his Trade; and,
Father, his Wife is a very Tidy Woman, for she is
a Bobbin-Filler, she brings up her Boy to fill
Pipes, and her Girl to knit: And now, O Lord,
lest thou shouldst mistake, behold there is a
great Stone lying at his Door. We pray thee,
Father, that thou wouldst be pleased to call upon
him and visit him in thy Mercy &c.[6]

Now it would be an utter travesty of the great

heights to which extemporary prayers can reach, if I

indicated that such bathos was general among the

Congregational churches of the century. To correct any

---

[5]David Bogue and James Bennett, *The History of
Dissenters from the Revolution to the Year 1808*, 2d ed.
(London, 1833), 2:634.

[6]Lewis Thomas, *English Presbyterian Eloquence
&c. in a Collection of Remarkable Flowers of Rhetorick,
By an Admirer of Monarchy and Episcopacy* (London:
Bickerton, 1736), 16.

such impression, I wish to cite part of a Communion
Meditation penned by B. H. Draper, an Independent
minister in Isaac Watts's town of Southampton:

> See they crown that sacred head with thorns, which
> is now encircled with the rainbow and crowned with
> glory and honour; they place a reed in that hand
> in mockery of his claims of sovereignty, which now
> really holds the sceptre of universal dominion;
> that blessed countenance is defiled with shame and
> spitting, which is clearer than the light of
> heaven, and brighter than the meridian sun. [7]

Nonetheless, if extemporaneous prayers were occasionally pentecostal, they were probably much more commonly
purgatorial.

It was precisely this state of affairs that the
most devout and thoughtful minds in the ministry set
out to improve. Pre-eminent among the Congregational
ministers of this century in the field of worship were
two friends: Thomas Binney and John Hunter. Binney was
the pioneer and Hunter the accomplished practitioner of
an improved worship of God. These remarkable men had a
great deal in common: each was minister of the King's
Weigh-House Chapel in the West End of London; each was
a pioneer in the use of prose psalms and chants in
Dissenting praise; each was in the forefront of the
movement to liberate and liberalize theology from the
conception of God as the arbitrary Calvinistic Poten-
tate of the Divine decrees, and from the thought of the
future life as substance and the present as shadow.
The liturgical conclusion they came to was one in which
Thomas Cartwright, the Elizabethan Puritan, had

---

[7]B. H. Draper, *Solemn Recollections before, at,
and after the Celebration of the Lord's Supper*
(Southampton, 1825).

anticipated them by almost three hundred years.[8] They
were forestalled even in their own century in *A New
Directory for Nonconformist Churches* which pled for the
use of a combination of fixed forms and free prayers.
The distinction of Binney and Hunter, however, was the
place they occupied in the respect and affection of the
denomination as eminent preachers and pastors, and in
the moving exemplification of their theories in their
own charges. Moreover, by their preaching and by their
books, as well as in fraternal discussion, they
promoted the reform of worship. It was the great
distinction of Dr. John Hunter that he produced the
first Congregational Liturgy worthy of the name in
1882. It was entitled *Devotional Services for Public
Worship*. The first edition comprised twenty-eight
pages, while the edition of 1901, which represents the
final form, consisted of 328 pages. The only previous
Congregational liturgy known to me is that of one
Thomas, minister of the Independent Chapel in Stock-
well, which appeared in the century's middle decade and
was known as *The Biblical Liturgy*. This is a pauper's
liturgy compared with Hunter's princely fare.

Now the revolutionary nature of these proposals
must be insisted upon. Hitherto, worship was either
liturgical or free, but never were the traditions
combined in the same service. The anonymous authors of
the *New Directory* of 1812 recommend the use of both
types of prayer and say that, if someone should object
that reading a precomposed prayer is like writing a
letter to another and then going to read it to him,
they must insist "it is rather like drawing up with
care a humble petition to the King, and then going in a

---

[8]Cf. A. F. Scott Pearson, *Thomas Cartwright and
Elizabethan Puritanism* (Cambridge: The University
Press, 1925), 406-7.

body to present it to Him."[9] They further recommend
that prayers of adoration, thanksgiving, confession,
and general intercession and supplication be offered
through precomposed forms,[10] and that responsive
orders of prayers should be printed for the use of
congregations.[11] They suggest as source-materials
Matthew Henry's *Method of Prayer*, Watts's *Guide to
Prayer*, and William Smith's *A System of Prayer*. These
and many other practical suggestions are offered for
the consideration of the ministry in general and for
tutors in theological academies in particular, because
their authors are so aggrieved by the improprieties of
Dissenting worship.

The admirable Thomas Binney made his views known
either in the celebrated sermon, *The Service of Song in
the House of the Lord*, or in his influential edition of
C. W. Baird's *A Chapter on Liturgies, Historical
Sketches* (1856) to which he prefixed an introductory
essay and added a brilliant appendix. Binney hopes
that it will come as a complete surprise to many of the
ultra-free-prayer school to find that the incontestably
Protestant John Knox prepared a fixed liturgy which was
adopted by the Church of Scotland, that many of the
Puritans and earliest Separatists used a Genevan
liturgy in their clandestine meetings, that later
Nonconformists objected not to the idea of a liturgy as
such, but to the particular liturgy which the Established Church imposed, and that one of them, Richard
Baxter, had prepared his own *Reformed Liturgy* for
general use. Binney declares that congregations show a

---

[9] *New Directory for Nonconformist Churches*, 10.

[10] Ibid., 57-58.

[11] Ibid., 101-2.

yearning for

> deeper devotion and richer song--something too in
> which the people shall take a prominent and active
> part,--not in psalmody only but in supplication;--
> -in which they shall be called vocally to utter
> some portion of the Church's common prayer,--so
> that by audible repetition and appropriate
> response, and other modes of united action, they
> shall feel that they positively do pray, as well
> as listen to another praying.[12]

Binney was a visionary, but no fanatic. So he con-

tented himself by prescribing a reasonable modicum of

improvement. This would take the form of a responsive

reading of the Psalms, vocal confession of sin, or the

Lord's Prayer, or the Apostles' Creed. To understand

how reverent the man's soul was we have only to cite

one verse of his great hymn, "Eternal Light:"

> O how shall I, whose native sphere
> Is dark, whose mind is dim,
> Before the ineffable appear,
> And on my naked spirit bear
> The uncreated beam?

In the same way a sublime short hymn can take us

to the beating heart of John Hunter's devotional

concern. Dr. Erik Routley describes it as "a perfect

example of the Christian lyric-epigram".[13] It reads:

> Dear Master, in whose life I see
> All that I would, but fail to be,
> Let Thy clear light for ever shine
> To shame and guide this life of mine.
>
> Though what I dream and what I do
> In my weak days are always two,
> Help me oppressed by things undone,
> O Thou, whose deeds and dreams were one.[14]

---

[12]Thomas Binney, preface to *A Chapter of Liturgies*, by C. W. Baird (London, 1856), xxiv.

[13]Erik Routley, *Hymns and Human Life* (London: John Murray, 1952), 154.

[14]No. 462 in *Companion to Congregational Praise*, ed. K. L. Parry (London: Independent, 1953).

Hunter's theory and practice of worship are concentrated in three publications: *Devotional Services
for Public Worship* (first edition, 1882), *Hymns of
Faith and Hope* (first edition, 1889), and the treatise
A Worshipful Church (1903). In the 1901 edition of the
first of these he wrote: "The two ways of worship
(liturgical and free) have each proved their right to
exist, and they may exist side by side." To this he
added in *A Worshipful Church* this sentence:

> Opportunity ought to be given in every service for
> the introduction of free prayer when the minister
> is moved thereto; but it is good that the larger
> part of the prayers should be before the eyes and
> in the hands of the people, that they may be able
> directly to participate in the worship, and that
> their worship may be saved from the unregulated
> and unchastened individualism of one man.[15]

In my own deliberate judgment I would state that
the book which has done more than any other for Free
Church worship, *The Methodist Hymn-Book* excepted, is
Hunter's *Devotional Services*. What is it that makes
this book so outstanding? It is not merely that it is
the first dignified Congregational liturgy in English,
nor even that its language is as aspiring as it is
chaste, nor even again that the people are given their
responsive rights in worship, important as all these
factors are. The secret of its success does not even
lie in the princely ruthlessness with which Hunter
raids the devotional treasures of the past. It lies in
the unusual combination of the traditionalist and the
modernist in Hunter. Technically he is a traditionalist, using the techniques of the collect and the
litany, steeped in the thoughts and the phraseology of
Catholic and Anglican liturgy and devotions. Equally
he is an advanced social thinker of his own day and

---

[15]John Hunter, *A Worshipful Church* (n.p.,
1903), 52.

sets his prayers firmly in the context of nineteenth-
century industrial society, remembering the needs of a
variety of vocations. The social reformer could pen
these incisive words:

> From all inordinate cares amd ambitions; from
> maxims of cunning and greed; from the godless
> pursuit of pleasure and gain; from wronging the
> poor and from envying and flattering the rich;
> from keeping back the price of labour and from
> rendering eye-service; Good Lord deliver us.

Yet the same author writes these mystical words:

> Almighty and everlasting God, in communion with
> Thy saints in all ages, with patriarchs and
> prophets, apostles and martyrs, with our beloved
> dead who have fallen asleep in Thy peace; we, who
> are still striving to do and bear Thy blessed will
> on earth, adore Thee and offer to Thee our praises
> and supplications.[16]

Hunter had the liturgist's gift for true architec-
tonic, rhythmical and balanced phrasing, as in the
opening of this prayer recalling the Communion of
Saints: "O Lord God, the Life and Light of the faithful, the Strength and Hope of those who labour and
suffer, the Everlasting Refuge and Rest of the dead."
Moreover, he had the liturgist's gift for the monumental, unforgettable phrase. Some of these phrases of
his have become the prayer currency of the Free
Churches: "the sacred and tender ties that bind us to
the unseen world"; "for the tasks and trials by which
we are trained to patience"; "for the order and
constancy of nature, for the beauty and bounty of the
world"; "the sweet and solemn hopes that cluster round
the newborn"; "the secret and blessed fellowship of the
Cross"; "forgotten by us, but dear to Thee"; and,
perhaps, the profoundest of them all, "the strength to
do and bear the blessed will of God." As long as the

---

[16]Both citations are from the Fourth Order of
Service.

English tongue is spoken, so long will his Communion
invitation endure. It is so good that it might be
inserted as it stands before the Prayer of Humble
Access in the Communion Order of *The Book of Common
Prayer.* "Come to this sacred Table, not because you
must, but because you may. . . ." it begins, and it
ends, "Come not to express an opinion, but to seek a
Presence and pray for a Spirit."

Dr. John Hunter's enrichment of the prayers and
praises of the Free Churches warrants a chapter to
itself. What has been said, however, would serve to
substantiate the claim made by Dr. Leslie Hunter,
former Bishop of Sheffield, on behalf of his father:

> It has proved one of the most influential con-
> tributions . . . to pastoral theology in the non-
> episcopal churches. Ministers who would dislike
> to read or to be seen to read prayers from a book
> in their pulpits, have sought inspiration from its
> pages. Many men, too, who have made little use of
> it in the ordinary services of the Church, have
> made regular use of its special orders of ser-
> vices, . . . and the occasional prayers which it
> contains.[17]

How far we have traveled from the unpremeditated,
repetitive, chaotic, free prayers at the commencement
of the century to the profoundly reflective and
relevant, dignified, orderly and devout prayers of
Hunter.

II

Significant changes were also taking place in the
praise of the Congregational churches. At the start of
the century the theology of the hymns was almost
exclusively Calvinistic, with Watts reigning as the
unrivalled king of hymnodists. In the course of the
century the range of Congregational hymns was extended,

---

[17]Leslie S. Hunter, *John Hunter, D.D., A Life*
(London, 1921), 211-12.

if not deepened, by several important influences.

Methodism contributed the magnificent enrichment of Charles and John Wesley; Anglicanism contributed the original hymns of Reginald Heber and the splendid translations of John Mason Neale. American Congregationalism provided the translator, Ray Palmer, and the leavening (or, watering-down) of liberal hymns of the kingdom such as "Rise up, O men of God." English Congregationalism had its own contribution to make in the hymns of Binney, Conder, Gill, Hood, Mason, Rawson, Reed, Arnold Thomas, Silvester Horne and Elvet Lewis, all nineteenth-century hymnodists. The outstanding characteristics of nineteenth-century Congregational hymnbooks are interdenominationalism and contemporaneity. The latter only became possible because of an even greater change, which A. G. Matthews rightly defines as "the divorce of the union that wedded the hymnbook to the Bible."[18] Now it became possible to sing the glories of the present challenge, of the joys of social service, and to provide hymns suitable to the development and experience of children. An expansion of themes was accompanied by a thinning of the theology, and the objectivity of the mighty acts of God in creation, redemption and sanctification was sacrificed for the subjectivity and introspection of lyrical spiders forever examining their insides.

We should also recall that the nineteenth century saw the gradual disappearance of the clerk and the precentor and the advent of the organist and choirmaster. The violins, violoncellos, and flutes ceded their rights to the harmonium and the pipe-organ. In some conservative congregations the innovators had a

---

[18]General Introduction to the *Companion to Congregational Praise*, xxv.

hard struggle. Finding dates is difficult, but we know, for example, that in Rugeley, Staffordshire, there were three stages: in 1840 there was a choir accompanied by a violoncello; in 1850 they boasted a harmonium; and in 1859 they raised the roof at the inauguration of their pipe-organ.[19] In Handsworth, Birmingham, however, they had an organ as early as 1832. Manchester, as we might expect, boasted an organ in Mosley Chapel, as early as 1823, and, equally according to prediction, an obdurate deacon resigned because of this "intrusion." The diehards found a spokesman in John Adamson, minister of Charlesworth. Among his quaint objections to pipe-organs are the following: to urge Judaism as a precedent for organs would also require us to introduce dancing in worship in order to be consistent; instrumental music was excluded from worship during the first seven hundred years of the history of the Christian Church; and the final, conclusive and presumably irrefutable argument that "it is a custom derived from the idolatrous Church of Rome."[20] We may note, in passing, that a superstition against superstition has prevented or slowed liturgical progress throughout church history.

It appears that it was Thomas Binney who introduced chanting into Congregational worship, while Henry Allon popularized it in his chant-book of 1876. It is significant that Dr. Allon could write: "At the present time the prose psalms are more generally sung and Gregorian music is more extensively used in Nonconformist than in Evangelical Episcopalian

---

[19]A. G. Matthews, *The Congregational Churches of Staffordshire* (n.p., 1924), 207-8.

[20]Cf. Benjamin Nightingale, *The Story of the Lancashire Congregational Union* (Manchester, n.d.), 125-26.

Churches."[21] The denominational approval of chants was
given by implication in the offically sponsored
Congregational Church Hymnal of 1887, edited by Barret.
Anthems were also introduced at the same time as
chants. Both innovations were undreamed of at the
beginning of the century.

III

The third great area of change was in the setting,
the architecture of Congregational worship. Before the
double onset of the Gothic revival of architecture and
the Oxford revival of ecclesiology, the traditional
preference of churches in the Puritan tradition for
simple, classical, Georgian structures, with porticoed
fronts, was broken down. The two characteristic
features of the older meeting-houses of the Nonconformist tradition were the central pulpit, with the place
of honor given to the open Bible resting on the red
velvet pulpit cushion, and the full light passing
undimmed through the large, D-topped windows, stressing
the pedagogic character of Puritan worship, where the
congregation was essentialy an "audience" gathered to
hear the exposition of the will of God in the obedience
of faith. The Gothic, medieval, cruciform shape, on
the other hand, presupposed a sanctuary in which the
sacrifice of the Mass, said often in an unintelligible
tongue, was not to be heard, but to be "seen"; and this
properly required a high central altar, while the
element of proclamation, being subordinate, was
relegated to a side pulpit. If the functions of the
Puritan meeting-house and the medieval Catholic
sanctuary were so radically different, how are we to
account for the neo-Gothic craze in several Congrega-

----

[21]Henry Allon, introduction to *Sermons Preached
in King's Weigh-House Chapel, London, 1829-1869, Second
Series*, ed. Henry Allon (London, 1875), xxxix.

tional churches built in the nineteenth century?

Mr. Martin Briggs, Fellow of the Royal Institute
of British Architecture, son of a Congregational manse,
has a shrewd guess to make when he says:

> It probably dawned upon Free Churchmen of early
> Victorian days, conscious of their growing
> political power, that the sense of social infe-
> riority under which they had smarted so long might
> be removed, or at least mitigated, if their
> despised "chapels" were made to "look like
> churches" of the new Anglican kind. . . . It was
> thus that the starveling spires, the shoddy
> tracery, and the hideous coloured-glass of these
> mid-Victorian chapels came to be derided more
> bitterly than the solid, Georgian, classical
> chapels, or the squat and homely "Bethels" ever
> had been.[22]

It is not to be thought that the threadbare device of
the intransigent, "No Popery," was not raised. To
change the metaphor, it was the aptly named Mr. J. A.
Tabor from Independent Ipswich who beats the denominational drum in a pamphlet bearing the title, *A Noncon-
forming Protest against the Papacy of Modern Dissenting
Architecture imitative of Roman Catholic Churches*
(1863). The Tabors might thunder, but the ears of the
well-to-do middle-class merchants were attuned to the
haunting melodies of plainsong in the medieval mode.
They insisted upon having their "Nonconformist Cathedrals," as they proudly but inappropriately called
them. Indeed, the very titles showed that these were
the attempts of megalomaniacs to get even with the
Anglicans!

The first Nonconformist chapel to be furnished
with a chancel was the Mill Hill Unitarian Chapel in
Leeds, built in 1848. This honor was well deserved
because the Unitarians had been the pioneers in

---

[22]Martin S. Briggs, *Puritan Architecture and
Its Future* (London: Lutterworth, 1946), 38-39.

reforming liturgical worship for a good century before
the other Nonconformist denominations.[23] The first
large scale Congregational church to be erected in the
new manner was Christ Church in Westminster Bridge
Road, London, which was completed in 1872. Its
exterior was designed in the shape of a Greek cross,
three arms of which were occupied in galleries while
the fourth contained the Communion-table and the side
pulpit and was flanked by the choir seats and the
organ. It had an impressive exterior culminating in a
massive but finely proportioned stone spire. The
entire building was finished in stone at great cost.

Not far away the trustees of the future Westminster Chapel had caused a brick building to be erected
where an equal number of seats was provided at a
quarter of the cost, and possibly with a quarter the
distinction of style (1863-65). It would be unfair to
Gothic to describe the architectural speech-box as of
that manner; it is far better to accept the suggestion
of Martin Briggs that "a charitable critic might liken
its brick interior, rather vaguely, to some of the
Italian Romanesque Churches lauded by Ruskin."[24] A
more genuinely neo-Romanesque edifice was designed by
the Nonconformist architect, James Cubitt, for Union
Chapel, Islington. The Royal Academician, Alfred
Waterhouse, designed two unusual churches for Congregationalism. One was the King's Weigh-House Chapel
in the West End of London, built in 1891 at a cost of
L60,000 to provide seating accommodation for 600
persons, and soon to be renowned as the highest of high

---

[23]Cf. Elliott Peaston, *The Prayer Book Reform Movement in the XVIIIth Century* (Oxford: Blackwell, 1940).

[24]Briggs, *Puritan Architecture*, 49.

Congregational churches under the ministries of
Dr. John Hunter and Dr. W. E. Orchard. The other
sanctuary built by Waterhouse was Lyndhurst Road
Congregational Church, Hampstead, erected to accommodate the great congregation of Dr. R. F. Horton, who
was the first Congregationalist to be elected a fellow
of an Oxford College, since the days of the seven-
teenth-century Commonwealth. Neither Waterhouse
sanctuary was an appropriate sounding-board for the
"Nonconformist Conscience."

IV

The final section of this chapter will map the
important changes in the celebration of the Lord's
Supper or Holy Communion. The earliest change was due
to the temperance movement and it resulted in the
forsaking of fermented wine. It began before 1850 and
by 1900 approximately two-thirds of the ministers of
the Congregational Union approved of the change.

A more serious change, since it atomized the unity
desirable in a Communion service, was the rejection of
the common chalice and its replacement by trays of
individual mini-glasses carried by the deacons to the
pews, and each tiny glass was then placed in a ring
attached to the pew. An attempt to regain unity was
made by simultaneous eating of the broken bread and
later the simultaneous drinking of the wine. The
justification for this unlovely disruption of tradition
made it seem that the Communion honored the goddess
Hygeia rather than Christ, the eternal Son of God and
the Second person of the Holy Trinity. It was suggested that the new custom would provide safety from
imperfection, and devotion would be unhindered by
concern for purity, and both considerations would
increase attendance at the Lord's Supper. This radical
change in celebration took place at the end of the

nineteenth century.

The third change was due to the liberalization of doctrine. Hitherto the Lord's Supper had been restricted to members of Congregational churches. In the last decade of the century it was proposed, according to the Rev. J. Bainton, that the invitation should be: "Let all who love the Lord Jesus join with us in his Holy Communion."[25] This indicates a vast change from the early Independents who had insisted that the local church must consist of "visible saints" and such alone.[26] This change was justified on the grounds that members of the churches were seriously divided in doctrine, that Congregationalists had always preferred covenants to creeds, and that many sensitive persons who would not arrogate membership were still "good practicing Christians."

"From the bare barn to the King's Weigh-House" is the title of a journey that symbolizes in more than architectural terms the revolution that took place in nineteenth-century English Congregational worship. The prayers, the praises, the way of celebrating the Lord's Supper, and the very setting of worship had changed almost out of recognition; yet this fluidity and adaptability was a living proof of the experimental flexibility of the life of the Congregational churches.

---

[25]J. Bainton, *The Congregational Handbook* (London, 1897), 105.

[26]See Geoffrey F. Nuttall, *Visible Saints: The Congregational Way, 1640-1660* (Oxford: Blackwell, 1957), and Edmund S. Morgan, *Visible Saints: The History of a Puritan Idea* (New York: New York University Press, 1963).

PASTORALS FOR THE PEOPLE:
PASTORAL LETTERS IN THE METHODIST TRADITION

Kenneth E. Rowe

The unanimous vote of the United Methodist Council of Bishops, April 29, 1986, to issue a major pastoral letter on peace took the Methodist and the religious world--to say nothing of the political world--by surprise. Catholic bishops have been issuing such pastorals for centuries but it was a first for the people called Methodists. Or was it?

Historically pastoral letters have been sent out by bishops or church assemblies regularly on specific occasions, as in the Roman Catholic and Anglican traditions at the beginning of Lent each year to give the current rules for fasting. Other pastorals have been issued at the discretion of the bishop or church assembly in order to warn against particular dangers or to instruct on some point of Christian faith or social responsibility. Is there a precedent in Methodism's past for this practice? Since 1812 Methodist bishops have been giving an address at the beginning of their general conferences. Such "Episcopal Addresses," however, are not technically Pastoral Letters, that is, formal letters, doctrinal, devotional or disciplinary, to their pastors and people. Although on occasion episcopal addresses receive wide circulation throughout the church, they are primarily addressed to the

church's elected policy makers, serve as a keynote
address on the state of the church, and as such are
parcelled out paragraph by paragraph to appropriate
legislative committees of the conference.

Research in the church's archives shows that
indeed there have been pastorals in Methodism's past.
Although Francis Asbury fashioned a strong, if not
imperial, model of episcopacy for the new church in
America, addressing formal pastoral letters was not one
of the historic marks of episcopacy he chose to
recover. Instead, general conferences over which he
presided carried on the ancient tradition. Fifteen
such pastoral letters were issued by general conferences of the Methodist Episcopal Church, South between
1844 and 1882, the first two by general conferences and
the last five by the college of bishops. There is no
evidence that the Methodist Protestant Church continued
the practice after their exodus in 1830. Drafted
either by a committee of general conference delegates
as in the northern church or by the bishops at the
request of the general conference as in the southern
church, Methodist pastorals were read from the church's
pulpits, published in the church's newspapers, distributed as pamphlets, and in a few instances were
included in the book of discipline. At least one, the
1880 Methodist Episcopal pastoral letter, was published
in a handsome pamphlet complete with a letter from the
pastor:

> Beloved:
>
> In accordance with a time honored custom, the
> recent General Conference appointed a special
> committee to prepare an address to the ministers
> and members of the Methodist Episcopal Church.
>
> It is my pleasure to present you with a copy of
> the address which was unanimously adopted by the
> General Conference, and may I ask you to read it

carefully, *prayerfully*, and *frequently*, and may its suggestions and exhortations prove a blessing to you, and to the whole Church.

Affectionately,

Your Pastor

June 1st, 1880. [1]

It is this little known tradition of Methodist pastoral letters that this chapter seeks to explore.

I

The idea of sending a pastoral letter from the church's governing conference to pastors and layfolk back home may have originated with John Wesley himself. Only one pastoral letter was sent out during his lifetime--in 1788, when the British conference made an appeal for higher salaries for preachers. [2] The second such pastoral leter, sent out in 1792, the year following Wesley's death, tackled the tricky question of the administration of the sacrament of the Lord's Supper in Methodist Chapels. [3] By 1819 the British Methodist practice was formally agreed upon:

> Q.XXV. Can we adopt any further measure to promote the spiritual benefit of the Societies under our care?

> A. We deem it expedient and proper to address the

---

[1] "Pastoral Address to the Ministers and Members of the Methodist Episcopal Church from the General Conference of 1880" (Philadelphia: J. B. McCullough, 1880), 2.

[2] "To our Societies in England and Ireland, London, August 2, 1788," *Minutes of The Methodist Conferences from the First Held in London by the Late Rev. John Wesley in the Year 1744* (London: John Mason, 1862), 1:216.

[3] "To the Members of our Societies who desire to receive the Lord's Supper from the hands of their own Preachers," *Minutes of the Methodist Conferences* (London: John Mason, 1862), 1:273-74.

Societies annually in a Pastoral Letter from the
Conference. This practice shall be commenced at
the present Conference; and the Address now
prepared and approved, shall be immediately
printed, that it may be sent to the Circuits, and
be read forthwith in our Minutes, and in the
Methodist Magazine. [4]

The practice continues to this day in Great Britain.

II

This historical precedent set by the mother church
may have been in the minds of delegates to the 1800
general conference of the Methodist Episcopal Church
when the leaders agreed to issue their first pastoral
letter. Near the end of the long conference in
Baltimore, which Asbury dismissed with the comment
"much talk, but little work," [5] Ezekiel Cooper moved:

that a committee be appointed to prepare an
affectionate address to the Methodist societies in
the United States, stating the evils of the spirit
and practice of slavery, the necessity of doing
away with the evil as far as the laws of the
respective states will allow; and that the said
address be laid before the conference for their
consideration, and, if agreed to, be signed by the
bishops in behalf of the conference. Agreed to. [6]

Drafted by three clergy, Ezekiel Cooper, William
McKendree and Jesse Lee, the address was "agreed to" by
the conference, signed by the three bishops, Coke,
Asbury and Whatcoat, and published in broadside format,
since the church had not yet established either a
weekly newspaper or a quarterly review.

Never was there a more clearly defined position

---

[4] *Minutes of the Methodist Conferences from the
First Held in London by the Late Rev. John Wesley in
the Year 1744* (London: J. Kershaw, 1825), 5:59.

[5] *The Journals and Letters of Francis Asbury*,
ed. Elmer T. Clark (Nashville: Abingdon, 1958) 2:231.

[6] *Journals of the General Conference of the
Methodist Church*, (New York: Carlton & Phillips, 1855),
1:41.

opposing slavery in the church both from the view of
the natural rights of persons and from the spirit of
the Christian Gospel:

> WE have long lamented the great national evil of
> NEGRO-SLAVERY, which has existed for so many
> years, and does still exist in many of these
> United States. We have considered it as repugnant
> to the inalienable rights of mankind, and to the
> very essence of civil liberty, but more especially
> to the spirit of the Christian religion.
>
> FOR inconsistent as is the conduct of this
> otherwise free, this independent nation, in
> respect to the slavery of the Negros, when
> considered in a civil and political view, it is
> still more so, when examined in the light of the
> gospel. For the whole spirit of the New Testament
> militates in the strongest manner against the
> practice of slavery--and the influence of the
> gospel, wherever it has long prevailed (except in
> the many of these United States) has utterly
> abolished that most criminal part of slavery, the
> possessing and using of the bodies of men, by
> arbitrary will and with almost uncontrollable
> power.

The address intended that the Methodists would "give a
blow at the root of this enormous evil." The major
strategy of petitioning the state legislatures for
emancipation laws was to continue "till the desired end
be fully accomplished."[7]

The church's first pastoral letter was not warmly

---

[7]A full text of the address was reprinted in
Charles Elliott, *History of the Great Secession from
the Methodist Episcopal Church in the Year 1845*
(Cincinnati: Swormstedt & Poe for the Methodist
Episcopal Church, 1855), document 8, appendix pp.
845-46. A more authoritative text copied from an
original 1800 broadside in Lovely Lane United Methodist
Museum in Baltimore appeared in *World Parish* 7:2
(August 1959): 58-60. The text was not included in the
standard edition of the Journal of the General Conferences published in 1855. Curiously neither Jesse
Lee nor Nathan Bangs mentions this historic address in
the accounts of the 1800 general conference in their
histories published in 1810 and 1839 respectively.

received in some sections of the church, especially in the south. In Charleston copies of the pastoral were gathered and burned in the presence of the mayor.[8] Asbury himself had second thoughts about the wisdom of such tough talk. Six months after it was issued he wrote in his journal: "Nothing could so effectually alarm and arm the citizens of South Carolina against the Methodists as the *Address of the General Conference.*"[9] This statement marked the beginning of a long period of compromise on the matter of slavery. The letter marked the beginning of a long line of Methodist pastorals to come.[10]

Twelve years later (1812), at the end of their three week general conference in New York City clergy delegates representing nine annual conferences issued the church's second pastoral. Drawn up by the eight clergy "Committee on the Administration of Doctrine, Discipline and Practice" and signed by Bishops Asbury and McKendree, the pastoral letter was passed with amendments and ordered to be printed and circulated on the last day of the conference, May 22, 1812.[11] The "Address of the General Conference to the Members of the Methodist Episcopal Church in the United States of America" was printed in New York again in broadside

---

[8]Abel Stevens, *History of the Methodist Episcopal Church in the United States of America* (New York: Carlton & Porter, 1867), 4:176.

[9]Clark, ed., *Journal and Letters of Francis Asbury*, 2:281.

[10]The texts of the earliest pastoral letters are difficult to find since they were not included in the published journals of the general conference.

[11]*Journal of the General Conference of the Methodist Episcopal Church*, 1:121; cf. 111 and 117.

format.[12]

The second pastoral letter differs from the first
in two respects. First, it is addressed to church
members and not to the wider community, and second, its
purpose is to promote personal piety not social
transformation. Less controversial, it set the pattern
for pastorals to come, at least in the nineteenth
century. The 1812 letter begins on a triumphal note by
counting converts. "Favored with repeated manifestations of the power and grace of God," the conference
delegates note with pleasure, God had given "astonishing success" to their labors, enabling the church
annually to make "accessions of thousands."

> From the cold provinces of Canada to the sultry
> regions of Georgia--from the shores of the
> Atlantic to the waters of the Mississippi--in
> populous cities, improved countries, and dreary
> deserts, God has extended the triumphs of his
> grace. Infidelity trembles in the presence of
> the cross, superstition yields to the mild
> influence of the gospel, and ignorance vanishes
> before the auspicious beams of truth. In the
> revolution of a few years our number has amounted
> to two hundred thousand, exclusive of expulsions,
> withdrawings, and the many happy souls who have
> departed in the faith and gone to their reward in
> heaven. We have mutually participated in prosper-
> ity.[13]

Following a pledge to renew the covenant "to live
and die as servants of Jesus Christ," the conference

---

[12]*Address of the General Conference to the
Members of the Methodist Episcopal Church in the United
States of America* (New York, 1812). "Signed in behalf
of the Conference: Francis Asbury, William McKendree."
Excerpts in Nathan Bangs, *A History of the Methodist
Episcopal Church* (New York: T. Mason and G. Lane for
the Methodist Episcopal Church, 1839), 2:325-30. The
text is not included in the standard printed edition of
the journal of the general conference. The broadside
printing is dated May 28, 1812.

[13]Ibid.

delegates and the two bishops hope the Methodist people
will gladly receive their word of exhortation.
Reminiscent of the three-fold pattern of the church's
General Rules, the 1812 pastoral admonishes the people
called Methodists (1) to pursue "internal religion in
all its branches," that is, avoid evil; (2) to practice
"external religion," that is, do good, "let your light
shine before men that they may see your good works;"
and (3) to use all of the means of grace, specifically
read the Scriptures, receive the sacraments, keep the
sabbath, avoid strong drink, dress plainly, remember to
fast and instruct the children.

Agitation to introduce lay representation into the
church's governing conferences and to curb the power of
bishops in the next decade called forth the church's
third pastoral letter. In the face of a mounting
challenge from a reform-minded caucus, the 1824 general
conference approved a pastoral letter to be issued by
the bishops designed to squelch the reformers' chief
argument, that taxation without representation was as
wrong in the church as it was in the state.

> The rights and privileges of our brethren, as
> members of the Methodist Episcopal Church, we hold
> most sacred. We are unconscious of having
> infringed them in any instance; nor would we do
> so. . . . But if by "rights and privileges," it is
> intended to signify something foreign from the
> institutions of the Church, as we received them
> from our fathers, pardon us if we know no such
> rights, if we do not comprehend such privileges.
> With our brethren everywhere, we rejoice that the
> institutions of our happy country are admirably
> calculated to secure the best ends of civil
> government. With their rights, as citizens of
> these United States, the Church disclaims all
> interference; but, that it should be inferred
> from these, what are your rights as Methodists
> seems to us no less surprising, than if your
> Methodism should be made the criterion of your

rights as citizens.[14]
Called the "no such rights" pastoral by the reformers,
they would wait for one more general conference (1828)
before exiting to form a new, and from their point of
view, a more democratic and more American, Methodist
church (the Methodist Protestant Church), with lay
representation and without bishops.

The pattern of issuing pastorals was revived by
the general conference of 1832. Each of the twelve
general conferences that followed issued a pastoral
letter except 1844. The 1880 pastoral letter appears
to be the last for the denomination. Curiously, no
pastorals were issued in crisis years--1816 (the death
of Asbury), only one (1824) in the decade of agitation
to introduce lay representation into the troublesome
decade of the 1820's, and none in 1844 (the separation
of the church north and south over the twin issues of
slavery and episcopacy)--years in which one would think
preachers and people most needed reassurance and
guidance from their chief pastors.

All Methodist Episcopal pastorals were drafted by
the church's pastors, rather than by its chief pastors,
the bishops. With the introduction of lay representatives into the general conferences beginning in 1872,

_____

[14]The text of this 1824 pastoral, not included
in the standard printed edition of the journal of the
General Conference, may be conveniently found in
*General Conference of the Methodist Episcopal Church
from 1792 to 1896*, ed. Lewis Curts (New York: Eaton &
Mains, 1900), 95-97. For official action on the
matter, see *Journals of the General Conferences of the
Methodist Episcopal Church* (New York: Carlton &
Phillips, 1855), 1:297 and 300. The pastoral was
widely circulated at the time through its publication
in the church's official monthly journal, *The Methodist
Magazine* [New York] 7 (June 1824): 274-76, as well as
in the reformers' paper, *Mutual Rights of the Ministers
and Members of the Methodist Episcopal Church*, 1:1
(August 1824), 5-7.

the drafting committee continued to be all clergy, with
the exception of 1876 when one lay delegate, John B.
Cornell of New York, served as a member of the seven-
person committee. The practice of issuing a pastoral
letter was discontinued after 1880 with no apparent
fuss.

III

Even before the Methodist Episcopal Church, South
was formally organized, it issued a pastoral address.
On the day after the divisive general conference of
1844 adjourned, before leaving New York City the
southern delegation met to prepare a plan to gather the
judgment of the southern conferences on the matter of
separation and issued a lengthy "Address to the
Ministers and Members of the Methodist Episcopal
Church, in the Slaveholding States and Territories."
Signed by more than fifty delegates, including seven
future bishops of the church in the making, the address
was an apologia for the benefit of the home constituency, interpreting forcefully the Southern attitude
toward the events which had just transpired in New
York. The final paragraphs deal with the impending
separation.[15]

Consent was given by the southern conferences to
implement the plan of separation and a general convention was held in Louisville, Kentucky the following
spring (1845) to formally organize the Methodist

---

[15]*History of the Organization of the Methodist
Episcopal Church, South: Comprehending all the Official
Proceedings of the General Conference; The Southern
Annual Conferences, and the General Convention; With
Such Other Matters as are Necessary to a Right Under-
standing of the Case* (Nashville: Compiled and Pub-
lished by the Editors and Publishers of the South-
Western Christian Advocate, for the Methodist Episcopal
Church, South, by order of the Louisville Convention,
William Cameron, printer, 1845), 106-8.

Episcopal Church, South. Although the organizing
general convention of 1845 issued no pastoral letter,
the first general conference of the new church, meeting
the following year in Petersburg, Virginia, did. The
1846 conference requested the bishops to appoint a
committee of five clergy delegates "to draft a Pastoral
address, at their earliest convenience."[16] On the next
to the last day of the conference, the committee was
granted an extension of time to complete the address,
"provided, the signatures of one or more of the
bishops, and the Secretary of this conference, be
affixed to the same."[17] One of the longest pastorals
on record, it was not published until September when it
appeared in the *Nashville Christian Advocate*.[18] The
1846 pastoral letter began with a long historical
statement giving a rationale for the separation from
the northern church:

> As long as the church was content simply to
> declare its conviction of the evil of slavery, and
> regulate its abuses in the instance of church
> members, without bringing its interference in
> direct conflict with the laws of the land, the
> Southern portion of the church was disposed to
> submit, without murmur or remonstrance. . . . But
> when, in 1844, in utter disregard of these high
> pledges, the General Conference, in the cases of
> Harding and Andrew, proceeded to acts and deci-
> sions . . . directly subversive of the laws of the
> church . . . [we departed.]

---

[16]*Journal of the General Conference of the
Methodist Episcopal Church, South, Held 1846 and 1850*
(Richmond, VA: Published by John Early for the Method-
ist Episcopal Church, South, 1851), 26.

[17]Ibid., 93.

[18]"Pastoral Address of the General Conference
to the Ministers and Members of the Methodist Episcopal
Church, South," *Nashville Christian Advocate* 10:47
(September 18, 1846), 2-3. Signed: "Affectionately,
Joshua Soule, President; T.N. Ralston, Secretary,
Petersburg, Va., 23d May 1846."

The pastoral went on to repudiate any notion of
disloyalty to the inherited tradition:

> We repel the imputation of defection from the
> Methodism of our fathers. We regard ourselves as
> defamed, in every instance in which the charge has
> been made. We do not claim to be better, more
> devoted, more worthy of imitation as Christians,
> than our brethren of the North; but in every thing
> essential, every thing peculiar to Methodism, we
> believe the impartial evidence of history will be,
> that we have been not only equally, but, in fact,
> even *uniquely* loyal and true to the duties and
> hopes of our end and calling, as American Wesleyan
> Methodists.[19]

Slave members were admonished to be obedient and
faithful; masters were admonished to be just and kind.
The rest of the pastoral was the standard appeal to
promote personal piety and family religion, support
Sunday schools at home and missions abroad, "never
forget our true original vocation, as a people 'to
spread Scriptural Holiness' over every land in which we
may be found."[20]

Three general conferences later, in 1858, the
delegates requested the bishops to prepare a pastoral
letter to the ministry and members of their church.[21]
After a portion of the letter was read, the conference
adopted it and ordered it to be published in the
journal of the conference and in the church press.[22]
What northern general conferences reserved to themselves, southern general conferences handed over to the

---

[19]*Journals of the Methodist Episcopal Church,
South, Held 1846 and 1850*, 106 and 112.

[20]Ibid., 117-18.

[21]*Journal of the General Conferences of the
Methodist Episcopal Church, South, 1846-1858* (Nashville: Southern Methodist Publishing House, [1874?]),
440.

[22]Ibid., 582.

bishops. All future southern Methodist pastorals were drafted by the college of bishops.

Four months after the Civil War officially ended in April of 1865, the southern bishops sent out a pastoral letter on their own. The need for offical expression of attitude of the southern church on a number of problems, particularly the relationship with the northern church and the disposition of its black members, became urgent. Meeting in Columbus, Georgia, Bishops Andrew, Paine and Pierce drafted a pastoral letter to the church which would also be a notice to the world of the church's "will to live."

The address stated emphatically that the questions raised in the division of 1844 were not settled by the war. All suggestions of reunion were rejected. The continued invasion of southern territory and the take-over of southern churches and pulpits were severely denounced, while the annual conferences were urged to present a united front against the invasion. A large proportion, if not a majority, of Northern Methodists were labelled "incurably radical."

> They teach for doctrine the commandments of men. They preach another Gospel. They have incor-porated social dogmas and political tests into their church creeds. They have gone on to impose conditions upon discipleship that Christ did not impose. Their pulpits are perverted to agitations and questions not healthful to personal piety, but promotive of political and ecclesiastical discord, rather than those ends for which the Church of the Lord Jesus Christ, was instituted.[23]

Yet tolerance toward the former foes was advised,

---

[23]"Pastoral Address of the Southern Methodist Bishops," appendix in *Minutes of the Fiftieth Session of the Mississippi Annual Conference of the Methodist Episcopal Church, South, Held in Lexington, Miss., November 1-7, 1865* (Jackson, MI: Printed at the Book and Job Office of the Daily and Weekly Clarion, 1866), 28.

especially toward those in the border states. The
platform of the southern church was restated by the
bishops in these words:

> Preach Christ and him crucified. Do not preach
> politics. You have no commission to preach
> politics. . . . Keep in view that rule of our
> faith which declares that "The Holy Scriptures
> contain all that is necessary to salvation; so
> that whatever is not read therein nor may be
> proved thereby, is not to be required of any
> man."[24]

On the fate of the newly freed black members, the
bishops cautioned patience. Give them time to decide
where their spiritual home shall be: "If they elect to
leave us, let them go with the assurance that as
heretofore we have been, and will continue to be, their
friends, and in every suitable way aid their moral
development and religious welfare."[25] Finally, the
bishops admonish the faithful to be loyal citizens of
their new government, to cultivate personal holiness,
to keep up the "family altar," and to attend the public
worship of God.

The southern bishops' pastoral of 1865 may have
sufficed for the time being, for the general conference
which met in New Orleans eight months later did not
issue a pastoral letter of its own. Drafting the next
one proved troublesome. At the beginning of the 1870
general conference a resolution called for the pastoral
address to be drafted by a committee of five clergy and
five lay delegates together with the bishops.[26] In the
middle of the conference the bishops begged to be

---

[24]Ibid.

[25]Ibid., 26-27.

[26]*Journal of the Methodist Episcopal Church,
South, 1870* (Nashville: Publishing House of the M. E.
Church, South, 1870), 169.

excused from the committee, "they being unable to attend to that matter."[27] On the next to the last day of the conference the original joint drafting committe was discharged from their duty and the bishops alone were requested to issue a pastoral address. Within twenty-four hours Bishop Wightman on behalf of the "College" of Bishops read a pastoral letter to the conference.[28] Had the bishops balked because they were too busy or because they thought it their duty to draft pastoral letters as they had done since 1858?

In 1874 a long resolution signed by twenty-eight delegates invited the bishops to prepare a new pastoral letter and suggested several themes they wished the bishops to address.[29] In effect, this was the southern church's last pastoral, since the 1878 general conference issued none and the 1882 general conference voted to republish the address of 1874.[30] No further pastoral letters were issued by general conferences or the bishops of the Methodist Episcopal Church, South, at least in the nineteenth century.

IV

The second pastoral letter of 1812 rather than the first of 1800 set the pattern for pastorals to come. After the first pastoral on slavery, successive nineteenth-century pastorals, whether drafted by clergy delegates or bishops, whether addressed to Methodists in the north or in the south, followed a familiar

---

[27]Ibid., 212.

[28]Ibid., 334-36.

[29]*Journal of the General Conference of the Methodist Episcopal Church, South* (Nashville, 1874), 437.

[30]*Journal of the General Conference of the Methodist Episcopal Church, South, 1882*, 83. See also the discipline of the M. E. Church, South for 1882, 351-62.

pattern. Each began with (1) a call to thank God for
members added, churches built, money given. Since
prosperity was considered the test of wise polity, then
came (2) a warning to guard the system and refrain from
making changes since the system was usually working
just fine. This was followed by (3) a call to support
the church's program agencies--establish Sunday
schools, give to missions, support our schools and
colleges, subscribe to our periodicals, buy our books.
Then, since a holy church demands a holy people,
successive pastorals called Methodists to seek personal
holiness by the three-fold pattern of the church's
venerable General Rules: (4) avoid evil, (5) do good,
and (6) use all the means of grace. Doctrinal matters
were rarely tackled in Methodist pastoral letters,
except for occasional reminders to (7) retain sanctification as the church's doctrinal distinctive. After
the first pastoral letter, social policy matters, such
as slavery and racism, sexism, war and peace, and
economic justice, if mentioned at all, were pronounced
political matters and therefore dangerous to true
religion and divisive to holy churches. Pointing to
the "purely spiritual" nature of the church the 1836
northern pastoral and the 1858 southern pastoral called
upon loyal Methodists to (8) shun politics altogether.

Give Thanks: Thanksgiving to God in Methodist
pastorals of the past bordered on boasting. An early
example of the exuberance came in the 1840 pastoral
following the celebration of the centenary of Wesleyan
Methodism in 1839.[31]

The first centenary of Methodism has brought with
it a state of great enlargement and prosperity.

---

[31]Both British and American Methodists
celebrated the centenary of the formation of the first
Methodist societies in 1839 in a big way.

The pious zeal which you exhibited in the appropriate celebration of this new era in our history,
and the liberal offerings you presented to the
church, exhibit a praiseworthy regard for her
institutions, and doubtless a sacrifice with which
God is well pleased. . . . Having brought your
tithes into the store-house of the Lord, and
proved him therewith, he has poured you out a
blessing that there is scarcely room to contain.[32]

Thirty-four years later revivals were still reaping a
host of converts and the southern bishops in their
pastoral letter of 1874 bragged unabashedly:

We render devout thanks to Almighty God for the
signal displays of his grace to us as a Church
during the past four years in the enlargement of
our course, in the increase of our numbers, in our
material prosperity, and in that agreement in the
faith, that unity in the Spirit, and in that
harmony and tranquility which have everywhere
pervaded our Zion. Extensive revivals of religion
have crowned the labors of our preachers, and the
life-giving energy of the gospel in the conversion
of sinners and in the sanctification of believers,
has been seldom more apparent amongst us.[33]

Guard the System: Convert counting was usually
followed by an appeal to guard the system. The third
pastoral letter (1832), following a decade of internal
turmoil over conference rights for laity and local
preachers and the status and role of Presiding Elders
and Bishops which led to the exodus of the Methodist
Protestants, confidently asserted:

Aroused by an attack which threatened the
integrity of [our] institutions, we carefully

---

[32]"Pastoral Address," in *Journals of the
General Conference of the Methodist Episcopal Church*
(New York: Carlton & Phillips, 1855), 2:158-59. The
full text of the address was also published in the
Christian Advocate [New York] 14:46 (July 32, 1840),
181, cols. 1-2; and in the *Methodist Quarterly Review*
[New York] 22:3 (July 1840), 351-55.

[33]*Journal of the General Conference of the
Methodist Episcopal Church, South, 1874* (Nashville:
Southern Methodist Publishing House, 1874), 568.

re-examined them; and, having satisfied ourselves
of their correctness and utility, we, with our
whole charge, have embraced them the more firmly.
. . . We consider it as now placed beyond question, that our system of government is too highly
appreciated by ourselves, as well as too firmly
supported by the hand of Heaven, to be shaken by
designing men.[34]

In scarcely no place had membership been "sensibly

diminished," reported the delegates. The seats of the

"malcontents" in the churches "have been filled by

occupants of a different and a better spirit."[35]

Subsequent pastorals north and south prided themselves

in not yielding in the slightest degree to the spirit

of innovation in church polity. The 1840 letter is

typical:

It affords us great pleasure to witness the strong
tendency which develops itself among the Methodists to adhere to the peculiar principles which
have characterized them from the beginning, and to
remain one and indissoluble. Though some have
entered into "doubtful disputations," and a few of
our societies have been hurtfully agitated, yet,
to the honour of our enlightened membership, and
to the glory of God, would we at this time express
our solemn conviction, that the great mass of our
people have remained "firm as a wall of brass"
midst the commotions of conflicting elements . . .
Indeed, brethren, we have no doubt but if we all
continue to "walk by the same rule, and to mind
the same things," in which in the order of God we
have been instructed, "the gates of hell shall not
prevail against us," and the enemy who would
divide and scatter, in order to destroy us, will
be disappointed.[36]

Thirty years later a divided Methodism's southern

pastoral (1874) made the same point:

---

[34]"Pastoral Address," *Christian Advocate* [New
York] 6:43 (June 23, 1832), 170, col. 2.

[35]Ibid.

[36]"Pastoral Address," *Journals of the General
Conference of the Methodist Episcopal Church* (New York:
Carlton & Phillips, 1855), 2:159.

We have abundant evidence of the continued power
and presence of the Holy Ghost in our ministra-
tions, and that the boon of Wesleyan Methodism, as
we received it from our fathers, has not been
forfeited in our hands. Regarding it as the
purest existing type of Christianity, and as a
priceless heritage of doctrine and discipline
committed to our keeping, we rejoice to believe
that we retain it in all its essential features.[37]

Support our Agencies: Pleas to support the
church's agencies increase as they grow in number and
importance in the life of the church: buy "our" books,
subscribe to "our" periodicals, use curricula produced
by "our" Sunday School Union, distribute "our" religious tracts (including, of course, pastoral letters
which were often issued as tracts), support "our"
expanding missionary enterprise.

Avoid Evil: Since a holy church demands a holy
people, each pastoral letter in its own way called
loyal Methodists to practice personal holiness by
keeping the church's General Rules. At least two evils
were regularly on the "to be avoided" list: alcohol and
amusements. The largest single paragraph in the 1848
Methodist Episcopal pastoral was devoted to temperance.
That was the year the northern general conference
restored Wesley's "general rule" on this subject, which
prohibited buying and selling, as well as using,
spirituous liquors as a beverage. Since this was a new
rule, the address recommended "kindness and gentleness
in its modes of enforcement" both for Methodists who
drank ("Be mild and gentle, yet decided, with of-
fenders") or Methodists who owned or invested in the
liquor business (". . . allow them a reasonable time to

---

[37]*Journal of the General Conference of the
Methodist Episcopal Church, South, Held in Louisville,
1874*, ed. Thomas O. Summers (Nashville: Publishing
House of the Methodist Episcopal Church, South, 1874),
568.

withdraw their capital, and invest it in some other occupation").[38] Although mentioned in many, one pastoral, the 1870 southern pastoral, was solely devoted to the danger of "worldly" amusements. Calling "the eager rush of Southern society after amusements . . . one of the startling signs of the times," the letter pronounced them inconsistent with the Baptismal vows of their members when they "renounced the devil and all his works" and vowed "not to follow or be led by them." The letter went on to warn their flock that

> the book of discipline provides not only against crimes and gross immoralities, but there is process laid down for cases of "imprudent conduct, and sinful tempers or words." We are persuaded that where that process is faithfully, firmly, but kindly, followed, these growing evils may be arrested.[39]

An earlier pastoral, 1840, singled out the reading of novels. Avoid the "dreadful tide of froth and corruption which is making such ravages upon the intellectual and moral character of the age, under the general tide of *novels*."[40] Warnings against worldly amusements were more strident in southern pastorals than in northern pastorals, especially after mid-century.

Do Good: Not wanting to accentuate the negative, nineteenth-century Methodist pastoral letters were never at a loss to prescribe decent deeds. Appeals to practice family religion, to instruct the children, to

[38]*Journal of the General Conference of the Methodist Episcopal Church, 1848*, 175.

[39]"Pastoral Address to the Members of the Methodist Episcopal Church, South," *Journal of the General Conference of the Methodist Episcopal Church, 1870* (Nashville: Publishing House of the M. E. Church, South, 1870), 334-35.

[40]"Pastoral Address," *Journal of the General Conference of the Methodist Episcopal Church* (New York: Carlton & Phillips, 1855), 2:160-61.

form Sunday schools, to support common school (the best
antidote to Romanism and infidelity), to build academies and colleges, and, of course, to extend missions
at home and abroad were regularly presented. Pre-Civil
War southern pastorals included a special section on
the duty of masters to their slaves. The 1858 southern
pastoral put it this way:

> The relation of master and servant is recognized
> in the New Testament, and the duties of each
> prescribed. The observance of these moral rules
> we regard as integral to the morality and piety of
> our members. The benign spirit of our holy
> religion not only demands that masters should
> render to their servants that which is just and
> equal in wages, as to food, raiment, and shelter,
> but that religious instruction should be provided
> alike for servants as for children. The gospel is
> God's gift to the black man as well as to the
> white, and Christian masters should see to it that
> all their dependents are regularly supplied with
> the preaching of the word, and all the privileges
> of the Church of God.[41]

Use the Means of Grace: To aid Methodists on their
pilgrimage from self-love to perfect love, all Methodist pastorals beginning with that of 1812 recommended
using the ordinary (instituted) means of grace (the
sacraments of Baptism and the Lord's Supper, Scripture
reading, private and public prayer, and fasting) as
well as those special (prudential) means of grace
obligatory on Methodists, that is, class meetings, love
feasts, and what was often called "Christian conference."

Seek Christian Perfection: Not surprisingly, the
one doctrine most frequently singled out in nineteenth-
century Methodist pastorals was holiness or Christian
Perfection. The rhetoric of the 1836 northern pastoral

---

[41]"Pastoral Address, 1858," *Journal of the
General Conferences of the Methodist Episcopal Church,
South, 1846-1858* (Nashville: Southern Methodist
Publishing House, [1874?]), 586.

is typical:

> The doctrine of *entire sanctification* constitutes
> a leading feature of original Methodism. But let
> us not suppose it enough to have this doctrine in
> our standards: let us labour to have the *experi-*
> *ence* and the *power* of it in our *hearts* . . . .
> When we fail to do this, then shall we lose our
> pre-eminence; and the halo of glory which sur-
> rounded the heads, and lit up the path of our
> sainted fathers, will have departed from their
> unworthy sons [and daughters].[42]

That the state in which God is loved with all the
heart, and served with all the power was considered to
be the goal of every Methodist. Pastorals hoped class
meetings and love feasts to come would be cheered by
stories of folk who sought pardon for their sins and
redirection for their love.[43] As the century wore on
this theme fades in northern pastorals but is picked up
again by southern pastorals after the civil war.

Shun Politics: Social policy matters did not come
up often after 1800, but when they did, as in the 1836
pastoral, they were to be shunned. Loyal Methodists
were to "abstain from all abolition movements and
associations," which were described as "fruitless
efforts which, instead of lightening the burden of the
slave, only tend to make his condition the more irksome
and distressing."[44]

> From every view of the subject which we have been
> able to take, and from the most calm and dispas-
> sionate survey of the whole ground, we have come
> to the solemn conviction that the only safe,
> Scriptural, and prudent way for us, both as
> ministers and people to take, is wholly to refrain

---

[42]"Pastoral Address," *Christian Advocate* [New
York] 10:43 (June 17, 1836), 171.

[43]Ibid., 170, col. 3.

[44]*Journals of the General Conference of the
Methodist Episcopal Church* (New York: Carlton and
Phillips, 1855), 1:443.

from this agitating subject, which is now
convulsing the country, and consequently the
Church, from end to end, by calling forth inflam-
matory speeches, papers, and pamphlets. While we
cheerfully accord to such, all the sincerity they
ask for their belief and motives, we cannot but
disprove of their measures as alike destructive to
the peace of the Church, and to the happiness of
the slave himself.[45]

Not meaning to deprive ministers or members of their

civil and political rights guaranteed by the nation's

constitution, the pastoral simply wished to

guard you against allowing yourselves to be drawn
aside from paramount duties, to mix in that angry
strife of political contests which tends to
disturb the peace of society, to alienate the
affections of brethren from each other, and to
interrupt the harmony of feeling which is essential to our prosperity.[46]

Clergy are admonished to stick to their "peculiar work"

("he that ministereth at the altar must be a partaker

of the things of the altar").[47] The 1858 southern

pastoral, pointing to the "purely spiritual" nature of

the church, proudly boasted, "Southern Methodism at

last stands dissentangled from this vexed and vexing

question [slavery], erect upon a scriptural basis. . .

We have surrendered to Caesar the things which are

his."[48]

V

Pastorals there have been in Methodism's past.

Whether issued by bishops or general conferences, their

---

[45]"Pastoral Address to the Member and Friends of the
Methodist Episcopal Church," *Christian Advocate* [New York] 10:43
(June 17, 1836), 171, col. 4.

[46]Ibid.

[47]Ibid.

[48]"Pastoral Address of the [1858] General Conference,"
*Journals of the General Conference of the Methodist Episcopal
Church, South, 1858*, 586.

rhetoric suggests that Methodism's leaders were not so
much impressed by the social evils from which their
flocks suffered as by the vices to which they suc-
cumbed. Although the first (1800) and last (1986) were
single-issue pastorals, drafted to rouse the church to
action on the most pressing social issue of the time,
slavery then and peace now, the twenty pastorals in
between preferred to promote personal piety and defend
denominational interests. Their repeated call in one
form or another to pray, pay and obey make them
quadrennial pep talks for the folks back home. It is
ironic that the practice of issuing pastoral letters
was abandoned in the 1800's just when American Methodism's social conscience was beginning to be aroused.
Stimulated by the emerging social gospel, Methodists
especially in the north began to pair again social
responsibility with personal piety. The denomination's
first modern declaration on social policy (the plight
of labor) was issued in 1908, not in a pastoral letter
but in a social crede.

Whether read from the pulpit or in the home,
pastoral letters shaped the spirituality of four
generations of American Methodists. Overlooked by
latter day historians, they constitute an important
resource for understanding Methodism's sense of
Christian faith and social responsibility in its most
expansive century.

A CATHOLIC AND REFORMED LITURGY
Howard G. Hageman

In 1978 Charles Yrigoyen and George Bricker
published a collection of the theological writings of
John Williamson Nevin under the title of *Catholic and
Reformed.*[1] For the most part, the articles chosen
represent Nevin's ideas about the Church, including
such well known items as his *Anxious Bench, The Sect
System* and in 1867, at the request of a number of
elders, Nevin published his *Vindication of the Revised
Liturgy.*

The Provisional Liturgy, published by the Committee in 1857, had started a vigorous discussion of the
liturgical question in the German Reformed Church. In
an effort to bring some peace to the troubled ecclesiastical scene, the General Synod of 1863 had re-
submitted the liturgy to the Committee, instructing it
to make revisions for presentation to the General Synod
of 1866. The result was the publication in 1866 of *The
Order of Worship for the Reformed Church in the United
States.*

Far from bringing peace, however, the submission

---

[1] *Catholic and Reformed, Selected Theological
Writings of John Williamson Nevin,* ed. Charles Yrigoyen
and George Bricker (Pittsburgh: Pickwick, 1978).

of the revision produced another furious debate at the
Synod of 1866 which finally voted by a small majority
to "allow the usage of the *Order of Worship* in the
congregations and families of the Reformed Church
without interfering in any way with the freedom of
pastors and congregations not to use it."[2] The leader
of the opposition to the adoption of the revision was
Dr. J. H. A. Bomberger who before the Synod meeting had
published a violent attack on it. Nevin's article was
an answer to Bomberger, but also contained replies to
some of the objections to the revision which were
uttered on the floor of the Synod.

Our interest in this article, however, will not
involve Nevin's tract as much as it will be focused on
the revised liturgy, the *Order of Worship* itself, for
it would be difficult to find a better example of what
is meant by "Catholic and Reformed" than is afforded by
this liturgy. Yrigoyen and Bricker could hardly have
included it in their collection because it was the work
of many people beside Nevin, though, as we shall see,
his theological hand can be seen in parts of it. But
it certainly provides an excellent illustration of what
Mercersburg theology understood by "Catholic and
Reformed."

I

The foundation for this had been laid in the
instructions given to the Committee by the Synod which
had met in Baltimore in 1852. These had included the
preparation of a liturgy which should reflect not only
Reformed liturgies of the sixteenth century but also
liturgies of the Greek and Latin churches of the third

---

[2]Ibid., 312.

and fourth centuries.[3] These instructions clearly
reflect the influence of Philip Schaff who was one of
the most active members of the Committee. It was in
response to these instructions that the Committee
produced the *Provisional Liturgy* of 1857 which was
revised as the *Order of Worship* and presented to the
General Synod of 1866.

Our examination of the *Order of Worship* as a
Catholic and Reformed document will be limited to the
liturgy which it provides for the Holy Communion.[4] It
might be noted at the outset that the use of the title
The Holy Communion is a nod if not in a Catholic
direction certainly an Anglican one. Any other
Reformed liturgy of the time would have carried the
title *The Administration of the Lord's Supper*.

The unfolding of the liturgy which follows clearly
indicates how seriously the Committee took its instruction that the liturgical life of the early Greek and
Latin Churches should be the general basis of its work.
For the first time in Reformed liturgical history, here
is a complete service of Word and Sacrament containing
all of the traditional elements of Christian worship
including such things as the Nicene Creed, the Gloria
in Excelsis, the collect, epistle and gospel for the
day.

The provision made for the eucharistic section of
the service reveals an even more catholic inclination.
Here we find the *Sursum Corda*, a fairly long invariable
preface (prayer of thanksgiving) culminating in the
singing of the *Sanctus and Benedictus Qui Venit*. The

---

[3]Ibid., 327.

[4]*Order of Worship for the Reformed Church in
the United States* (Philadelphia: Publication Board of
the Reformed Church in the United States, 1944), 132ff.

recitation of the narrative of institution with the
accompanying manual acts is followed by an epiclesis,
an anamnesis, a series of intercessions, a commemo-
ration of the departed and the Lord's Prayer. After
the people have communed there is a short prayer of
thanksgiving followed by the chanting or responsive
reading of the *Te Deum*. Small wonder that Dr. Bomberger and his friends felt compelled to raise the cry
of *Popery*!

I can still remember sharing the *Order of Worship*
with a friend who was a priest in one of the Orthodox
Churches and watching his eyes open more widely as he
read the eucharistic prayer, pointing out to me its
derivation from various Eastern liturgies. When it
comes to following Catholic antecedents, more eastern
than western, the *Order of Worship* in its eucharistic
liturgy is unique in Reformed liturgical history. Only
in modern time has the same kind of ecumenical influence made itself felt in any of the liturgies of
churches in the Reformed tradition.

The impression of its Catholic heritage is so
overwhelming that one wonders what aspects of the *Order
of Worship* can be considered Reformed. They may be
somewhat less obvious, but they are certainly there as
an integral part of the service.

II

The liturgy begins almost immediately with a
prayer of confession in which the congregation joins.
This was also the way in which the service in Calvin's
Form of Prayer began. Having done away with private
confession, the reformers made it a public prelude to
the Sunday Service. In Luther's case it was not as
corporate as in Calvin's whose prayer of confession was
always in the first person plural and an invariable
part of the Sunday service, the way in which the gates

of Prayer are opened, as he once said.

The language of the prayer of confession in the
Order of Worship is not the same as that of the prayer
in Calvin's service, but theologically they are almost
identical.

> We have sinned against thee. . . . provoking most
> justly they wrath and indignation against us. The
> remembrance of our transgressions and shortcomings
> fills us with sorrow and shame.[5]

These phrases are from the prayer of confession in the
Order of Worship, but in spirit they could just as well
have been from Calvin's *Form of Prayer*. At its very
beginning the *Order of Worship* sounds recognizably
Calvinistic notes!

After the pastor has recited some appropriate
words from Scripture, the confession in the *Order of
Worship* is followed by a Declaration of Pardon. Once
again, this is following exactly the sequence used by
John Calvin in his liturgy. It is true that when
Calvin took his liturgy from Strasbourg to Geneva in
1542, the congregation there objected to the absolution
so strongly that the reformer finally removed it from
the liturgy, but there can be no question that he
preferred the Strasbourg usage.

If we compare the language of Calvin with that of
Mercersburg, there is virtually no difference. Each
one is clearly an absolution that unhesitatingly
declares the forgiveness of sin. Those who objected to
the popish (sic) character of the Declaration of Pardon
in the *Order of Worship* evidently did not know the
liturgy of John Calvin which was equally high church!

The use of Scripture and sermon at this point in
the service is not necessarily Reformed, but it is
certainly Protestant. Living in a post-Vatican II era,

---

[5]Ibid., 143.

we are likely to forget that the proclamation of the
Word was from the point of view of the Reformation a
central part of worship.

It could be argued that the use of a lectionary
was more Catholic than Reformed. Certainly the lectionary was rejected by both Zwingli and Calvin who
followed the equally ancient tradition of *lectio
continua*. Neither reformer would have understood the
popular Protestant custom of free text-choice.

Though there can be no question that Zwingli and
Calvin advocated *lectio continua* for the proclamation
of the Word, there is good evidence that in parts of
Germany and in the northern Netherlands the use of the
lectionary continued after the Reformation. In fact
one of the German hymnals printed in Pennsylvania in
the mid-eighteenth century for use in the Reformed
churches contained all the Sunday gospels and epistles.
That fact may have been known to some of the members of
the Committee. In any event, the use of the lectionary
was not totally outside the Reformed tradition.

If we ask why the conservative Reformed critics of
the *Order of Worship* did not recognize the Reformed
antecedents of these items that we have discussed, the
answer is that under the influence of the pietism which
had blanketed the German Reformed Church in this
country things like confession, absolution and lectionary had just about disappeared from Sunday worship. Dr.
Bomberger, the new liturgy's fiercest critic was
acquainted the Palatinate Liturgy but it takes a much
lower ground than Calvin's liturgy which the Committee
obviously was using as its model.

Once we turn to the eucharistic section of the
Sunday liturgy we seem to have entered the Catholic
rather than the Reformed tradition. The long invariable preface is where my Orthodox friend felt so much

at home. This is because much of the text was borrowed
from the Liturgy of the Catholic and Apostolic Church
with which Dr. Schaff was very familiar and which
itself had borrowed generously from the liturgies of
eastern Orthodoxy, especially the Liturgy of St. James.

Following the reading of the words of institution
there is an epiclesis, again something to gladden the
heart of my Orthodox friend. The invocation of the
Holy Spirit has a very central role in the eucharistic
liturgies of the eastern Churches, but has disappeared
from the Latin mass. Was it their acquaintance with
eastern liturgies or with that of the Catholic and
Apostolic Church that led to the Mercersburg fathers to
restore it in their *Order of Worship*? It would clearly
seem to be another mark for the Catholic side of this
liturgy.

But the question is not quite that simple. If we
examine the liturgies of the Reformation beginning with
Calvin's, we discover a form of epiclesis in all of
them. The Dutch Reformed liturgy of 1566 will serve as
an example.

> O most merciful God and Father, we beseech thee
> that thou wilt be pleased in this Supper (in which
> we celebrate the glorious remembrance of the
> bitter death of thy Son Jesus Christ) to work in
> our hearts through the Holy Spirit that we may
> daily more and more with true confidence give
> ourselves up unto thy Son Jesus Christ that our
> afflicted and contrite hearts, through the power
> of the Holy Ghost, may be fed and comforted with
> his true body and blood; yea, with him, true God
> and man, that only heavenly bread; and that we may
> no longer live in our sins, but he in us and we in
> him. [6]

It will be noticed that in these Reformed epicleses, of
which this is one example, the presence of the Holy

---

[6] *The Liturgy of the Reformed Protestant Dutch Church* (New York: n.p., 1860), 70.

Spirit is sought not for the transformation of the elements, as in Orthodox usage, but for the transformation of the communicants. H. O. Old has described the Reformed epicleses in this way:

> It is characteristic of the Reformed Communion Invocation that Christ is asked to take up his dwelling in the hearts of the faithful to the end of their sanctification and God's glory. The sacrifice of praise is the fruit of the consecration of the congregation.[7]

With that much by way of introduction, we should now look at the epiclesis in the 1866 *Order of Worship*, asking ourselves whether it basically belongs in the Catholic or Reformed tradition. This is the full text of it:

> Almighty God, our heavenly Father, send down, we beseech thee, the powerful benediction of thy Holy Spirit upon these elements of bread and wine, that being set apart now from a common to sacred and mystical use, they may exhibit and represent to us with true effect the body and blood of thy Son Jesus Christ; so that in the use of them we may be made, through the power of the Holy Ghost, to partake really and truly of his blessed life, whereby only can we be saved from death and raised to immortality at the last day.[8]

It would seem that such a prayer does include a consecration of the elements as well as of the congregation, subtly combining both Catholic and Reformed traditions. Fortunately, however, we have an expert exegete of the prayer in no less a person than Dr. Nevin himself. In his 1867 *Vindication of the Revised Liturgy*, there is a section in which he takes up some of the specific objections raised in the debate at the General Synod of 1866. Evidently someone had claimed

---

[7]Hughs Oliphant Old, *The Patristic Roots of Reformed Worship* (Zurich: Theologischer Verlag, 1975), 291.

[8]*Order of Worship for the Reformed Church*, 151.

that the prayer we are examining teaches the doctrine
of transubstantiation. In his printed reply Dr. Nevin
claims that the prayer in question is not Popish and
not Lutheran but strictly Reformed. The rather preju-
diced claim of his opponent is enough to bring the
theological professor into action, almost as though he
were instructing a slow student in the classroom.

> Now it is (the) old Reformed doctrine. . . . and
> no other which is involved in the consecratory
> prayer of the Liturgy. Anyone familiar with the
> Calvinistic terminology in regard to it can see
> that it is faithfully followed at every point. It
> would be hard indeed to give the doctrine more
> succinctly or exactly in the same compass.
> God is called upon to "send down the powerful
> benediction of his Holy Spirit" upon the elements,
> "that being set apart from a common to a sacred
> and mystical use, they may exhibit and represent"
> --these being the very terms made use of by Calvin
> to distinguish the Reformed doctrine from the
> Lutheran; may *exhibit and represent* "to us with
> true effect"--that is not corporeally, and yet not
> simply in sign or shadow either, but with the
> energy of actual presence--"the body and blood of
> his Son, Jesus Christ; so that in the *use of them*"
> --mark again the distinction; not in the elements
> themselves outwardly considered, but in the use of
> them, that is, in the sacramental transaction "we
> may be made, through the power of the Holy Ghost"
> --again the Calvinistic or Reformed qualification
> --"to partake really and truly of his blessed life
> whereby only we can be saved from death and raised
> to immortality at the last day." [9]

If we compare the theology of this prayer with
that of any of the Calvinistic confessions (such as the
Gallic or the Belgic, both produced in Calvin's life
time), we shall see that Dr. Nevin's exegesis is
correct; the prayer is a liturgical expression of the
eucharistic theology of John Calvin. Only one thing
has been changed; the fruit of this communion is no
longer a life lived as a sacrifice to God's glory, but

---

[9] Yrigoyen and Bricker, *Catholic and Reformed*, 401.

immortality. There is no reason to suppose that Calvin
would have objected to this, but he might have been
critical of the omission of sanctification. Otherwise
the prayer might have come from his own pen, as many of
its phrases in fact did.

III

Why then did the appearance of the *Order of
Worship* (and of its predecessor in 1857) raise such
excited accusations of Romanism? Probably the basic
answer is the one which Nevin himself gave. Many parts
of the Reformed Church no longer recognized its
Calvinistic heritage in liturgy or in the doctrine of
the eucharist. The forces of pietism had taken over
(which Nevin often called the forces of puritism).
Probably if John Calvin had presented his *Form of
Prayer* to the General Synod of 1866, he would have
encountered the same kind of opposition!

But in fairness to that same opposition, it has
too be said that the Reformed parts of the *Order of
Worship* were presented in such a Catholic framework
that many in the Reformed Church were confused. Not
only had such Reformed elements as confession, absolution, lectionary, and epiclesis disappeared from
their usual patterns of worship, but when they made
their reappearance in 1857, it was in connection with
such strange companions as the *Gloria in Excelsis*, the
Te Deum and the *Seraphic Hymn*, to say nothing of
numerous responses which just about everyone thought to
be unreformed, even though liturgy as a corporate
activity was certainly one of the strong emphases of
the Protestant Reformation.

The positive vote by the Synod of 1866 by no means
quieted the liturgical struggle in the German Reformed
Church. It continued heatedly, often dividing congregations, until a Peace Commission was appointed in

1878 which in a few years published a *Directory of Worship* which became the official liturgy of the Church, although the *Order of Worship* was continued as a permissive use. That use must have continued in some numbers because my personal copy of the *Order of Worship* was issued by the Denominational Publishing House in 1944, almost eighty years after the original publication! There are still a few congregations which use it regularly and many more that use a somewhat abbreviated version.

Over the years the mortality rate in Reformed liturgies has been very high. Bits and pieces of them have survived for longer periods of time, but there are few that have survived in their entirety for more than a century as has been the case with the *Order of Worship*. There are doubtless many factors involved in this survival which is itself worthy of further study. But one factor which certainly needs to be considered is the way in which this liturgy carried the Reformed understanding of worship in a Catholic setting.

And in these days of ecumenical liturgical interest and endeavor, the *Order of Worship* deserves to be better known as an early but still significant attempt to create a liturgy which would be both Catholic and Reformed.

PART TWO:
THE CHURCH AND MODERN THOUGHT

MERCERSBURG: A REFORMED ALTERNATIVE FOR THE TWENTIETH CENTURY

Charles A. Jones III

A small village in southern Pennsylvania on the
Mason-Dixon line provided a home for a significant
theological movement in nineteenth-century America.
Between 1840 and 1870 the German Reformed Seminary,
originally located in the hamlet of Mercersburg,
produced a distinct expression of Reformed
Christianity. The Mercersburg Theology has been called
"the most celebrated theological development in the
German Reformed Church in the nineteenth century."[1] In
the wake of the Second Great Awakening and in the midst
of strong nativist fervor, the Mercersburg Theology
espoused an anti-Puritan, anti-revivalistic, Christological, ecclesiological, liturgical and sacramental
interpretation of the Reformed tradition. Operating in
such a climate, the Mercersburg school "tended to
create difficulties for both simple anti-Catholicism
and uncritical non-denominationalism."[2] It spurred
such a debate both within the German Reformed

---

[1]Charles Yrigoyen, Jr., "Emanuel V. Gerhart:
Apologist for the Mercersburg Theology," *Journal of
Presbyterian History* 57:4 (1979): 485.

[2]Sydney E. Ahlstrom, *A Religious History of the
American People* (New Haven: Yale University Press,
1972), 619.

communion in particular and American Protestantism in
general that the positive points of the Mercersburg
position tended to be obscured in theological wran-
gling. The questions then arise: what specifically is
the Mercersburg Theology, and how is one to understand
the uniqueness of the Mercersburg perspective within
the nineteenth-century American milieu?[3]

I

The 1840's saw the meteoric rise of a nascent
seminary of an immigrant church which drew response
from all quarters of American Protestantism.[4] But
within fifty years, Mercersburg faded into the land-
scape as another thread in the rich tapestry of
American religious history. Was Mercersburg just an
aberration or did it have any lasting impact upon
America? It was not until the middle of the twentieth
century that the Mercersburg Theology would emerge for
reconsideration.[5] Since that time Mercersburg has been
seen as offering new alternatives for ministry in the
modern Reformed family in America.

---

[3]For good introductory essays covering the
basics of the Mercersburg theology see James H.
Nichols, ed. *The Mercersburg Theology* (New York: Oxford
University Press, 1966), 3-30; and Jack M. Maxwell,
*Worship and Reformed Theology: The Liturgical Lessons
of Mercersburg* (Pittsburgh: Pickwick, 1976), 9-48.

[4]James H. Nichols, in his book *Romanticism in
American Theology: Nevin and Schaff at Mercersburg*
(Chicago: University of Chicago Press, 1961), provides
a good survey of the reactions that the Mercersburg
school drew from other leading American theologians of
the day.

[5]Two articles which spurred a new interest in
the content and implications of the Mercersburg
theology are George W. Richards' "The Mercersburg
Theology--Its Purpose and Principles," *Church History*
20:3 (1951): 42-55; and Scott Francis Brenner's "Nevin
and the Mercersburg Theology," *Theology Today* 12
(1955): 43-56.

Four major figures led the Mercersburg movement
and played key roles in its development: Frederick
Augustus Rauch (1806-41), the founder and philosopher
of the school; John Williamson Nevin (1803-86), a
Princeton Seminary educated Presbyterian, its theologian; Philip Schaff (1819-93), a Swiss who trained in
Germany, its historian; and Emanuel Vogel Gerhart
(1819-1904), son of a German Reformed pastor, its
systematizer and apologist.[6] The works of these men
constitute the heart and soul of the Mercersburg
Theology. This chapter contends that the Mercersburg
Theology can best be understood as a Christological
reformation which manifested itself in a sacramental
and churchly theology. It sought to reclaim certain
Calvinistic commitments with an evangelical,
"catholic," romantic spirit. And while it was not
fully appreciated in nineteenth-century America, it
offers the contemporary church a distinct Reformed
theological alternative for ministry. Nevin and
Schaff, who are the most noted of the Mercersburg
leaders, are the focus of this article.[7]

Nevin and Schaff emphasized the objective,

---

[6]Other people who figured prominently in the
Mercersburg school were John H. A. Bomberger (1817-
1890), Henry Harbaugh (1817-1867), and Bernard C. Wolff
(1794-1870). They served on the liturgical committee
of the German Reformed Church and played leadership
roles in the parish and educational institutions of
their denomination.

[7]Theodore Appel's work, The Life and Work of
John Williamson Nevin (Philadelphia: Reformed Church
Publication House, 1889), and David S. Schaff's The
Life of Philip Schaff (New York: Charles Scribner's
Sons, 1897) remain the authoritative biographies of
these two men. A recent monograph by George Shriver,
Philip Schaff: Christian Scholar and Ecumenical Prophet
(Macon, GA: Mercer University Press, 1987), offers a
more recent but limited perspective on Schaff and his
place in American Church History.

sacramental, and liturgical factors in theology over
against the subjective, revivalistic, and rationalistic
elements which are congenial to the American mindset. [8]
Sydney Ahlstrom identified Mercersburg's major focus as
"its persistent effort to achieve a Christ-centered
theology. The chief purpose of both Nevin and Schaff
was to make the 'person' of Christ the center of
theology and church life." [9]   James Nichols claimed that
it was the "catholicizing tendency within the framework of German idealism and historical thought which is
the characteristic note of Mercersburg Theology." [10]   He
then notes that "a second major tendency was a
reverence for tradition as expressing the continuity of
the Church." [11]   These two major tendencies were
manifested in a movement for liturgical renewal within
the German Reformed Church. As Nichols points out: "In
its practical effect . . . the Mercersburg movement was
primarily a Eucharistic revival." [12]   It held that "the
historical development of the Church reveals by its
richness and diversity how Christian faith fulfills and
culminates every human or historical tendency." [13]

The context in which the Mercersburg movement

---

[8]George W. Richards, "The Mercersburg Theology:
Its Purpose and Principles," *Church History* 20:3
(1951): 44.

[9]Sydney Ahlstrom, "Theology in America," in *The
Shaping of American Religion*, ed. James W. Smith and A.
Leland Jamison (Princeton: Princeton University Press,
1961), 271.

[10]Nichols, *Mercersburg Theology*, 11.

[11]Ibid., 13.

[12]Ibid.

[13]Ahlstrom, *Religious History of the American
People*, 618.

gained exposure was through the effort in the German
Reformed Church to devise a new liturgy. As was
typical in that era, worship had fallen into confusion
and disarray. Some services were held in German,
others in English. Little form or reason undergirded
the activity of worship. As Schaff admitted, "The
Mercersburg controversy did not originate the liturgical movement in the German Reformed body, but it gave
it new impulse and direction and carried it to a
practical result."[14] Howard Hageman also notes that it
was the liturgical reform that provided Mercersburg the
vehicle for expression:

> What made the liturgical movement there [in the
> German Reformed Church] remarkable was not the
> Order of Worship, despite its high degree of
> liturgical skill. It was rather that it was the
> first liturgy in the Reformed Church to articulate
> a theology. Indeed, it was at Mercersburg that
> there was worked out, often in the heat of battle,
> for the first time in the Reformed Churches what
> could be called a theology of the liturgy.[15]

The presentation of the Liturgy to the Eastern Synod of
the German Reformed Church in 1857 articulated the
major commitments of the Mercersburg school. The
chairperson of the liturgical committee, and the chief
architect of its work, was Philip Schaff, and John
Nevin served as one of its members.[16]

Nevin himself provided the most concise definition
of the Mercersburg Theology when he stated the following in 1867:

---

[14]Philip Schaff, "The New Liturgy," The
Mercersburg Review 10 (1858): 208.

[15]Howard G. Hageman, Pulpit and Table: Some
Chapters in the History of Worship in the Reformed
Churches (Richmond: John Knox, 1962), 92.

[16]Jack M. Maxwell covers the development and
work of this committee in detail in Worship and
Reformed Theology.

In the first place, it is Christological, or more
properly perhaps Christocentric; in the second
place, it moves in the bosom of the Apostles'
Creed; in the third place, it is Objective and
Historical, involving thus the idea of the Church
as a perennial article of faith.[17]

Nevin believed that Christ was the starting point of
all thelogy. Theology "must plant itself boldly and
broadly on the proposition, that Jesus Christ is the
principle of Christianity, and that the full sense of
the Gospel is to be reached only in and through the
revelation which is comprehended in His glorious
Person."[18] For Nevin this was a self-evident first
principle in theology.[19] Nevin's convictions were
grounded in the belief that "all sound Christian
feeling and experience, flow from the sense of Christ
formed in us as the hope of glory."[20] Luther Binkley
noted that for Nevin and Schaff, "Christ was the
meaning of history and a spiritual force active in the
world through his ongoing incarnation in the Christian
Church."[21] Ultimately, all of the Mercersburg Theology
hinges upon its Christocentric nature. Christ is the
clue to the meaning of history, for he is the incarnation of the divine purpose in human history.[22] And for
both Nevin and Schaff,

---

[17]John W. Nevin, "Theology of the New Liturgy,"
The Mercersburg Review 19:1 (1867): 28.

[18]Ibid., 28-29.

[19]Ibid., 31.

[20]Ibid., 33.

[21]Luther Binkley, *The Mercersburg Theology*
(Manheim, PA: Franklin and Marshall College, 1953), 40.

[22]Philip Schaff, *Moral Character of Christ*
(Chambersburg, PA: Office of the Weekly Messenger,
1861), 53.

A theology which is truly Christocentric must
follow the Creed, must be objective, must be
historical; with this, must be churchly; and, with
this again, must be sacramental and liturgical.[23]

Thus, Christology is the lens through which to grasp
the meaning of the Mercersburg Theology. By stressing
Christology, the Mercersburg men aligned themselves
with the developments in liberal nineteenth-century
Protestantism.

From this conviction, the Mercersburg Theology
stressed the incarnation rather than the atonement as
the central Christian doctrine. Nevin maintained,
"What we call the atonement in its more special sense,
as wrought out by [Christ's] sufferings and death, was
nothing more . . . than the irresistible, inevitable
movement of the incarnation itself out to its own
necessary end."[24] The incarnation pointed to a new
order of humanity, and was the keystone in the arch of
sacramental doctrine. It was through the incarnation
that Nevin sought to highlight the organic link between
Christ and the church.

> The Church is the body of Christ, only as it
> serves to reveal Christ, under a truly living and
> historical form, in the history of the world; in
> which view all the power it has to propound Christ
> as an object of faith, is found in the fact of its
> being itself an object of faith through Christ and
> from him, the form in which his life completes
> itself among men.[25]

The sacrifice of Christ does not relate solely to the
Cross, but includes all which transpires from the

---

[23]Nevin, "Theology of the New Liturgy," 44.

[24]John W. Nevin, "Undying Life in Christ," in
Tercentenary Monument of the Heidelberg Catechism
(Chambersburg, PA: Office of the Weekly Messenger,
1863), 36.

[25]John W. Nevin, "Brownson's Quarterly Review,"
Mercersburg Review 2 (1850): 71.

incarnation through Christ's continuing priestly
intercession as manifested in the church.

Schaff and Nevin believed that "religion was a
life." The influence of German theology was seen as
they maintained that religion was "a matter of sentiment more than of mere intellection." Moving away from
Reformed scholasticism, they argued that "life" conveyed the idea of gradual change, growth and development. Faith embraced not simply the notion of supernatural things, but the very power and presence of the
things themselves. The invisible was felt to be truly
actual and real, while the outward and visible was
regarded as being its empty shadow projected on the
field of space.[26] Joseph Berg, a Mercersburg critic,
summarized the sense of Mercersburg's organic tendency
in the action of salvation when he stated:

> In regeneration, the person of the Lord Jesus
> Christ in the fulness of his glorified humanity,
> body and soul, is infused into the believer; this
> participation in the nature of Christ constitutes
> the germ, as it were, of the new creation, and is
> finally consummated in the resurrection of life.
> Thus believers in this life, by virtue of their
> union with Christ, have in themselves the germ of
> the resurrection body. . . . The person of Christ
> is regarded not merely as individual and single,
> but as generic also, and Christ's glorified
> humanity is in his people, just as Adam's humanity
> is in the whole human race.[27]

In this way Christ takes the initiative by being
present in a person before salvation has an effect.
From this vantage, faith is a kind of intuition, the
"organ of spiritual vision," while sense is the
perception of the material world. Nevin held that
faith was not opposed to reason but was above it:

---

[26]Richards, "Mercersburg Theology," 44.

[27]Joseph F. Berg, "Mercersburg Theology,"
Protestant Quarterly Review 3 (1846): 77.

> Faith is the capacity of perceiving the invisible
> and supernatural, the substantiation of things
> hoped for, the certification of things not seen;
> which, as such, does not hold on the outside of
> reason, any more than this can be said of sense,
> but opens to view rather a higher form of what may
> be called its own proper life, in which it is
> required to become complete, and without which it
> must always remain comparatively helpless, blind
> and dark.[28]

Faith is that vision or sensibility by which, in the
words of the Bible, we hear the living God or in nature
constantly sense God's providential rule always
encircling us in the events of our practical existence.[29] For Schaff, faith and knowledge were organically united in Christianity. It was an exercise of
the mind and of reason as well as of the heart and
will.

The Mercersburg Theology was also creedal by
nature, thus linking it to the more orthodox expressions of Calvinism. Unlike the transcendentalists'
total rejection of creedal formulations and Horace
Bushnell's relativizing of religious language, Nevin
accepted the *Apostles' Creed* as "the deepest, and . . .
most comprehensive of all Christian symbols." For him,
it lay "at the foundation of all evangelical unity; it
is the last basis and bond of comprehension in the
conception of the Church."[30] Nevin believed that the
Apostles' Creed articulated the Christocentric nature
of theology. "Starting in Christ, it [*The Apostles'
Creed*] follows the order in which the facts of religion
unfold themselves with necessary connection from His

---

[28]Nevin, "Brownson's Quarterly Review," 67.

[29]Nichols, *Romanticism in American Theology*,
39.

[30]Nevin, "Theology of the New Liturgy," 34.

person."[31] Creeds and confessions are evidence of the
church's attempts throughout its history to set forth
and clarify, in concise statements, the object of
faith, Jesus Christ. As the church experienced new
truths, creedal expressions were open to revision, thus
embodying the Reformation conviction that the Reformed
church is "always reforming and being reformed."
Creeds then represented

> the necessary form of the Gospel, as this is first
> apprehended by faith; a direct transcript . . . of
> what the Gospel is to the contemplation of the
> believer, turned wholly upon the Person of
> Christ.[32]

Creeds served as a testimony of Christ's presence in a
faith community, and as such were formative for the
ministry and life of the church.

From this conviction, Nevin declared that the
Mercersburg Theology was "objective and historical."
Nevin carefully delineated what he meant by this when
he stated that his theology

> . . . is not a system simply of subjective
> notions, a metaphysical theory of God and religion
> born only of the human mind, a supposed apprehen-
> sion of supernatural verities brought into the
> mind in the way of abstract thought; but it is the
> apprehension of the supernatural by faith under
> the form of an actual Divine manifestation in and
> through Christ, which, as such, rules and governs
> the power that perceives it, while it is felt also
> to be joined in its own order to the natural
> history of the world onward through time.[33]

"All revelation is primarily something that God
does--an objective, supernatural manifestation, which

---

[31]Ibid., 35.

[32]Ibid., 34-35.

[33]Ibid., 39.

causes His presence to be felt in the world."[34] The
objective is always first in the order of "true"
revelation, followed by the subjective perception which
defines what God has revealed. The focal point of this
objective and historical approach to Christianity is,
again, the incarnation of Jesus from which the rest of
religion receives its content. The objectivity of the
incarnation means that it has entered permanently into
the activity of daily living. For Nevin, "the Gospel
is supernatural; but it is the supernatural joined in a
new order of existence to the natural; and this, it can
be only in the form of history."[35] Through the
objective fact of Christ's incarnation and its expression in history, the supernatural is brought into union
with the natural. Nevin writes,

> The Incarnation constitutes the gospel--being in
> its very nature a new revelation of God in the
> world, by which the life of heaven is made to
> unite itself with the life of earth, in a real and
> abiding way, so as to bring the supernatural home
> to men in a form fully answerable to their inmost
> wants.[36]

In the incarnation, Nevin saw the supernatural as "the
proper complement or filling out of the natural."[37] On
this point, he agreed with Bushnell that the two
together constitute "the one system of God."[38]

---

[34]Ibid.

[35]Ibid., 40.

[36]John W. Nevin, "Natural and Supernatural,"
Mercersburg Review 1 (1859): 203.

[37]Ibid., 196.

[38]In *Nature and the Supernatural* (New York:
Scribner's, 1858), Bushnell espoused a view similar to
that of Nevin. It is difficult to determine whether
Bushnell directly influenced Nevin on this point since

Finally, the Mercersburg Theology can be described as "churchly." The medium of communication between Christ and his people, between the supernatural and the natural, is the church. "Salvation is of the Church, and not of the world."[39] The incarnation produced the church through which Christ continues to be active and present in the world. Thus churchly theology is of necessity sacramental.[40] "Where the idea of the Church involves the conjunction of the supernatural and the natural continuously in one and the same abiding economy of grace, its sacraments are outward signs of what they represent."[41]

II

The two works that catapulted the Mercersburg Theology into the national limelight were Schaff's *The Principle of Protestantism*, published in 1845, and Nevin's *The Mystical Presence, A Vindication of the Reformed or Calvinistic Doctrine of the Holy Eucharist*, published in 1846. These works set forth the early expression of the basic tenets of the Mercersburg school which confronted nineteenth-century American theology with new formulations of traditional topics.

As Nevin interpreted it, our participation in the second Adam and the New Creation is concentrated and actualized most dramatically in the Lord's Supper. Nevin's Christocentric, incarnational theology leads inexorably to his doctrine of the "spiritual Real Presence" of Christ in this sacrament. He readily

---

Bushnell's book preceded Nevin's article by only a little over eight months.

[39]Nevin, "Theology of the New Liturgy," 43.

[40]Ibid.

[41]Ibid., 48.

acknowledged this fact which other churchmen were
decrying as heresy.

> To my own mind, all that is great and precious in
> the gospel may be said to center in this doctrine.
> Without it, I must feel that the whole Christian
> salvation would be shorn of its glory and force.
> I have no hope, save on the ground of a living
> union with the nature of Christ as the resurrec-
> tion and the life. Both for my understanding and
> my heart, theology finds here all its interest and
> attraction. For no truth am I more willing to
> suffer contradiction and reproach, if such be the
> will of God. . . . The fact that the Christian
> life holds in an actual communication with the
> humanity of Christ, and that this, in particular,
> forms the soul of the Lord's Supper, may never be
> relinquished.[42]

Nevin sought to reclaim what he believed to be the
central teaching of Calvin on the Lord's Supper. To
Nevin most of American evangelical Protestantism had
slipped into a Zwinglian understanding of the Lord's
Supper, which he felt robbed the sacrament of its
vitality as a means of grace. He was convinced that

> the sacramental doctrine of the primitive Reformed
> Church stands inseparably connected with the idea
> of an inward living union between believers and
> Christ, in virtue of which they are incorporated
> into his very nature, and made to subsist with him
> by the power of a common life. In full correspon-
> dence with this conception of the Christian
> salvation, as a process by which the believer is
> mystically inserted more and more into the person
> of Christ, till he becomes thus at last fully
> transformed into his image, it was held that
> nothing less than such a real participation of his
> living person is involved always in the right use
> of the Lord's Supper.[43]

The mystical presence of Christ in the Lord's Supper

---

[42]John W. Nevin, "The Mystical Union," *The
Weekly Messenger*, October 8, 1845; quoted in James
Hastings Nichols, *The Mercersburg Theology* (New York:
Oxford University Press, 1966), 197.

[43]John W. Nevin, *The Mystical Presence* (Philadelphia: J. B. Lippincott, 1846), 54.

was a distinctive ingredient for the church's work
and worship.

The key issue for Nevin was the nature of the real
"mystical" union that took place in the sacrament. Did
it depend upon the recipient taking the elements in
faith? Was there a corporal presence in any way? How
did Nevin's concept differ from the Roman Catholic,
Lutheran or Zwinglian views? Nevin was very clear on
this point, which few of his detractors fully comprehended. He held that:

> The union of believers with Christ is not simply
> that of a common humanity . . . but on the ground
> of our participation in his own nature as a higher
> order of life. Our relation to him is not
> circuitous and collateral only; it holds in a
> direct connection with his person.[44]

Nevin drew upon Calvin's doctrine of the Holy Spirit to
make the connection in this mystical union. "We
communicate . . . with the living Saviour himself, in
the fulness of his glorified person, made present to us
for the purpose by the power of the Holy Ghost."[45] He
believed that in the Lord's Supper one participated in
Christ's "true and proper life." The Holy Spirit was
the medium through which union occurred. One is united
with Christ in this sacramental act in both a real and
spiritual way. Nevin denied that Christ's body was
located in the elements in any local or corporate
manner. It was through the action of the Spirit that,

> while the outward symbols are received in an
> outward way, the very body and blood of Christ are
> at the same time inwardly and supernaturally
> communicated to the worthy believer, for the real
> nourishment of his new life.[46]

---

[44]Ibid., 55.

[45]Ibid., 57.

[46]Ibid., 61.

Where the Church is understood as involving the
conjunction of the supernatural and the natural
continuously in one and the same abiding economy of
grace, the sacraments cannot be regarded as outward
signs only of what they represent.

In *The Principle of Protestantism*, Schaff presented a new understanding of the historical connectedness
of the church. He rejected both the common Protestant
view that the Reformation was an attempt to return to
the "primitive" church of the New Testament, and the
Anglican notion that Protestantism was a revival of the
patristic church. Schaff proposed that the Protestant
Church was connected to both the New Testament Church
and the church fathers by historical development.
Church history is organic, with a continuous flow of
life in which every succeeding age is a true development of its own organic will from the life preceding.[47]
In an era when anti-Catholic sentiment was running high
in America, Schaff suggested that the Protestant Church
was a development from the good forces within Catholicism before the Reformation. Schaff revealed the
influence of German Idealism as he maintained that this
developmental character would continue until Protestantism and Catholicism would approach a unity. This
left Schaff open to the charge of Romanizing.

In summary, for Nevin and Schaff Christianity was
properly understood as:

> a perpetual fact, that starts in the Incarnation
> of the Son of God, and reaches forward as a
> continuous Supernatural reality into the end of
> time. The Bible was neither the principle of

---

[47]James I. Good, *History of the Reformed Church
in the U.S. in the Nineteenth Century* (New York: Board
of Publication of the Reformed Church in America,
1911), 215. Good's work also has a detailed account of
the controversies that Mercersburg caused within the
German Reformed church, 202-304.

Christianity nor the rock on which the church was
built. Rather, Jesus, his actual living revelation, was the foundation. The human race was not
an aggregate of people, but the power of a single
life, inwardly bound together. The redeemed were
mystically unified to this life and drawn to its
center in Christ. Christianity was organically
and temporally expressed in the traditions of the
church, in its institutions, patterns of worship
and creeds. [48]

This concept removes Christianity from the context of

propositional theology and sees it more as a mode of

life. Contrary to more orthodox approaches, Nevin

contended that "theology can never be a science except

as it has to do with the whole of Christianity, and is

thus at once both churchly and historical."[49]   Old

School Presbyterians, particularly Charles Hodge of

Princeton, took issue with this notion.[50]

III

The Mercersburg school introduced new principles

which would serve as building blocks for theology in

the twentieth century. An idealistic view of the world

with an emphasis on divine immanence, the conception of

the universe as an organism, the genetic relation of

---

[48]John W. Nevin, "The Apostles' Creed," in *The
Mercersburg Theology*, ed. James H. Nichols (New York:
Oxford University Press, 1966), 71 and 310.

[49]John W. Nevin, "The Sect System II," *The
Mercersburg Review* 1 (1849), 525.

[50]Nevin was a student of Hodge in the early
1820's and was so admired by Hodge that he was appointed to take Hodge's place while Hodge spent two
years (1826-28) in Europe. But Hodge took issue with
Nevin in the pages of the *Biblical Repertory and
Princeton Review*. George H. Shriver wrote a short
article which reviewed the correspondence between Hodge
and Nevin, "Passages in Friendship: John W. Nevin to
Charles Hodge," *Journal of Presbyterian History* 58:2
(1980): 116-22. He shows that Nevin always maintained
a respect for his teacher, while Hodge turned Nevin a
cold shoulder.

nature and history, the recognition of the principle of
development of all forms of life, the primacy of the
generic in the life of the individual, and the objective reality of universal concepts were formative
contributions. It demarcated a distinct place in the
romantic movement with its stress on historic tradi-
tionalism. As Bruce Kuklick has pointed out:

> Mercersburg formulated its views within the
> framework of communitarian traditionalism that
> dramatically contrasted with the ahistoric
> individualism of New England. . . . Emerson shared
> with Mercersburg an idealist organicism, but with
> New England Unitarians and Trinitarians he shared
> a static individualism. Mercersburg emphasized an
> historical community, augmenting ideas only
> implicit in Bushnell. Nevin and Schaff believed
> that the spiritual and moral life had no meaning
> aside from history, whereas Emerson attacked
> traditional Christianity and divested the spirit
> from the past. . . . Nevin and Schaff thought the
> essence [of Christianity] was revealed only in
> historical study. For Transcendentalists, the
> intuitive powers of reason grasped truth, which
> was immediately and directly available to the
> individual and independent of society. For Nevin
> and Schaff, truth was incorporated in tradition
> and could be comprehended only in the society of
> the elect, that is, the temporally extended
> institutions of the church.[51]

As theologians of the "mediationalist" school, the
Mercersburg theologins attempted

> to harmonize dogmas with the conclusions of phil-
> osophy, and religion with culture by putting old
> truths into new forms. They recognized the right
> of reason by giving it a formative function rather
> than a creative one in relation to revelation and
> religion. They made room for emotion in the
> Christian life, without yielding to fanaticism.[52]

What made their theological endeavor so different from
others of their time was the practical implications it

---

[51]Bruce Kuklick, *Churchmen and Philosophers*
(New Haven: Yale University Press, 1985), 176-77.

[52]Richards, "Mercersburg Theology," 45.

had for the life of the church, particularly in the
formation of liturgy and worship. With their emphasis
on the incarnation and the place of the church in
history, theological expression had natural consequences for contemporary ministry. They had an appreciation for history as being critical to spiritual life in
the present. They understood the church as the organic
revelation of the divine. They restored a sense of
dignity and reverence to worship which had been lost
during the Second Great Awakening. They reclaimed
Calvin for their day by offering a living and vital
Christology as the foundation for theology in place of
a rational bibliolatry.

Unfortunately, Mercersburg's theology ran contrary
to the current of American individualism of the day.
Nevertheless, by articulating basic principles of the
Reformation it has precipitated a revival in
Mercersburg studies in the latter half of the twentieth
century. Howard Hageman provides a clue to the
lingering appeal of the Mercersburg school:

> Repelled by the sterility of a fossilized Cal-
> vinism, appalled by the success of a mindless
> evangelicalism, and discouraged by the emptiness
> of classic liberalism, [pastors] are looking for a
> fresh understanding of the Reformed tradition.
> Mercersburg, with its emphasis on incarnation,
> church, sacraments, and ministry as essential
> elements of that tradition, seems to offer an
> interesting possibility. [53]

In an age of the "electronic church," the "Jesus-for-
me" religion, and the "gospel of success," Mercersburg
offers an authentic Reformed perspective of Christ's
presence in the world at a time when Calvinism has been
all but dismissed as a viable theology for modern
times. It challenges parochial sectarianism with a

---

[53]Howard G. Hageman, "Back to Mercersburg," *The
Reformed Journal* 35:8 (1985): 6.

broad view of the church. It calls for a reclamation of the traditional Reformed balance of "Word and Sacrament" in the liturgy. And finally, it provides a rationale for both a reverence for God in worship as well as personal communion with God, combining practice with piety. In many respects, the Mercersburg Theology was ahead of its time. Perhaps its full impact is yet to be made. The churches of the Reformed family would do well to reconsider the implications of Mercersburg for today's ministry.

THEODICY IN THE WORK OF WALTER RAUSCHENBUSCH

Henry F. French

> The words "Deliver us from the evil one" have in
> them the ring of battle. They bring to mind the
> incessant grapple between God and the permanent
> and malignant powers of evil in humanity. To the
> men of the first century that meant Satan and his
> host of evil spirits who ruled in the oppressive,
> extortionate and idolatrous powers of Rome. Today
> the original spirit of that prayer will probably
> be best understood by those who are pitted against
> the terrible powers of organized covetousness and
> institutionalized oppression.
>
> Walter Rauschenbusch
> "The Social Meaning of the Lord's Prayer"

Walter Rauschenbusch, who has been called "the
major architect of American Protestant social
thought,"[1] and whose influence has extended through his
own time to subsequent generations, was born in 1861
and died in 1918. His life spanned that tumultuous
period between the American Civil War and World War I,
a period marked by rapid, unprecedented industrial and
economic growth, labor and management turmoil, and the
spreading blight of urban poverty and immigrant
ghettos. It was also the period of progressive social
Christianity and that movement which came to be known

---

[1]Shelton H. Smith, *Changing Conceptions of
Original Sin* (New York: Scribner's, 1955), 199.

as the "Social Gospel." It was this movment that
provided the practical and theological agenda of Walter
Rauschenbusch.

Rauschenbusch is noted for his advocacy of the
Kingdom of God, but it is clear that the problem of
evil also had a prominent place in his theological
program. Fully six of the nineteen chapters in his
major work, *A Theology For The Social Gospel*, treat of
sin and evil, while only one deals directly with the
idea of the Kingdom of God.

From 1886 to 1897, a period of eleven years during
which time he turned down several calls to teach at his
denominational seminary in Rochester, New York,
Rauschenbusch served a German Baptist parish in Hell's
Kitchen on New York's West Side. His personal experience as an underpaid pastor to working-class im-
migrants during a time of severe economic distress led
to Rauschenbusch's "social awakening." His awakening
to the "social problem" marked the beginning of his
life-long confrontation with the realities of sin and
evil in the modern world. Rauschenbusch finally left
Hell's Kitchen and his parish in 1897 to accept a
teaching assignment at the Rochester Theological
Seminary. He continued in this position until his
death from cancer in 1918.[2]

---

[2]The best sources of bibliographic material on
Rauschenbusch are *Walter Rauschenbusch* (New York:
Macmillan, 1942), the somewhat hagiographic biography
by his personal secretary Dores Sharpe; and Vernon
Bodein's *The Social Gospel of Walter Rauschenbusch and
its Relation to Religious Education* (New Haven: Yale
University Press, 1944), which, despite its title, is
quite biographical in content. Cf. also the recent
works by Paul Minus, *Walter Rauschenbusch: American
Reformer* (New York: Macmillan, 1988); Winthrop Hudson,
ed., *Walter Rauschenbusch: Selected Writings* (New York:
Paulist, 1984); and Max Stackhouse, "Rauschenbusch: The

If Rauschenbusch were to be typed theologically we would find him within the stream of evangelical liberalism, at home in the "New Theology." Rauschenbusch conceived of God's relationship to humanity and nature in terms of immanence rather than transcendence. He understood history in progressive terms and adopted an evolutionary understanding of creation with its implied moral analogy. He understood the Kingdom of God in moral terms and veered towards a purely instrumental view of the Church. Nevertheless, Rauschenbusch's work evidenced significant points of divergence from mainstream liberalism. Germane to this essay is the fact that, although he did reflect the predominant American mood of historical and cultural optimism, he did not believe that progress was inevitable. Furthermore, he tempered his optimism with a more realistic view of human nature than was commonly found among liberal theologians, anticipating the more realistic view of sin found in later neo-orthodoxy. As one historian notes, "because of his most atypical insistence on the power of the 'kingdom of evil,' he is also one of the few liberal theologians who could still be read after wars and depressions had dimmed men's vision of a perfected social order."[3]

I

Rauschenbusch had much to say about sin and evil, but very little to say, explicitly at any rate, about theodicy. His concerns were essentially empirical rather than metaphysical, pragmatic and pastoral rather than theoretical or philosophical. In his five major

---

Legacy of a Loving Prophet," *The Christian Century* (January 25, 1989): 75-78.

[3]Sydney Ahlstrom, *A Religious History of the American People* (New Haven: Yale University Press, 1972), 800-801.

books the word "theodicy" appears only twice, and that
within the space of two pages in *A Theology For The
Social Gospel*. Theodicy as an explicit theme occupies
a mere four pages in that work, but as an implicit
theme it is present throughout.

Rauschenbusch self-consciously modeled himself on
Jesus who, he claimed, "apparently was not interested
in the philosophical question of the origin of evil,
but accepted the fact of evil in a pragmatic
way."[4] Rather than spend his energy on the unresolv-
able problem of the ultimate origin of evil,
Rauschenbusch, like Jesus, was concerned with "only
those sources of sin which he saw in active work around
him."[5] He was quite content to leave the question of
the first origin of evil to God and follow the examples
of Jesus and the Hebrew prophets who "concentrate[d]
their energies on the present and active sources of
evil."[6] By so limiting his area of concern, Rauschenbusch essentially reduced theodicy to anthropodicy,
that is, he attempted to account for evil in terms of
human rather than divine agency, and thus tended to
replace theological categories with biological and
sociological categories.

II

During the few times when Rauschenbusch did
approach the problem of evil as a metaphysical problem,
he approached it from the perspective of suffering. He
was quite frank in admitting that "the existence of

---

[4]Walter Rauschenbusch, *The Social Principles of
Jesus* (New York: Association, 1916), 157-58.

[5]Walter Rauschenbusch, *A Theology for the
Social Gospel*, reprint ed. (Nashville: Abingdon, 1978),
40.

[6]Ibid., 44.

innocent suffering impugns the justice and benevolence of God, both of which are essential in a Christian perception of God."[7] It is interesting that he did not entertain, at least explicitly, the possibility of impugning the divine omnipotence, a concept which, traditionally at least, has also been considered essential to a Christian understanding of God. Indeed, the word "omnipotence" is not a part of Rauschenbusch's vocabulary. On the one hand, the language of omnipotence is supplanted in Rauschenbusch's works with the language of democracy. His was a democratized God.[8] He understood the language of omnipotence to be related to monarchic and autocratic conceptions of God which were the theological correlates of the dominant, despotic and autocratic social institutions of ages long past.[9] For Rauschenbusch, then, to use the language of omnipotence would be atavistic. It is interesting to note that although he could readily see the cultural relativity of autocratic conceptions of God, he did not see himself as guilty of reading contemporary democratic ideas back into Scripture in such a way that they were then available as "scriptural" supports for his theological agenda.

Rauschenbusch noted that "when he [Jesus] took God by the hand and called him 'our Father,' he democratized the conception of God. He disconnected the idea from the coercive and predatory state and transferred it to the realm of family life, the chief social

---

[7]Ibid., 180.

[8]Ibid., 175.

[9]Ibid., 169-78; cf. p. 167, where he writes, "The conception of God held by a social group is a social product."

embodiment of solidarity and love."[10] Rauschenbusch,
an advocate of the historical-critical study of the
Bible, failed, however, to ask the crucial question of
the meaning of first-century family life, and simply
read back into the Scriptures his ideal of the sup-
posedly democratic and Christianized Victorian
family.[11] When he stated that "We have classified
theology as Greek and Latin, as Catholic and Protestant. It is time to classify it as despotic and
democratic,"[12] he effectively eliminated the language
of omnipotence.

There is, however, another reason why Rauschenbusch avoided the language of omnipotence. The
traditional problem of evil is understood in terms of
the following Epicurean triad: (1) God is wholly good;
(2) God is all powerful; (3) there is evil in the
world. Those who argue that it is an inconsistent
triad point out that the problem can only be solved by
giving up, in whole or in part, one of the three
statements. Rauschenbusch would not give up either the
reality of evil or the goodness of God. It can be
argued, however, that although he did not explicitly
solve the problem of evil by giving up omnipotence on
the temporal plane, practically speaking that is
exactly what he did.

In his early works he appealed to the self-

---

[10]Ibid., 174.

[11]Walter Rauschenbusch, *Christianizing the
Social Order* (New York: Macmillan, 1912), 134. For a
detailed study of the social gospel's paradigmatic use
of the Victorian family see Janet Fishburn, *The
Fatherhood of God and the Victorian Family* (Philadelphia: Fortress, 1981).

[12]Rauschenbusch, *Theology for the Social
Gospel*, 175.

limitation of God. He argued that,

> In all the dealing of God with men the human
> factor is the variable quantity. God has so
> conditioned himself that within certain limits he
> allows us free action, and the fulfillment of his
> counsel is hastened or retarded according to our
> obedience or disobedience.[13]

This is a clear departure from the confessional
documents of Rauschenbusch's Baptist tradition which
acknowledged no contingency on the part of the Creator,
and maintained the total independence of the Creator
vis-a-vis the creature.

In his later work, Rauschenbusch had recourse to
the way God is present in history, a mannner of
presence which limits omnipotence. He entertained the
idea that God "come(s) to consciousness in the spiritual life of men."[14] He argued:

> God is not only the spiritual representative of
> humanity; he is identified with it. In him we
> live and move and have our being. In us he lives
> and moves though his being transcends ours . . .
> He works through humanity to realize his purposes,
> and our sins block and destroy the reign of God in
> which he might fully reveal and realize himself.[15]

Although Rauschenbusch did not deny God's ability to
terminate history, and thus exercise ultimate omnipotence, clearly he did not expect this to happen. "An
eschatology which is expresed in terms of historic
development has no final consummation."[16] As long as
the temporal plane exists, God is limited by history.

---

[13]Walter Rauschenbusch, *The Righteousness of
the Kingdom*, ed. Max Stackhouse (Nashville: Abingdon,
1968), 107.

[14]Rauschenbusch, *Theology for the Social
Gospel*, 264.

[15]Ibid., 49.

[16]Ibid., 227.

III

Rauschenbusch recognized that the simplest
solution to the problem of evil was to deny the
existence of unjust suffering.[17] Although God would
still bear ultimate responsibility as Creator, this
approach to the problem of evil would eliminate the
charge that he is responsible for undeserved suffering.
Rauschenbusch quickly rejected this solution, however,
for reality simply will not support it.

He even more quickly rejected the dualistic
solution which "exculpated the good God by making the
evil God the author of this world, or at least its
present lord."[18] Such a solution would affirm the
reality of unmerited suffering, suffering which
Rauschenbusch saw all around him, but it is not a
Christian solution.

Two other responses to the problem of evil that
Rauschenbusch could not endorse were (1) "the hope of a
public vindication of the righteous in the great
judgment, and of an equalization of their lot by their
bliss in heaven and the suffering of the wicked," and
(2) the idea that "God allots suffering with wise and
loving intent, tempering it according to our strength,
relieving it in response to our prayer, and using it to
chasten our pride, to win us from earthliness to
himself, and to prepare us for heaven."[19] At this
point, Rauschenbusch clearly rejected an instrumental
view of evil.

Rauschenbusch recognized that these ultimately
unacceptable responses to the problem of evil may have

---

[17]Ibid., 180.

[18]Ibid.

[19]Ibid., 180-81.

significant pastoral efficacy. Nevertheless, he
concludes that "they are shaken by the bulk of unjust
suffering in sight of the modern mind."[20] Here, of
course, lies the crux of the modern problem of evil.
Whereas these unacceptable responses to evil may appear
both plausible and defensible given a provincial
world-view and the realities of a small village or
agricultural community, they lose their attractiveness
and effectiveness given the realities of the highly
urbanized, laissez-faire capitalist, industrialized and
militarized modern world which confronted Rauschenbusch.

Rauschenbusch noted that

> today entire social classes sit in the ashes and
> challenge the justice of the God who has afflicted
> them by fathering the present social system. The
> moral and religious problem of suffering has
> entered on a new stage with the awakening of the
> social consciousness and the spread of social
> knowledge.[21]

In coming to this conclusion Rauschenbusch narrowed his
concern with the problem of evil to concern with the
social problem of evil. In so doing, he made a
significant advance in theological thought. Before
turning to this issue, however, we must take a brief
look at his understanding of natural evil in order to
round out our study of his treatment of the problem of
evil.

Rauschenbusch took an essentially pragmatic rather
than philosophical point of view with respect to the
individual experience of natural evil. Rather than ask
why such evil exists at all under the aegis of a
benevolent and all-powerful God, he simply acknowledged
that it does exist and implied that its existence is

---

[20]Ibid., 181.

[21]Ibid.

not an insurmountable obstacle to theistic faith. The
pain of birth and death and the physical infirmities
that come between cradle and grave are the price we pay
for biological existence, while accidents and an
occasionally angry Mother Nature "are the price we pay
for the use of a fine planet,"[22] that is, for an
ordered and scientifically explainable rather than
chaotic world. Furthermore, instances of individual
suffering such as "the mental anguish of unrequited
love . . . [or] foiled ambition" are the necessary and
acceptable price we pay "as possessors of a highly
organized personality amid a world of men."[23] The
nature of human-being-in-the-world (not an expression
Rauschenbusch would have used) demands such instances
of "evil."

Rauschenbusch did not ask why things are as they
are--they simply are--for the reason remains hidden in
the mystery of God. Nevertheless, given the contingent
nature of reality-as-it-is, Rauschenbusch asserted that
we may still affirm "a joyful acceptance of the present
life," a life that may be experienced as meaningful and
as "worth having."[24]

IV

Now let us turn from natural to moral evil.
According to Rauschenbusch, "the problem of evil
becomes far more complicated when evil is social-
ized."[25] The "bulk of unjust suffering" which con-
fronts the Christian with the need for an adequate

[22]Ibid., 182.

[23]Ibid.; cf. *Christianizing the Social Order*, 126.

[24]Rauschenbusch, *Christianizing the Social Order*, 97.

[25]Rauschenbusch, *Social Principles of Jesus*, 160.

theodicy finds its roots in the social organization of human life. It is an organization of life that finds "poor and laborious people being deprived of physical stature, youth, education, human equality, and justice, in order to allow others to live luxurious lives."[26] Rauschenbusch noted the empirically obvious, that "these conditions [are] perpetuated by law and organized force, and palliated or justified by the makers of public opinion."[27] To say that this observation is empirically obvious is perhaps a bit anachronistic. The depth of Rauschenbusch's recognition of systemic or institutionalized evil represents an ethical and empirical breakthrough.

Rauschenbusch identified systemic evil as the proximate cause of the great bulk of excessive, unjust and innocent suffering which he saw as challenging theistic faith. He was quick to deny the challenge by denying any divine intent or sanction with respect to the contemporary social order. He was unequivocal in his assertion:

> To interpret the sufferings imposed by social injustice in individualistic terms as the divine chastening and sanctification of all individuals concerned is not only false but profoundly mischievous. . . . A conception of God which describes him as sanctioning the present social order and using it in order to sanctify its victims through the present order, without striving for its overthrow, is repugnant to our moral sense.[28]

We have here the roots of a creative theodicy of protest and involvement which seeks not merely to explain but also to undermine the reality of evil by

---

[26]Rauschenbusch, *Theology for the Social Gospel*, 182.

[27]Ibid.

[28]Ibid., 183-84.

enlisting men and women in a pragmatic conflict with
the structures which promote it. While natural evil
may be seen as both within the creative vision of God
and as serving the dialectic of historical growth and
development, moral evil cannot be so understood.
Rooted in sin, understood essentially as selfishness,
moral evil is an offense to God which must be protested
against and radically opposed. But to whom is the
protest directed? Most certainly not to God. Theodicy, via the concept of solidarity, becomes anthropodicy.

The key to Rauschenbusch's theodicy is the concept
of solidarity. It is not a concept unique to Rauschenbusch. In his well-known 1884 essay, "The New Theology," which served as a manifesto of American theological liberalism, Theodore Munger wrote that "the New
Theology seeks to replace an excessive individuality by
a truer view of the solidarity of the race."[29] Horace
Bushnell, who provided a formative influence in the
development of American liberal theology, had done much
long before Rauschenbusch to spread the idea of the
organic unity of the race. Furthermore, Rauschenbusch's understanding of solidarity shows the
influence of Schleiermacher to whom he acknowledged his
debt in *A Theology For The Social Gospel*.[30] Rauschenbusch's understanding of solidarity, however, cannot be
simply reduced to historical influences. The mark of
Rauschenbusch's original thought is found in the
centrality which he gave to the idea.

In one of the two times in which Rauschenbusch

---

[29]Theodore Munger, *Freedom and Faith* (Boston:
Houghton, Mifflin, 1884), 22.

[30]Rauschenbusch, *Theology for the Social
Gospel*, 92-93.

actually used the word "theodicy," he stated that "the
idea of solidarity, when once understood, acts as a
theodicy."[31] It was empirically evident to Rauschenbusch that, just as God had chosen to create an
ordered, and thus scientifically explainable and
controllable, world in which the structure of reality
necessitates events which we interpret as natural evil,
he has also chosen to create the structure of human
existence as an "organic community of life."[32] When
one individual does good others benefit, and when one
group or class of persons does good other groups or
classes benefit. Conversely, when one sins others
suffer, and when groups or social classes sin the
concomitant suffering falls on others. "These sufferings are not vicarious, they are solidaristic."[33]

Solidarity is a conductor of both sin with its
concomitant evils and rightousness with its concomitant
blessings.[34] Echoing Marx, whom he had read with some
approval, and anticipating the sociology of knowledge,
Rauschenbusch noted that "those who have learned to
understand the organic unity of sociology know how
profoundly the individual is conditioned in all his
acts and thoughts by the social life that makes and
molds him and sets his goals and limits."[35]

Solidarity is clearly the "beneficent part of
human life" in that it is the source of the social good

---

[31]Ibid., 183.

[32]Ibid.

[33]Ibid., 182.

[34]Cf. Rauschenbusch, *Social Principles of
Jesus*, 179.

[35]Rauschenbusch, *Theology for the Social
Gospel*, 200.

that enriches and secures the lives of all. Solidarity
can, however, be twisted and perverted so that the
lives of the many are effectively wasted:

> If our community is organized in such a way that
> permits, encourages, or defends predatory prac-
> tices, then the larger part of its members are
> through solidarity caged to be eaten by the rest
> and to suffer what is both unjust and useless.[36]

Solidarity acts as a theodicy in that it frees God
from the charge of direct complicity in unjust suffering. Solidarity is an element in the structure of
human existence which can swing either way, towards the
extension of righteousness or the extension of evil.
The choice is ours, although, as Rauschenbusch noted,
the cumulative effects of racial, solidaristic sin
limit the boundaries of human freedom.

Rauschenbusch developed the concept of the Kingdom
of Evil to represent the dynamics of systemic evil. He
argued that "our theological conception of sin is but
fragmentary unless we see all men in their natural
groups bound together in a solidarity of all times and
all places, bearing the yoke of evil and suffering."[37]
In calling for a solidaristic and organic conception of
the power and reality of evil in the world, Rauschenbusch pointed to the reality of evil collective forces
or super-personal personalites which transcend and
determine the individuals who are identified with them.
These super-personal forces assimilate individuals to
themselves. Rauschenbusch clearly saw that "there is
more to sin than our own frailty and stupidity, and the
bad influence of other individuals. There is a

---

[36]Ibid., 182-183.

[37]Ibid., 81; cf. Friedrich Schleiermacher, *The
Christian Faith*, trans. H.R. Mackintosh and J.S.
Stewart (Philadelphia: Fortress, 1928), 288, for the
possible root of this idea.

permanent force of organized evil . . . ."[38]

It is important to remember that Rauschenbusch
asserted that super-personal forces are discrete
personalities with a mental life every bit as real as
that of individuals. Where did he get the idea? The
question may be answered from both biblical and
philosophical sources. Biblically he credited the idea
to the Old Testament Hebrew tradition which presents
the nation of Israel as a corporate personality. He
also referred to the concept of the Church found in the
New Testament Pauline tradition of the "body of Christ"
as "the first and classical discussion in Christian
thought of the nature and functioning of a composite
spiritual organism."[39]

Philosophically, Rauschenbusch credited the
idealist philosopher, Josiah Royce, with developing the
concept of super-personal personalities. In *The
Problem of Christianity*, Royce stated:

> . . . there are in the human world two profoundly
> different grades, or levels, of mental beings--
> namely, the beings that we usually call human
> individuals, and the beings that we call com-
> munities. . . . The communities are vastly more
> complex, and in many ways are also immeasurably
> more potent and enduring than are the individuals.
> Their mental life possesses, as Wundt has pointed
> out, a psychology of its own which can be sys-
> tematically studied. Their mental existence is no
> mere creation of abstract thinking or of metaphor.
> . . . As empirical facts, communities are known to
> us by their deeds, by their workings, by their
> intelligent and coherent behavior, just as the
> minds of our individual neighbors are known to us
> through their expressions. Considered as merely
> natural existences, communities, like individuals,
> may be either good or evil, beneficent or

---

[38]Rauschenbusch, *Social Principles of Jesus*,
155; cf. Schleiermacher, *Christian Faith*, 286-89.

[39]Rauschenbusch, *Theology for the Social
Gospel*, 69-70.

mischievous. The level of mental existence which belongs to communities ensures their complexity; and renders them, in general, far more potent, and for certain of their activities, much more intelligent than are the human individuals. . . . A community may be as base and depraved as any individual man can become, and may be far worse than a man.[40]

Rauschenbusch's mature thought was certainly influenced by Royce, but the idea of composite personalities with the power to assimilate individuals to themselves can be found germinally in the early *Righteousness of the Kingdom*. In this unpublished manuscript, written some twenty years before Royce's work, Rauschenbusch noted that "it is not enough to Christianize individuals, we must Christianize societies, organizations, nations, for they too have a life of their own which may be made better or worse."[41] Most likely, Royce's work simply provided further support for an idea which was readily available to Rauschenbusch from the idealist ambience that surrounded liberal theology.

Be that as it may, Rauschenbusch's concept of super-personal forces, coupled with his acceptance of evolutionary theory and its moral analogy, enabled him to argue for the development of corporate evil in much the same way that other theologians have accounted for individual evil as, in part, a function of survival.[42] "All human organizations develop a kind of corporate egotism, a collective hunger and self-assertion that

---

[40]Josiah Royce, *The Problem of Christianity* (New York: Macmillan, 1912), 1:164-68.

[41]Rauschenbusch, *Righteousness of the Kingdom*, 102.

[42]See John Hick, *Evil and the God of Love* (New York: Harper and Row, 1966).

endangers the higher ends for which they were created."[43]

V

Rauschenbusch's understanding of original sin is integral to his theodicy--or perhaps we should say anthropodicy--of solidarity. Unlike the vast majority of liberal theologians, Rauschenbusch did not abandon the concept of original sin, although he did significantly modify the doctrine.

Original sin has a twofold meaning in Rauschenbusch's theological reconstruction. First, he conceded that original sin may, on one level, be understood biologically:

> Evil does flow down the generations through channels of biological coherence. Idiocy, feeble-mindedness, neurotic disturbances, weakness of inhibition, perverse desires, stubbornness and anti-social impulses in children must have had their adequate biological causes somewhere back on the line, even if we lack the records.[44]

The biological transmission of original sin, however, was not what interested Rauschenbusch. His interest lay in the social transmission of evil. He saw that "evil runs down the generations not only by biological propagation but also by social assimilation."[45] In a telling metaphor, Rauschenbusch noted:

> Just as syphilitic corruption is forced on the helpless foetus in its mother's womb, so these hereditary social evils are forced on the individual embedded in the womb of society and drawing his ideas, moral standards, and spiritual ideals

---

[43]Rauschenbusch, *Christianizing the Social Order*, 78.

[44]Rauschenbusch, *Theology for the Social Gospel*, 58.

[45]Ibid., 61.

from the general life of the body.[46]
Both biologically and socially sin comes with the human
condition and is thus original. Given the structure of
existence, however, sin is a possibility only, not a
necessity. Rauschenbusch regards evil as a "variable
factor in the life of humanity, which it is our duty to
diminish for every young life and for every new
generation."[47]

Rauschenbusch conceived of persons as having a
lower and a higher self. The lower or sensual self is
that of powerful animal impulses and appetites. The
higher self, however, is "gifted with high ideals, with
a wonderful range of possibilities, with aspirations
and longing . . . ."[48] The conflict between the natural
impulses and spiritual ideals and potentialities is the
field of sin. Sin arises out of an inner conflict
between the sensual and the spiritual. This conflict,
however, is not an even-handed one because the higher
self is weakened through "ignorance and inertia." This
fact, which for Rauschenbusch was empirical, was
accounted for by recourse to evolutionary theory. The
sensual, animal, natural impulses of the lower self
which have been necessary for survival, "run far back
in the evolution of the race and are well established
and imperious, whereas the social, altruistic, and
spiritual impulses are of recent development and
relatively weak."[49]

Looked at in developmental terms, then, it is the
relative weakness of the spirit and not its depravity

---

[46]Ibid., 60.

[47]Ibid., 43.

[48]Ibid., 45.

[49]Ibid., 58.

that accounts for sin and its concomitant evils. Evil
is variable simply because its intensity and prevalence
depend not upon the static notion of depravity, but
upon the dynamic notion of moral development. "This
sensuous equipment, this ignorance and inertia, out of
which our moral delinquencies sprout, are part of our
human nature."[50] This fact, rather than some primal
fall, is the ground of sin. The "sensual equipment"
comes through biological inheritance, whereas the
inertia and ignorance, to the extent that they are
institutionalized, come to us not biologically but
through social inheritance.

Rauschenbusch separated the doctrine of original
sin from the myth of humanity's primal fall. Like most
liberal theologians of his time, he abandoned the
doctrine of the contemporary person's complicity and
guilt with respect to some ancient first sin. With
respect to sin, guilt enters in only "in the degree
intelligence and will enter."[51] To recognize the
powerful and yet variable and transient reality of evil
and to do nothing to diminish it is an act of the will
which hinders the self-revelation and self-realization
of God, leaving the sinner with genuine guilt.

Unlike the older theology which understood grace
primarily in terms of forgiveness, Rauschenbusch saw
grace ultimately in terms of power, the power set
moving in history by the life of Jesus which aims at
the realization of the Kingdom of God and the assimilation of individuals to it. Grace is the power to live
the life of faith in conformity with the reign of God.
"It is faith to see God at work in the world and to

---

[50]Ibid., 45-46.

[51]Ibid., 46.

claim a share in his job."[52]

Rauschenbusch viewed the work of God in the world primarily in ethical categories. He insisted that in everything that was religious there must be an immediate ethical nexus and effect. He was interested in separating the nonethical from the religious in order to encourage the Church to align itself more closely and faithfully with the work of God in the world, a world clearly not bounded by the Church.

Rauschenbusch unequivocally stated that "the Kingdom of God is not confined within the Church and its activities. It includes the whole of human life."[53] Indeed, he was so convinced that the field of God's historical activity exceeded the boundaries of the Church that he wrote a short book, *Unto Me*, which anticipated the modern concept of the "anonymous Christian." In this small book, Rauschenbusch argued that social workers who have no conscious faith commitments, and no connection with organized Christianity, are, nevertheless, "in the direct line of apostolic succession." To the degree that secular social workers struggle to ameliorate the conditions and consequences of evil "they are treading step by step in the footsteps of Jesus of Nazareth."[54]

VI

Jesus of Nazareth is the linch pin of Rauschenbusch's clarion call to confront evil. Echoing Schleiermacher, he saw Jesus as having achieved perfect God-consciousness. "The personality which he achieved was a new type in humanity. Having the power to master

---

[52]Ibid., 102.

[53]Ibid., 144-45.

[54]Walter Rauschenbusch, *Unto Me* (Boston: Pilgrim, 1912), 12-13.

and assimilate others, it became the primal cell of a
new spiritual organism."[55] The significance of this
statement becomes clear if, remembering what he said
about our sensuous equipment, ignorance and inertia, we
read it together with his assertion that "an overpower-
ing consciousness of God is needed to offset and
overcome the tyranny of the sensuous life and its
temptations."[56] The similarity to Schleiermacher's
assertion that "the Redeemer assumes believers into the
power of his God-consciousness and this is his redemptive activity" is obvious.[57]

Jesus' achievement was the first foothold of the
Kingdom of God in human history, and it set in motion a
historical force which has overflown the boundaries of
the Church.

> Jesus not only achieved the kind of religious per-
> sonality which we have tried to bring before our
> memory and imagination, but he succeeded in
> perpetuating his spirit. What was personal with
> him became social within the group of the dis-
> ciples. His life became a collective and assim-
> ilating force and a current of historic tradi-
> tion.[58]

The whole thrust of Rauschenbusch's work may thus
be seen from the perspective of his theodicy of
solidarity. It is a theodicy which accounts for evil
more in sociological and historical categories than in
theological categories and is, therefore, more properly
an anthropodicy. Evil is variable and transient, and
the structures of evil which may appear to be intrac-

---

[55]Rauschenbusch, *Theology for the Social Gospel*, 152.

[56]Ibid., 154.

[57]Schleiermacher, *Christian Faith*, 425.

[58]Rauschenbusch, *Theology for the Social Gospel*, 164.

table are, in fact, not immune to the power of the
human will and the historical forces of redemption set
in motion by Jesus of Nazareth. In a revealing statement, Rauschenbusch asserted,

> We now have such scientific knowledge of social
> laws and forces, of economics, of history that we
> can intelligently mold and guide the evolution in
> which we take part. . . . We have reached the
> point where we can make history make us. Have we
> the will to match our knowledge?[59]

The question for Rauschenbusch, of course, is not so
much have we the will as will we use it?

VII

A final word needs to be said regarding eschatology, normally an important component in any theodicy.
Given Rauschenbusch's tendency to reduce theodicy to
anthropodicy, it is not surprising that eschatology has
diminished importance in his work. What he did have to
say, however, is interesting in that it reflects a
general attitude of turn-of-the-century theological
liberalism in America.

In the opening pages of *A Theology For The Social
Gospel*, Rauschenbusch asked an interesting question:

> Can personal forgiveness settle such accounts as
> some men run up with their fellow men? Does
> Calvinism deal adequately with a man who appears
> before the judgment seat of Christ with
> $50,000,000 and its human corollaries to his
> credit, and then pleads a free pardon through
> faith in the atoning sacrifice?[60]

It is clearly a rhetorical question; however, if such a
pardon would impugn the justice and morality of God, so
would eternal punishment. Any punishment following
death must be educational and redemptive, not retribu-
tive. The words of the 1897 Ingersoll Lecturer at

---

[59]Rauschenbusch, *Christianizing the Social
Order*, 41.

[60]Ibid., 19.

Harvard, George Gordon, would have been endorsed by
Rauschenbusch: "The old theologies, whether of the
remnant, or election, or the restriction of moral
opportunity to this life, rend asunder the ethical idea
of God."[61]

In a passage worth quoting at length, Rauschenbusch argued that, even in a future life, we want the
possibility of growth:

> We cannot conceive of finite existence or of human
> happiness except in terms of growth. It would be
> more satisfactory for modern minds and for
> Christian minds to think of an unlimited scale of
> ascent toward God reaching from the lowest to the
> highest, and each could advance as it grew . . . .
> This idea would also satisfy our Christian faith
> in the redeeming mercy of God. In this unending
> scale of beings, none would be so high that he
> could not be drawn still closer, and none so low
> that he would be beyond the love of God. God
> would still be teaching and saving all . . . .
> Rather than a simple universalist doctrine where
> all enter salvation at death, a concept unequal to
> the reality of sin, the idea of a scale of life in
> which each would be as far from God and in as much
> narrowness and darkness as he deserved, would
> constitute a grave admonition to every soul.[62]

This passage approximates what John Hick has termed an
"Irenaean theodicy." In Irenaeus we find the same
principles of continuity and dynamism which we find in
Rauschenbusch. According to Gustav Wingren, Irenaeus
insisted that ". . . even after Christ's parousia and
the resurrection of the just, man will still have to
grow. The resurrection continues and intensifies man's
communion with God. . . . As long as human life

---

[61]George A. Gordon, *Immortality and the New
Theodicy* (Boston: Houghton, Mifflin, 1897), 80.

[62]Rauschenbusch, *Theology for the Social
Gospel*, 233ff.

continues, it is still a life of growth and development."[63]

Irenaeus' central concept of growth would certainly have appealed to Rauschenbusch and, as a church
historian in an age when the profession was not
specialized, we might safely assume that Rauschenbusch
knew Irenaeus. Nevertheless, Rauschenbusch's eschatological ideas were certainly not unique in late-
nineteenth and early-twentieth-century America. In an
interesting article, "The Erosion of Postmillennialism
in American Religious Thought, 1865-1925," James
Moorhead noted that most late-nineteenth-century
liberals

> preferred to believe in a future punishment from
> which the wicked might be ultimately released. . .
> Heaven, too, was assuming a new appearance, one of
> continuity with the present life. . . . The new
> view of individual destiny implied an abhorrence
> of dichotomies of any sort. Humans did not face
> the choice of two eternally opposed futures so
> much as they encountered a moral continuum with an
> almost infinite number of gradations. Accord-
> ingly, the passage from evil to good did not
> transpire as if by a sudden leap from one state to
> another. Like all life, religious existence
> proceeded by the slow organic law of growth.
> Similarly, this life and the next could not be set
> against each other too sharply. The deity was a
> God of continuity and thus would not arbitrarily
> work a miraculous transformation in persons at the
> moment of death. They would commence their
> spiritual pilgrimage on the other side precisely
> where they had left off here.[64]

Rauschenbusch's eschatological ideas were clearly
not out of step with prevailing liberal attitudes;

---

[63]Gustav Wingren, *Man and the Incarnation: A
Study in the Biblical Theology of Irenaeus* (Philadelphia: Muhlenburg, 1959), 186-87.

[64]James Moorhead, "The Erosion of Postmillennialism in American Religious Thought, 1865-1925,"
Church History 53:1 (1984), 71.

however, he left his mark on those attitudes by
socializing them, by complementing the hope for a
higher life for the individual with the hope for a
higher life for the race. "The desire for heaven gets
Christian dignity and quality only when it arises on
the basis of that solidaristic state of mind which is
cultivated by the social gospel."[65] The significance
of such eschatological notions for Rauschenbusch and
the other advocates of the social gospel is that they
allowed the religious mind to focus on this life
instead of the next life. If the fate of individuals
after death could be safely left in the hands of a
moral God, then the Church could devote its energy and
resources to the more pressing task of establishing a
more moral social order.

VIII

There is much to be said for a theodicy such as we
find in the works of Walter Rauschenbusch, a theodicy
of solidarity. It demands a prophetic protest against
the structures of evil in the world, a protest supported by critical social analysis and legitimated by
collective action. It is a theodicy which offers hope
in that although it does not expect a final consummation of the Kingdom of God within history it does
expect ever greater approximations to the ideal. By
recognizing the possibility of regression, that is, the
advance of institutionalized evil, as well as the
possibility of progress, Rauschenbusch invested his
work with a sober-minded realism which encouraged men
and women to take the call to protest and action with a
high level of seriousness.

---

[65]Rauschenbusch, *Theology for the Social
Gospel*, 230.

It remains to be said, however, that the major
problem with Rauschenbusch's theodicy of solidarity is
the threat of the loss of God. To the degree that
theodicy is replaced with anthropodicy in his approach
to the problem of evil, Rauschenbusch set in motion a
tendency to reduce the cross to a symbol and Jesus to a
moral example while raising the notion of God to such a
high level of abstraction that he need no longer be
taken with much seriousness. That is to say, in
Rauschenbusch's theodicy of solidarity we find a logic
which anticipated Bonhoeffer's "man come of age," and
the "God is dead" celebration of the 1960's.

RELIGIOUS TOLERATION:
POINT OF ARRIVAL OR POINT OF DEPARTURE?

Charles Courtney

Religious toleration has been praised as one of
the highest achievements of modern public life, a near
miracle worked, for example, in England between Henry
VIII's reform and, a century and-a-half later, The Act
of Toleration under William and Mary of 1689. This
prize was carried over to the United States, for ours
was the first government specifically to refrain from
having authority over religious matters. But toleration has had its detractors as well. Oliver Wendell
Holmes, seeing that the idea of toleration springs from
the theory that the civil power has inalienable and
absolute prerogatives, declared it to be an insult to
mankind.[1] E. C. Dewick contends that "tolerance is, at
best, a negative and nerveless virtue. It leads to no
decisions; it inspires no enthusiasms."[2] The limitations of tolerance are made clear by the following
notice that I saw posted in the entry to an apartment
building in Fresnes, a Paris suburb: Les chiens ne sont

---

[1]Wilbur K. Jordan, *The Development of Religious
Toleration in England*, 4 vols. (Cambridge: Harvard
University Press, 1932-40), 1:17-18.

[2]E. C. Dewick, *The Christian Attitude to Other
Religions* (Cambridge: The University Press, 1953), 160.

que toleres et doivent obligatoirement etre tenus en laisse (Dogs are only tolerated and must be on leash). Thus, the issue posed in my title. Is toleration a point of arrival, a modest value that once served a purpose but leads us no farther? Or is it a point of departure, an idea capable of carrying us on to new insights?

I

No doubt the meaning of all concepts is determined by the context, but this is especially the case for "toleration." Toleration, even the word,[3] issued from the wars of religion in the sixteenth century. Before that, it was a matter of religious intolerance and persecution, first of the Christians by the Roman emperors, then of non-Christians by the alliance of Church and Christian emperors after Constantine's victory in 312.

Since Judaism was a subordinated minority under both the Romans and the Christians, it will serve as an informative example. Judaism enjoyed a special protected status in pagan Rome and it was the only dissenting and non-Christian faith that was to remain legal in Christendom.[4] This limited freedom was precarious, however, because the laws of the Christian empire increasingly reflected a theological image of the Jew. The Jew was to be a living proof of divine reprobation. Therefore, although the Jewish community was not proscribed, it was systematically demoted. Jews were physically preserved, but in a state of misery. The constant anti-Jewish rhetoric from

---

[3]F. Mentre, in A. Lalande, *Vocabulaire technique et critique de la Philosophie*, 9th ed. (Paris: Presses Universitaires de France, 1962), 1133.

[4]Rosemary R. Ruether, *Faith and Fratricide* (New York: Seabury, 1974), 185.

religious and political leaders established the
conditions for violent persecution of the Jews in times
of crisis. Surprising as it may seem to us, the
establishment of ghettos, beginning in the sixteenth
century, was not resisted by Jews for it gave them
security and a dedicated place for Jewish activity.[5] A
later sign that the Jews were beginning to have a new
status is that Cromwell treated them as he did Catholics and dissenting Protestants. Still, the Jew was
special, and Lawrence Danson, writing about Shylock,
the character in Shakespeare's *The Merchant of Venice*,
puts it this way:

> The Jew was a dramatic idea derived from myth and
> derived from a theological idea. The Jew repre-
> sents a denier among other things--he refuses
> festivity and music, he refuses young love. For
> Shakespeare in his age, the Jew was a man who had
> refused: the Jews had refused Christ and so had
> willfully turned down salvation. From our point
> of view, their attitude was anti-Semitic, but then
> we believe in pluralism--that's our ideology. It
> was not the Elizabethan ideology--they didn't
> think it was a bad thing to think they were right
> and the Jews were wrong.[6]

John Courtney Murray says that "in the Christian
commonwealth the Christian faith was the basis of
citizenship."[7] In Western Europe Jews did not attain
full citizenship until the period 1848-70.

   In contrast, Christianity's relations with other

---

[5]Jacob Katz, *Exclusiveness and Tolerance*,
Scripta Judaica, (Oxford: Oxford University Press,
1961), 3:133.

[6]Lawrence Danson, quoted in Michiko Kakutani,
"Leisure and Arts," *New York Times*, February 22, 1981,
p. 30. Below, I will discuss what is good and bad
about making religious judgments and whether pluralism
must be an ideology.

[7]John Courtney Murray, *The Problem of Religious
Freedom*, Woodstock Papers, No. 7 (Westminster, MD:
Newman, 1965), 48-49.

religions during the period of Christendom were
outright hostile. The chief example is Islam. Islam
approached Christian Europe as a conquering invader and
we know how close it came to succeeding. The favor was
returned with the monstrous effort of the Crusades to
liberate the holy places of the Faith from the infidel.

Across the centuries, many Christian heretical
movements were successfully eradicated. But the
Protestant Reformation of the sixteenth century was not
to be put down so easily. The resulting intramural
wars of religion precipitated the crisis which led to
the emergence of toleration.

II

Toleration is not, however, a creation of the
Protestants. Protestant authorities, religious and
civil, were every bit as intolerant as the Roman
Catholics. Toleration came about not because of what
Protestants taught or believed but simply because
they persisted in existence. Many people, observing
the rival claims of exclusive possession of the truth,
began to be skeptical about those claims. But many
others killed and were killed for their version of the
Christian truth. To some, like Voltaire, "intolerance
is absurd and barbaric. It is the right of the tiger;
nay it is far worse, for tigers do but tear in order to
have food, while we rend each other for paragraphs."[8]

Toleration was forged by civil authorities, among
whom Elizabeth I is exemplary, because they judged that
society paid an unacceptably high price when it tried
to root out a religious minority. The modern religious
wars involved killing not Jews or infidels but our very
own. Moreover, this extraordinarily painful killing

---

[8]Francois-Marie A. Voltaire, *Toleration and
Other Essays*, trans. Joseph McCabe (New York: G. P.
Putnam's, 1912), 30-31.

yielded an unstable result. The state is not made
secure after all because the subdued minority may rise
up again at any time. Toleration is an act of state
which rules that persecution or coercion will not be
allowed in religious matters. It is an act of state
for reasons of state. W. K. Jordan says that Elizabeth
I's policy made the religious question subordinate to
the requirements of Statism.[9] The sovereign of the
modern nation was no longer going to allow the nation
to be destroyed by religious disputes.

John Locke, in his letters On Toleration, gave the
classic apology for toleration. Locke says that it is
crucial to distinguish between the business of civil
government (a society constituted to procure and
advance such civil interests as life, liberty, health,
and possessions) and religion (a voluntary society for
worship of God leading to the salvation of souls).[10]
He says that the one who would try to control belief by
persecution is trying the impossible because religious
assent is an interior matter that cannot be commanded
but must be freely given according as the mind is
persuaded. Locke also reminds magistrates that if they
try to command the impossible they will encourage the
very uncivil and dangerous sin of hypocrisy. Locke,
writing in the 1680's, shows how far opinion had
advanced and also its limitations. He, as all since
him, is intolerant of those who would bring about
serious civil strife; he would not tolerate Roman
Catholics (because they owe allegiance to a foreign
prince) and atheists (because their oath could not be

---

[9]Jordan, *Development of Religious Toleration*,
4:471.

[10]John Locke, *A Letter Concerning Toleration*,
trans. William Popple, 2nd ed. (Indianapolis: Bob-
bs-Merrill, 1955), 17 and 20.

trusted in court). Locke shows the rationalistic bias
of his time when he asserts that we should be tolerant
about religion because even though there is only one
true position in these matters we fallible humans
cannot know with certainty *which* it is.

The theory and practice of toleration developed
slowly over the next 300 years. A few major advances
may be mentioned: the First Amendment to the Constitution of the United States (1791); John Stuart Mill's *On
Liberty* (1859); the writings of the American Jesuit,
John Courtney Murray, notably, *We Hold these Truths*
(1960); and the Declaration of Vatican II on Religious
Liberty and The Relation of the Church to Non-Christian
Religions (1965). Since this brief essay does not
allow me to do justice to the various concepts and
distinctions put forward in these texts, I will, by way
of summary, connect the history of toleration to my
guiding image of arrival and departure. At the
beginning, toleration was a matter of the civil
sovereign, in association with a dominant and established religion, granting permission for minority or
opposition religions to exist. From the sixteenth
century to the present, we see a process of increasing
and finally complete dissociation of civil power and
religious authority. The civil body, referring to no
particular religion and disclaiming any competence in
religious matters, declares and protects religious
liberty for all citizens. Since the chief characteristic of toleration, namely, a relation of dominance and
subordination among religious communities, no longer
exists, the question can be raised whether the term
"toleration" is rightly applied to the current situation. It seems that toleration, a hard-won civil
accomplishment, has been transcended. The toleration
train, in taking a track from the point of departure,

came to the point of arrival with changed markings.
What, at the beginning, had little to do with liberty
became a fully developed civil doctrine of religious
freedom which serves to promote civil peace and
increasingly to respect the distinctiveness and
inviolability of religious life.

Philip Schaff, writing a century ago, said that

> toleration is an intermediate state between
> religious persecution and religious liberty. . . .
> The theory of medieval Europe was intolerance and
> persecution; the theory of modern Europe is
> toleration; the theory of North America is
> religious liberty and equality.[11]

Considered with reference to the state of war that
existed before, toleration is a point of arrival--a
precious haven of security. Considered with reference
to the civilly protected religious freedom to which it
led, toleration is a point of departure. If, on the
civil side, we have gone from war to truce to peace,
what is the state of affairs on the religious side?

III

In choosing to explore the religious side of the
question, we enter relatively new territory. John
Courtney Murray, who helped prepare the Vatican II
Declaration on Religious Freedom, relates that the
process was confused and blocked until a clear distinction was made between what he calls the moral-
ecumenical dimension of the problem of religious
freedom and the juridical dimension. The third and
final schema, which came to be adopted, "took up the
issue of religious freedom as a formally juridical
concept." It left aside the moral-ecumenical dimension
which has to do with "the higher order of charity and

---

[11]Philip Schaff, *The Progress of Religious
Freedom, As Shown in the History of Toleration Acts*
(New York: Charles Scribner's Sons, 1889), 2.

love between persons."[12]

But is the higher possibility of love often realized? Even though citizens in a society affording religious freedom obey the law and do not think of trying to use civil power to coerce or restrain the religion of others, they may "personally" be intolerant or merely tolerant. Many, following on the conviction that their religion is true, hold that society and its members would be better if everyone adhered to their religion. In the terms previously used, this is a state of war--perhaps not a hot war, but a cold one. We have traced a movement in the civil realm from war to truce to peace. What sort of movement is appropriate for interreligious relations of persons and communities?

The civil or juridical order, after moving away from establishment, decides that it cannot properly make judgments on religious matters. Is it correct to generalize and conclude that judgments should not be made about religious matters, even in the religious realm? No, because the differentiation of religion from the state marked an important advance in our understanding of the state. Something alien to the state's nature was eliminated; the state thereby became more nearly itself. It seems that the very existence of a religious community implies the judgment on the part of its adherents that it is true. In saying this, we have made no commitment as to the location of religious truth. But it does seem correct to say that if a religion failed to "assert" itself it would cease to be itself.

---

[12]John Courtney Murray, "The Declaration on Religious Freedom: A Moment in Its Legislative History," in *Religious Liberty: An End and a Beginning*, ed. John Courtney Murray (New York: Macmillan, 1966), 27.

But do certain individuals have the luxury of avoiding judgments about religious matters? It would seem so. Someone acquainted with several different religious options may remain content to know about them and choose none of them. This description fits someone who has been an adherent of religion. Such a person has become a spectator of the religious scene. Whereas the scholar's distance is methodical, rule directed, and goal oriented, the indifferent person seems not to care very deeply. The religions are seen as all good or all bad or irrelevant or merely interesting. Such a person is not religious in a strong sense and would not be prominent in an inquiry into the types of inter-religious understanding. This is not to say that the number or significance of religiously indifferent people is negligible. Quite the contrary is the case. Many historians of modern Western history say that when religions, faced with a pluralistic situation, left intact their exclusivist and absolutist claims the stage was set for widespread indifference to and defection from religion. In fact, indifferentism was one of the chief objects of attack by the Roman Catholic Church in the nineteenth century.

W. K. Jordan, to whose great *The Development of Religious Toleration in England* we are all indebted, said in his conclusion that even those who attempted to make pure tolerance a central Christian virtue tended to see doctrines as vehicles of moral sentiment, tended to be individualistic and rationalistic, were led, in short, to "a fundamental reconsideration of the entire structure of Christian thought."[13] Some would question whether the result is recognizable as Christian.

---

[13]Jordan, *Development of Religious Toleration*, 4:488.

But perhaps the issue was posed so as to lead
inevitably to indifference or fundamental reconsideration. Consider, that at the very time the freedom and
inviolability of religious life was gaining support,
religious truth was still regarded as attaching to
correct doctrine and belief. The new situation of
religious freedom did not lessen the harshness of
doctrinal disputes, for the assumption was that serious
commitment required sharp definition and closedness.
Moreover, in contrast to disputes in science, there
seemed to be no prospect of rationally resolving the
differences. Thus indifferentism, with people turning
their backs on an apparently hopeless conflict. Fundamental reconsideration was undertaken by those who
remained religious adherents but were driven by the
intractability of doctrinal disputes to give centrality
to the moral meaning of beliefs.

Let us look at the matter from the point of view
of the orthodox believer. This person, adopting the
position that his or her religion is the only true one,
may want to persecute those who hold false beliefs or,
at the very least, will reject all other religions as
untrue and pernicious. A tolerationist, one who
prescribes Voltaire's medicine of gentle and humane
reason, proposes that since authoritatively pronounced
dogma is the basis for religious exclusivism, dogma
should be eliminated from religion. This would leave a
minimalist religion, one which is tolerant, but one
which is so changed that it could be dubbed a religion
of toleration. To the orthodox believer, it appears
that the price of toleration is the heart of religion.
This believer feels justified in turning aside from
toleration and continuing to include doctrinal exclusivism as a central mark of true, vital, and robust
religion.

None of the three options reviewed--indifferent-
ism, fundamental reconsideration, orthodox exclusivism
--seems to be satisfactory. Is there any other possibility? I think there is. Notice that the tolerationist of the preceding paragraph made a double move. The
first was to see the link between exclusivism and
dogma; the second was to propose the excision of dogma.
But is such radical surgery indicated? What if dogma
is to religion as eyes are to sight? Would not the
removal of the eyes be a poor way to correct faulty
vision? Are not corrective lenses or cataract surgery
more reasonable procedures? Thus, rather than removing
dogma or reducing its meaning to moral sentiment, would
not it make better sense to try viewing it in another
way? Or, to put the matter more generally, is it
possible to eliminate exclusivism from religion while
retaining its expressive fullness? That is the
possibility I would like to pursue in a concluding
section.

IV

Toleration theory has achieved *for* religions civil
peace, but in the absence of a parallel theory of
relations *among* religions, we have, at best, a state of
cold war. Theories of toleration and religious freedom
could be called exo-therapies. That is, they offer
principles, developed outside religion, to overcome
strife in the civil arena. The medicine offered has
cured a disease that once was rampant in the public
order. Religious disputes are no longer to be civil
disputes. A distinct space has been dedicated for
religion. We have yet to think through how the
religions are to coexist in this space.

From the perspective of the state, all the
inhabitants of the religious space are equal. But the
inhabitants do not see themselves this way. In fact,

they have very little experience in dealing with other
religions as equals. Uniformity or dominance and
subordination, rather than coexistence, has been the
norm. Theologizing (theorizing) has occurred as if the
religions were alone or dominant or subordinate.
Because religious communities have not profoundly
acknowledged that "religious pluralism is theologically
the human condition,"[14] they have not yet produced a
"theology of religious pluralism."[15] Can they do so?
Are there resources for treating the problem of
exclusivism by means of endo-therapy, a cure from
within?

In a passage cited above, Lawrence Danson said
that pluralism is the contemporary ideology. This
ideology leads us to regard the Elizabethans as
anti-Semitic because they did not think it was a bad
thing to think they [Christians] were right and the
Jews were wrong (see n. 6). I prefer, following Jay
Newman, to begin with the point that "though it ends
with the suffix '-ism,' religious *pluralism* is not just
a theory or ideology; it is a fact, a state of
affairs."[16] The fact of pluralism does not by itself
dictate any theory or ideology. In particular, it does
not require that religious persons must become indifferent or less committed. Nor does it require that
religious persons or students of religion refrain from
making evaluative judgments about religious pluralism.
Of course, some theories and theologies of religious

---

[14]Murray, *Problem of Religious Freedom*, 109.

[15]Robert Bellah, "Commentary and Proposed
Agenda: The Normative Framework for Pluralism in
America," *Soundings* 61:3 (1978): 371.

[16]Jay Newman, *Foundations of Religious Tolerance* (Toronto: University of Toronto Press, 1982), 86.

pluralism have done these things. But the fact of
religious pluralism leaves room for the possibility of
developing another kind of theory. I want now to take
some first steps toward one.

Let us begin by comparing so-called particular or
ethnic religions with universal religions on the
question of toleration. It has been suggested by some
(Georg Simmel[17] and Gustav Mensching[18]) that particular
or ethnic religions are by nature tolerant. The people
of a city or tribe who have a particular god devoted to
their welfare readily acknowledge that their god, who
is completely identified with them, must be paralleled
by the gods of other cities and tribes. We have our
god and they have theirs. It seems that tolerance
emerges here because a modest claim (X is *our* god)
leaves room for generosity toward others (Y is *their*
god and Z is *their* god). So far so good, at the
abstract level. But what is the concrete religious
situation? First, the particular religions are and
must be fiercely intolerant at home; the identification
of society and god leaves no room for questioning nor
for the worship "here" of a god from "there." Second,
the gods of other peoples would be regarded benignly
only from a distance; as soon as two peoples and their
gods approached each other, it would be a question of
competition and conflict. Mensching reports that each
Roman city had formulae for calling out the god from
another city so as to domesticate the god and leave the
city open for conquest. Abstract tolerance seems to be

---

[17]Georg Simmel, *Sociology of Religion*, trans.
Curt Rosenthal (New York: Philosophical Library, 1959),
67-68.

[18]Gustav Mensching, *Tolerance and Truth in
Religion*, trans. H. J. Klimkeit (University, AL:
University of Alabama Press, 1971), 14-17.

coupled with, and outweighed by, concrete intolerance,
as generals from different countries regard one
another. It proves to be so limited as not to be
helpful in solving our problem.

Simmel and Mensching also hold that universal
religions, those that worship the one God who is the
God of the universe, are by definition intolerant. The
God of radical monotheism allows no other gods before
or along side. The bond between society and divinity
is broken so that it is finally the individual who
faces God and the question of spiritual destiny. And
if the God appears to and deals with an individual,
that God could appear to and deal with any and all
individuals and is, therefore, universal. There is no
decisive interposition of society between the individual and God. So goes this account of a jealous and
intolerant God who leaves no room for tolerance.

But has the correct conclusion been drawn about a
transcendent and universal God? I suggest, to the
contrary, that it is only with such a transcendent God
that we can come to appreciate the gap between God and
the human comprehension of God, between the forms of
revelation, ritual, and religious expression. If God
resists all domestication, then no religious forms can
claim exclusive possession of truth about God, and no
religious forms can a priori be ruled invalid or false.
The God of the universe is intolerant because abso-
lutization of religious forms is forbidden, and this
intolerance is experienced first and most strongly "at
home" by the worshipper. But just as God tolerates the
incomplete but adequate forms of one's religion, so
must the worshipper be led to be tolerant, to allow for
the possibility that other religious forms are valid.
Accordingly, other religions are not regarded as
competitors to be overcome but as potential siblings in

the religious family.

What I have just presented is endo-therapy, not exo-therapy. I have teased out a case for toleration from an experience at the very core of universal and dogma-creating religions, namely, the experience of the transcendence and intolerance/tolerance of the wor- shipped God.

With Gustav Mensching as our guide, we can go further with our exploration of "living religiousness." He is unwilling to grant that absoluteness attaches to intellectual or institutional claims; rather, he finds it in what he calls the intensive religious experience of absoluteness.[19] A student of Rudolf Otto, Mensching regards the experience of the sacred as the originary ground of religion. He views doctrines and institu- tional forms as *expressions* of the initiating experi- ence of the divine and as vehicles offering ongoing recourse to that experience. The forms, rather than standing between persons and God, rather than absorbing energy in order to be preserved, should serve as instruments of communication. The trouble begins when we absolutize either the expressions of the experience or the convictions about it. This is illustrated by two examples only indirectly related to religion. James Billington, in his study of the revolutionary mind, cites a Frenchman who says that since profound convictions are intolerant, revolutionaries must maintain the severity of the exclusive spirit.[20] Later, he quotes a German who encourages a comrade by saying that

---

[19]Ibid., 152-55.

[20]James Billington, *Fire in the Minds of Men: Origins of the Revolutionary Faith* (New York: Basic Books, 1980), 177.

> Islam was invincible as long as it believed in
> itself. . . . But the moment it began to com-
> promise . . . it ceased to be a conquering force.
> . . . Socialism can neither conquer nor save the
> world if it ceases to believe in itself.[21]

We fall into idolatry if we forget that there is no
direct translation from the intensive experience to
worldly action. Absoluteness is better applied to
Moses' experience at the burning bush than to his
career as leader of the Hebrew people. The molten
steel of the experience must be cooled and shaped
before it is available for use in the world of human
intercourse. The endo-therapeutic application of this
is as follows: intensive religious experience relativi-
zes all things and objects, including religious ones,
and rules out an intolerance which would make the
boundary of any one religion the boundary between the
sacred and the profane.

Reinhold Niebuhr, in the pages devoted to toleration in *The Nature and Destiny of Man*,[22] bases a case
for toleration on the ground that we both have and do
not have the truth, that our doctrines are ambiguous,
that we should have only a broken confidence in the
finality of our own truth, and that we can be forgiving
and tolerant because we are not sure of our own virtue.
I do not disagree, but I do not find here the basis of
my case for toleration. Niebuhr seems to have discovered that his spiritual glass is half empty, that he
knows why it is not fuller, that he had better sip
rather than gulp, and that he, with his half-empty
glass, has no reason for feeling superior to others.
Granted, but another articulation of the same situation

---

[21]Ibid., 383.

[22]Reinhold Niebuhr, *The Nature and Destiny of Man*, vol. 2, *Human Destiny* (New York: Charles Scribner's Sons, 1943), 213-43.

is possible. I, recalling that the forms are grounded
in the intensive experience of absoluteness, say that
the glass is half full, that I know who did the
pouring, that I have enough and more, that it is
reasonable to suppose that many others also have
half-full glasses, and that still others can be invited
to bring their glasses to the sources.

If it is in the initiating religious experience of
absoluteness that persons discover their solitary
weakness and the source of their strength, how could
they use the forms of religion to make a priori
judgments on others? Is the one who is continually
judged by God to become judgmental? Is the one who is
adopted by a Lord to lord it over others? Is the one
who is forgiven to be unforgiving? Is the one whose
enmity is overcome to preserve enmity? Once any flaw
is religiously overcome, can it ever again appear the
same when it appears in ourselves or in others? This
series of questions leads me to refer to two New
Testament texts which use a word close to toleration,
anechomenoi, which is translated as "forbearance." In
Ephesians 4:2 the people are urged to be forbearing
with one another in love;[23] Colossians 3:13 links
forbearing with forgiving and the godly marks of
compassion, kindness, lowliness, meekness, and
patience. Toleration, which can mean bearing or
enduring an other to whom we are opposed, can also mean
forbearing and bearing with an other who shares our
existence. It appears that whatever else the encounter
between a Christian and another person may be, it is

---

[23]"Forbearance in Love" was a motto of the
United Presbyterian Church of North America in which I
was confirmed. Being alive to this meaning is just one
of the many things for which I am ever grateful to my
parents, Charles and Marie.

always an occasion for the Christian to be christian
(i.e., compassionate, patient, loving, etc.) toward the
other.

These observations lead me to suggest that we
probably have pushed the concept of toleration to its
limit and have moved over to respect and sympathy. And
perhaps with that we have reached the point where we
have the possibility of interreligious peace. Philip
Schaff summarizes the historical and theoretical
process in the public order in terms of persecution,
toleration, and liberty. A parallel summation for
religious space would go like this: triumphalist
Christianity will be at war with other faiths; civil-
ized Christianity will exist in a state of truce with
them; chastened Christianity will bear with them in
love, sharing both joys and sorrows.

V

My conclusion can be drawn quickly. In both the
civic and religious orders toleration is a point of
arrival, for it is an achievement with a background of
persecution, ignorance, and ill will. But it is also a
point of departure, a concept that invites being
transcended. In the civic order, the development is
toward discrimination of the orders and full religious
liberty. In the religious order, it is toward mutual
sympathy of the religions generated from an endogenous
critique of exclusivism. (I illustrated endo-therapy
with Christianity; other illustrations could be
provided.)

The next to last word goes to M. F. Abauzit who
said to those who criticized the idea of tolerance:

> If you recommend tolerance to generous spirits,
> they will sense on their own that they must rise
> above this first level. Respect will be born in
> them and sympathy will rise in their hearts.
> Moreover, the more spontaneous such sentiments
> are, the more they are worth. As for ordinary

> spirits, if you preach to them tolerance pure and
> simple, using good arguments, if you even succeed
> in showing them that tolerance is in their
> interest, you have done a good work. If you
> preach higher virtues to them, they will not
> listen to you; you will be speaking in the
> desert.[24]

My response is simply that all our speaking is in the
desert, more or less, and that the endo-therapeutic
approach to philosophy of religion can keep us from
ever forgetting it and from ever despairing over it.

---

[24]M. F. Abauzit, in Lalande, *Vocabulaire*, 1134.

EMIL BRUNNER'S
TWOFOLD UNDERSTANDING OF TRUTH

Kenneth J. Collins

Even as a young man, Emil Brunner had the remarkable ability to see through the multifarious changes
descending upon European culture in the early twentieth
century--in terms of new political ideologies, advances
in science, and the increasing secularism-- in order to
discern the leading question of his age: How does one
find a place for value in a world of fact? To be sure,
this question is a perennial one, at least since the
time of Descartes and the advent of modern philosophy,
but it has been posed by the contemporary Church with a
new sense of urgency and by Brunner in particular in
the form: How can one have a scientifically satisfying
formulation of the Christian faith?[1] Such a concern
led the early Brunner to explore the epistemology of
Kant and the phenomenology of Husserl as he searched
for the intellectual apparatus requisite to respond to
the disappearance of transcendence in modern European
culture.

It was not until the middle of the 1930's,
however, that is, *after* his famous debate with Karl

---

[1]Emil Brunner, "Intellectual Autobiography," in
The Theology of Emil Brunner, ed. Charles W. Kegley and
Robert W. Bretall (New York: Macmillan, 1962), 5. For
the German original, "Autobiographische Skizze," see
Reformatio 12 (1963): 631-46.

Barth over natural theology, that Brunner refocused his growing apologetic concerns and began to see, to use his own words, "that the root of the whole problem was the question of anthropology."[2]

During this period, then, he began a serious and critical reading of the works of Ferdinand Ebner and Martin Buber who together helped this Swiss theologian to see not only the difference between the I-Thou world (*Ich-Du-Welt*) and the I-It world (*Ich-Es-Welt*)--in other words, that human existence is different from all other kinds of existence--but also, and more important-ly, that this distinction was at "the heart of the biblical conception of man."[3]

By 1937 Brunner's anthropological studies had led him to a reevaluation of the nature of humanity and to a reformulation of the biblical conception of truth.[4] Thus, his anthropological interests soon flowed quite naturally into epistemological ones. And again in that same year,[5] his assessment of the limits and extent of human knowledge was further clarified by his prepara-

---

[2]Brunner, "Intellectual Autobiography," 11.

[3]Ibid.

[4]Ibid., 12.

[5]There is a discrepancy here concerning the date of the lectures and the book, *Wahrheit als Begegnung*, which followed. Brunner's autobiography, for example, indicates that the lectures were delivered in 1936 and the book was published in 1937. However, the foreword to the Second Edition of *Wahrheit als Begegnung*, written by Brunner himself, maintains that the lectures were delivered in 1937 and that the book was published in 1938. Since the publication of the book by a Berlin press can easily be determined as having occurred in the year 1938, the latter chronology is to be preferred as more reliable. Cf. Emil Brunner,

Truth as Encounter (Philadelphia: Westminster, 1943), 3; and "Intellectual Autobiography," 3.

tion for a series of lectures he was to deliver at the
University of Uppsala on the topic of the relation
between the objective and the subjective in the
Christian faith. By means of this task, he was able to
see more clearly that there is a marked difference
between the biblical understanding of truth, on the one
hand, and the Greek conception of truth which is
presupposed by Western philosophy and science, on the
other.

Equipped with this insight, the Zurich professor
began to retool, theologically speaking, and hereafter
all his work in dogmatics was done from this new
vantage point. Indeed, in his own estimation at least,
this distinction between truth--biblical and otherwise
--was to become his "most important contribution to the
theological concept of knowledge."[6] The purpose of
this study, therefore, will be to consider the nature
of these truths enunciated and distinguished by
Brunner, their relation to each other, and the question
of whether they are parts or at least could possibly
become parts of some greater unity. In other words,
must the duality of truth always remain or is there
some basis for a transcendent unity in the theology of
Emil Brunner? But even before these pertinent questions can be addressed a few points concerning Brunner's method are in order.

I

The epistemological project that is undertaken in
Truth as Encounter is not as broad and extensive as one
might initially expect. The focus here is on theological rather than philosophical knowledge; that is, the
work itself evidences the Anselmic perspective of *credo
ut intelligam* and is, therefore, written from the

---

[6]Brunner, "Intellectual Autobiography," 12.

viewpoint of faith, "from within the church, not from
without."[7] This means, no doubt, that the larger
question of the relation between biblical truth and
other truth is not specifically addressed here,
although Brunner does consider it later in his book
Revelation and Reason which is much more ambitious and
satisfying, at least from a philosophical point of
view.

Brunner's apparent reluctance to entertain these
kinds of questions at the outset most likely grew out
of his concern to present the biblical understanding of
truth untrammmeled by other considerations. Indeed, he
feared that if general epistemological or ontological
categories were introduced at an early stage, they
would inevitably reduce, transform, and actually
distort the biblical understanding of truth. Put
another way, Brunner believed he was dealing with
something *sui generis*, arising from Scripture itself,
and therefore no appeal could be made to any preliminary philosophical judgments, not even "those of
existential philosophy."[8] This does not mean, however,
that he did not consider the nature of the Greek
conception of truth at all in *Truth as Encounter*, for
he clearly did, especially in terms of its distortion
of biblical truth throughout history. The point,
though, and it is an important one, is that the former
truth must be understood in terms of the latter and not
the other way around.

II

In *Truth as Encounter*, Brunner claims that a
departure from the biblical understanding of truth--and

---

[7]Brunner, *Truth As Encounter*, 65-66.

[8]Emil Brunner, *The Divine Human Encounter*
(Westport, CT: Greenwood, 1943), 82-83.

of faith for that matter--occurred quite early due to
the inordinate influence Greek philosophy exercised
over the life and thought of the primitive church. Two
principal transformations, he contends, took place as a
result of such intellectualism: first, revelation was
now defined as "the communication of those doctrinal
truths which were inaccessible by themselves to human
reason,"[9] and second, "faith consisted in holding
these supernaturally revealed doctrines for truth."[10]

The chief paradigm, then, which engendered these
transformations and under which the genius of Christianity was subsumed was the object/subject antithesis.
By the first prong, objectivism, Brunner understands
the tendency of the individual to get something in his
or her power, to become a master of an object, to have
an "it" in one's control.[11] Here he cites the magical-
materialistic conception of the Lord's Supper and the
authoritarian concept of the obedience of faith
prevalent in the Roman Catholic Church of his day as
two instances of this deeper "sickness."[12] Beyond
this, he refers specifically to the doctrine of the
verbal inspiration of the Bible, as championed by
Protestant orthodoxy, in which the words of the Bible
are equated quite literally with the Word of God.

By the second prong, subjectivism, Brunner has in
mind the attempt to repudiate all fixed order in trying
to attain the highest possible, unlimited self-realiza-

---

[9]Brunner, *Truth as Encounter*, 68.

[10]Ibid.

[11]Ibid., 71.

[12]Ibid.

tion,[13] as depicted, for example, in the theology of
Friedrich Schleiermacher with its emphasis on human
subjectivity in terms of feeling and consciousness.[14]
In underscoring the priority of personal experience
under the freedom of the spirit, this second prong is
actually rooted just as deeply in the being of an
independent humanity, and therefore has just as
devastating an effect upon the church as objectivism
does. In short, the first prong highlights the
externality and objectivity of the faith, the second
its subjective appropriation, but both underscore human
autonomy.[15]

It should be apparent by now that one of the
foundational axioms in the theology of Emil Brunner is
that "the Biblical understanding of truth cannot be
grasped through the object-subject antithesis: on the
contrary, it is falsified through it."[16] Both prongs,
therefore, are rejected outright, and even the possibility of an imaginative dialectical resolution of
these poles is excluded as well, for there simply can
be no correct mean between two errors. The problem is
not within the antithesis but *with* the antithesis

---

[13]Ibid., 74.

[14]Ibid., 79-80. Observe that Brunner maintains
Schleiermacher emphasizes subjectivity in terms of
human self-consciousness with the result that religion
is defined not in terms of Word and Act, but in terms
of pure passive consciousness. See Emil Brunner, *Die
Mystik und Das Wort*, 2d ed. (Tübingen: Furche Verlag,
1924), 132ff.

[15]There is an excellent discussion of the
relation between the objective and the subjective as
two instances of rational knowledge in Kenneth Cauthen,
"Biblical Truths and Rational Knowledge," *Review and
Expositor* 53 (1956): 467-76.

[16]Brunner, *Truth as Encounter*, 69.

itself. Brunner writes:

> In any event the damage to the church did not lie
> in the onesided emphasis on either the objective
> or the subjective but, rather, in the fact that
> the Biblical revelation was brought under this
> antithesis. The Bible is as little concerned with
> objective as with subjective truth. The objectiv-
> e-subjective antithesis cannot be applied to the
> Word of God and to faith. It is a category of
> thought wholly foreign, not only to the way of
> expression in the Bible, but also to the entire
> content.[17]

It should be noted, however, that Brunner's
rejection of the object-subject antithesis as a
suitable vehicle for the understanding of Biblical
truth does not entail its repudiation in other important areas of human knowledge and endeavor. Certainly,
the object-subject paradigm is immensely valuable in
all those spheres where reason itself is competent such
as in logic, mathematics, empirical and rational
philosophy, and science, to name a few. Moreover, one
of the principal functions of reason, useful in so many
ways, is the actual demarcation of the limits of human
knowledge; it is able to mark out quite clearly the
bounds (*Die Grenzen*) of all that can become an *object*
of thought. To be sure, all *thinking*, as Brunner
readily concedes, "including theological"[18]--in the
sense that it is a reflection upon the divine/human
encounter--occurs within this antithesis. Its legitimate sphere, then, "is the things of the world,"[19] or,
to use Kantian language, the phenomenal realm to which
the categories of understanding may be suitably

---

[17]Ibid., 84-85.

[18]Brunner, *Divine Human Encounter*, 83.

[19]Emil Brunner, *The Christian Doctrine of Creation and Redemption* (Philadelphia: Westminster, 1952), 26.

applied.

Difficulties begin to emerge, argues Brunner, only
when reason becomes arrogant and sets itself up as the
sole arbiter, the principal criterion, in all matters
of truth. Whether it is expressed in the form of
realism or idealism, reason is simply not qualified to
judge in the crucial areas of biblical truth, faith,
and revelation. Here, the autonomy of reason, which
Brunner also refers to as a "sinful fundamental
axiom,"[20] can only result in distortion since it makes
humanity itself the measure of all things, and thereby
destroys at the outset the very possibility of a
revelation which transcends the limits and reach of
human competence. Thus, in order to understand
biblical truth properly, another quite different,
though not contradictory, model is required.

III

Emil Brunner is in basic agreement with Heim's
characterization of the discovery of "I-Thou" truth in
philosophy by Ebner and Buber as a "Copernican tur-
ning-point in the history of thought."[21] Yet, as
influenced as he was by these two thinkers, Brunner did
not confuse the issues of discovery and source. That
Ebner and Buber, through their reading of Soren
Kierkegaard, discovered or--better yet--rediscovered
this vital truth was allowed, but that they or their
philosophies were the source or origin of this truth
was flatly denied. Along these lines, Brunner insisted, interestingly enough, that his *Dogmatics* were
not an attempt to combine "I-Thou" philosophy with
Christian theology, as was often mistakenly supposed,

---

[20]Emil Brunner, *Revelation and Reason*, (Wake
Forest, NC: Chanticleer, 1946), 208.

[21]Brunner, *Doctrine of Creation*, v.

but were instead written to stress the importance of I-Thou truth, "I which is wholly derived from the Bible."[22] Brunner substantiated this significant claim by pointing out that the biblical understanding of truth, in a real sense, is simply the contents of the Bible considered in their "formal aspect,"[23] or what elsewhere he referred to as the "common denominator of all biblical proclamaion."[24] When he was more specific than this, he referred to the Prologue of John's Gospel, "Grace and truth came by Jesus Christ" (John 1:17), as perhaps the clearest expression of this truth, but this verse was certainly not to be viewed as a proof-text. Brunner knew all too well that such "proofs" would only indicate that an external paradigm had, in fact, been forced upon the Scriptures.

Throughout his many writings, Brunner employed a number of phrases to describe his new insight into the biblical understanding of truth, among which are "truth as encounter," "divine/human correspondence," "divine/ human encounter," and "personal correspondence." The last phrase is especially revealing because it suggests something of the double-sided self-giving which results in fellowship between Lord and creature,[25] while at the same time it highlights the personal nature of this relation. Properly speaking, however, the correspondence here is between the Word of God and faith which

---

[22]Ibid. Emphasis is mine. Leon Hynson finds this claim difficult to accept in light of the obvious influence of Buber on Brunner's thought. See Leon Hynson, "Theological Encounter: Brunner and Buber," *Journal of Ecumenical Studies* 12 (1975): 364.

[23]Brunner, *Divine Human Encounter*, 46.

[24]Ibid., 201.

[25]Ibid., 75.

can be analogously, but only analogously, understood in
terms of the encounter between human beings. Brunner
writes:

> . . . when God reveals Himself to me in His Word,
> we are not then concerned with a 'something.' In
> His Word, God does not deliver to me a course of
> lectures in dogmatic theology . . . but makes
> Himself accessible to me. . . . An exchange hence
> takes place here which is wholly without analogy
> in the sphere of thinking. The sole analogy is in
> the encounter between human beings, the meeting of
> person with person.[26]

Nevertheless, Brunner was not restricted to this
particular phrase, personal correspondence, nor did he
overwork it. In fact, when the issues were clearly
epistemological he preferred the expression "truth as
encounter."

One of the chief characteristics of I-Thou truth,
truth as encounter, is that the historical element
plays a crucial role. As such, this truth is "given"
truth; it is not in us but must come to us in a
decisive event. Again, this truth is not preceded by
the words, "I think"--in other words the Cartesian
Cogito is excluded--but by the words "here it is."[27]
To be sure, the historical nature of this truth,
especially in terms of its externality, underscores the
insufficiency of the self's resources apart from God.
And it is precisely this element, as Brunner aptly
notes, that is "most offensive to the autonomous
reason."[28] But the offense will and indeed must
continue, he adds, "so long as we are held captive in

---

[26]Ibid., 85.

[27]Emil Brunner, *The Christian Doctrine of God*
(Philadelphia: Westminster, 1949), 125.

[28]Brunner, *Truth as Encounter*, 21.

the 'Thouless' thinking of the solitary self."[29]

Second, truth as encounter is not an objective,
impersonal, or abstract conception of truth, but is a
"Thou" truth, a revelation of the Word of God, Jesus
Christ, in love. In no way, then, is this truth
superficial. Nor is it a thing of indifference, since
it engages humanity at the deepest levels of its being.
As such, this truth is dialogical, not monological,
personal,[30] not impersonal. It occurs only in a
relation when the speaking, revealing God addresses
humanity. Not surprisingly, then, it is exactly this
revelation of love which, for Brunner, constitutes the
meaning of human life.

The third characteristic flows immediately from
the second: truth understood as an encounter with the
Word of God is participatory; it cannot be known second
hand, like doctrines can, but only in an act of
personal surrender and decision, which is exactly what
Brunner calls faith. "We cannot possess this truth,"
he observes, "as we can possess other truth, but we
must be in the truth, we must live this truth, we must
do it."[31] In this setting, notice that truth is
principally defined not in terms of nouns but of verbs;
the substantive has for the most part dropped out of
Brunner's vocabulary. Biblical truth is not an "it," a

---

[29]Ibid.

[30]One of the accusations leveled against
Brunner's understanding of I-Thou truth is that it
overemphasizes the personal aspects of faith and,
therefore, lacks social breadth. But in light of the
entire Brunnerian corpus, especially in terms of
Justice and the Social Order, such criticism hardly
seems justified. Cf. Roger Hazelton, "Religion as
Encounter," *Journal of Religious Thought* 14 (1957):
134.

[31]Brunner, *Revelation and Reason*, 371.

thing, but an event, an encounter with the living God.

To attain an even clearer understanding of the
nature of biblical truth, it is imperative to give at
least a cursory account of the dialogical poles
involved in the revelatory event--namely, the Word of
God and faith.[32]   Concerning the former, it should be
noted that Brunner repudiated the possibility of the
knowledge of *Gott-an-sich*; God is neither the object of
our thought, nor the conclusion of a theological
syllogism. Abstraction and philosophical speculation,
based as they are on the "I-It" model of truth,
necessarily lead to secularization, to the "curse of
the law."[33] In other words, God is not an object, but
Absolute Subject,[34] and does not choose to be known
outside Christ, but to be clothed, as it were, in the
promises of the gospel. Brunner's dependence on
Luther's distinction between the hidden God and the

----

[32]Brunner, *Divine Human Encounter*, 76. Observe
that, strictly speaking, the correlation is between the
Word of God and *faith*. But concerning this last
element it should be added that Brunner probably had in
mind the *person* who has been freely given faith.

[33]Brunner, *Revelation and Reason*, 411.

[34]Ibid., 24. George A. Schrader suggests that
it is bad theology and metaphysics to consider God as
pure subject. But perhaps he has missed Brunner's
chief point here: knowledge of God as an object of
one's thought is always knowledge *about* God (doctrine),
not knowledge *of* God. That the latter will eventually
have to be expressed in the vocabulary of the former is
not denied so long as it is realized that a translation
is taking place. In fact, this is precisely the task
and difficulty of theologians who must walk in the
midst of two worlds. See George A. Schrader, "Brunner's Conception of Philosophy," in *The Theology of
Emil Brunner*, ed. Charles W. Kegley and Robert W.
Bretall (New York: Macmillan, 1962), 126.

revealed God,[35] and inferentially, God's strange work
and proper work, is obvious and is not at all surprising since both theologians had to contend with a
burgeoning philosophical and theological speculation
that was in danger of rendering the gospel opaque.
Brunner notes,

> In Jesus Christ alone, however, God makes Himself
> known as He really is. In Him God shows Himself
> to us 'as abyss of eternal love.' The revelation
> and the communication of this love, the work of
> free grace is 'God's proper work,' His *opus
> proprium*.[36]

Since valid knowledge of God can only be gained in
Jesus Christ, this indicates not only that Christ
Himself is the Word of God, *par excellence*, but also
that He is the content of faith and truth. This last
claim is, without doubt, a "radical departure from the
ordinary conception of truth with its emphasis on
universality and timelessness."[37] Yet Brunner remained
undeterred and stressed the particularity and the
"timefullness" of the Biblical understanding of truth
in its proclamation and exaltation of the person of
Christ. And to his critics, who charged that such
particularity was intolerant and for that reason even
offensive, Brunner responded,

> . . . all this generalization, this anti-in-
> tolerance, is nothing but a cloak for the circum-
> vention of the historical as event. 'History in
> general' is nothing more than just man himself
> once more, man the self-sufficient, man who needs
> nothing outside himself, the autarky and autonomy

---

[35]Martin Luther, "On the Bondage of the Will,"
in *Luther and Erasmus: Free Will and Salvation*, ed. E.
Gordon Rupp and Philip S. Watson (Philadelphia:
Westminster, 1969), 200-204.

[36]Brunner, *Doctrine of God*, 168.

[37]Brunner, *Divine Human Encounter*, 140.

of nonreceptive reason.[38]

Moreover, he asserted, once again, that Christ as the
content of truth is the perspective of the New Testament itself: "But grace and truth came into being
through Jesus Christ."[39] Simply put, truth is not
static, but dynamic; it comes into being; it is not an
object but a Person, Jesus Christ.[40]

With respect to faith, the second aspect of the
correlation, Brunner employed the imagery of a revolution, an overthrow of government to convey his meaning.
So understood, faith entails a change of hands, a
surrender of self, whereby a "lord of self becomes one
who obeys."[41] It is, to use Brunner's own words, "the
knowledge that I do not belong to myself, but that I
have a master, that I belong to another."[42] Faith,
then, is a total self-giving, an utter dependence upon
God which engages the whole being, not just the
intellect. It is a shift from the monologue of
existence, where self is supreme, to a dialogue of
existence, where humanity is addressed by and is

---

[38]Brunner, *Truth as Encounter*, 22.

[39]Brunner, *Divine Human Encounter*, 140.

[40]Richard A. Muller contends that Brunner makes
very little use of John 1:14 in his Christology.
However, in light of the large role the Johannine
prologue plays in Brunner's consideration of the
question of biblical truth, it is difficult to take
such criticism seriously. See Richard A. Muller,
"Christ--The Revelation or the Revealer: Brunner and
Reformed Orthodoxy on the Doctrine of the Word of God,"
Journal of the Evangelical Theological Society 26
(1983): 316.

[41]Brunner, *Divine Human Encounter*, 89.

[42]Emil Brunner, *The Christian Doctrine of the
Church, Faith, and the Consummation* (Philadelphia:
Westminster, 1962), 141.

responsible to the ever-revealing God.

Moreover, as noted earlier, Brunner believed that
the misunderstanding of faith as belief in doctrine--
-which received great impetus during the period of
Protestant scholasticism--was probably, "the most fatal
occurrence within the entire history of the Church."[43]
Given his theological stance, Brunner is not engaging
in hyperbole here, for when this type of error occurs
--in other words, when a doctrine of the Church, such
as justification by faith, becomes the object of faith
instead of pointing beyond itself to the gracious
God--the result can only be disastrous. Indeed, the
very possibility for God's lordship and fellowship with
us leaves us undisturbed in our self-isolation. The
referent of faith has become an "it" instead of a
"Thou." Brunner observes:

> This Biblical understanding of faith, which is
> tantamount to what has been said about personal
> correspondence, stands in sharp contrast to the
> popular conception of faith . . . . Once let dogma
> be the object of faith, and faith is then deter-
> mined by means of the Object-Subject antithesis,
> by means of the rational concept of truth, and
> remains thus . . . . [44]

That the words "historical," "given," "personal,"
"eventful," "participatory," and "dialogical" are all
apt in expressing what Brunner meant by the phrase
"truth as encounter" is readily granted by most
scholars who work in this field either as theological
admirers or as opponents. However, some scholars have
discovered in these words just cited the basis for a
serious indictment of Brunner's theology, especially in
terms of his understanding of revelation and faith.
These charges usually revolve around the central

---

[43]Brunner, *Divine Human Encounter*, 154.

[44]Ibid., 153.

question of whether the Word of God, as encountered in
the revelatory event, and doctrine, as recorded in the
Bible, are completely different. Another way of posing
this same question is to ask, Does the Word of God have
content, or, to entertain yet another query, is faith
knowledge?

A leading critic in this area has been Paul
Jewett, an evangelical scholar, who claims that the
Word of God conceived in the Brunnerian sense as the
content of "truth as encounter" cannot be talked about
at all, "for what is reduced to speech must be subject
to the laws of rational coherence,"[45] and these laws do
not apply to this "event." Naturally, this means that
the Word of God is irrational, indescribable, and
without form--or so it is claimed. But did Brunner
actually view the Word of God in this manner, in a
mystical amorphous sense? Is Jewett's assessment
really fair? More importantly, is it accurate?

In response to these questions, it appears, first
of all, that Jewett's position fails to do justice to
the complexity and subtlety of Brunner's theology for
it discerns little of the dialectical relation between
the Word of God and doctrine that he took such great
care in explicating. For instance, Brunner affirmed on
the one hand that all doctrine in the Bible points
beyond itself to the God who addresses us, but on the
other hand he maintained that "this address and this
response can take place only by virtue of Biblical
doctrine,"[46] which is related instrumentally to the

---

[45]Paul King Jewett, *Emil Brunner's Concept of
Revelation* (London: James Clarke, 1954), 96.

[46]Brunner, *Divine Human Encounter*, 108.

Word of God as *token* and *framework*.[47] In other words, Brunner not only defined the relation between doctrine and the Word of God in a negative way by emphasizing the difference between the two, but he also conceived the relation in a positive way by showing that the two are not *completely* different. Jewett acknowledged only the first movement, and this is part of the problem with his analysis, and with others like it.

Second, Paul Jewett and Richard Muller, another evangelical scholar, both misunderstand in what way and to what extent Brunner was dependent on the Kantian distinction between phenomena and noumena as it relates to the differentiation between I-It and I-Thou truth, and consequently, between doctrine and the Word of God. Muller, for example, argues:

> It is Brunner's conception of revelation as divine self-communication that appears a bit one-sided and restrictive . . . the rigid epistemological firmament separating the noumenal and phenomenal levels of the Kantian universe prevents him from revealing—even in Christ, the Word Incarnate—the supramundane truth concerning his transcendent Being.[48]

However, it is more accurate to note that Brunner did not appropriate the Kantian distinction in a straightforward way, but in a dialectical, yes/no fashion. First of all, Brunner, like Kant, asserted a sharp difference between the phenomenal and noumenal realms, especially when he wanted to indicate the

---

[47]Ibid., 111.

[48]Muller, "Revelation or Revealer," 318. Notice also in this piece that Muller is not content with the possibility of knowing God in Jesus Christ alone, but requires a knowledge of the transcendent God, God outside the revelation of the Word of God, the *Gott-an-sich* (p. 310). Luther and Brunner, however, are correct in pointing out that when this attempt is made, one knows not the *Gott-an-sich*, but the God of Wrath.

inability of reason to know God. Along these lines, he acknowledged that God is neither an object in the spatiotemporal realm nor a Being who can be grasped by the categories of understanding which are strictly limited to phenomena.[49] Thus, contrary to popular belief, Brunner excluded the possibility of a rational, natural knowledge of God,[50] in his claim that God is not an object at all, but instead is Absolute Subject.

Secondly, Brunner differed from Kant, not in considering God a noumenon which transcends phenomena-- notice the English language continually moves in the direction of reification--but in claiming that God as a noumenon could be known, not by theoretical reason to be sure, nor merely as a postulate of practical reason, but through the divine/human encounter. Again, if Brunner, like Kant, had claimed that God cannot be known at all, that is, if he had considered religion within the limits of reason alone, then revelation would have necessarily been precluded and the heart of Brunner's theology would have collapsed with it.

Thirdly, and this is perhaps most disturbing to

---

[49]Immanuel Kant, *Critique of Pure Reason*, trans. Norman Kemp Smith (New York: St. Martin's, 1965), 113.

[50]This may indeed come as a surprise to the Barthians who have been schooled on the idea that Brunner taught humanity has a natural capacity for revelation and the knowledge of God. Brunner taught no such thing. He did, however, uncautiously employ the phrase "Christian Natural Theology"--which he later regretted (the particular phrase that is)--to indicate that *after* one has been renewed by Christ, one is able to see, faintly perhaps, the revelation in Creation. For his part, Barth misinterpreted Brunner on several key points, some of which are being perpetuated even today, the principal one, of course, being Barth's substitution of the word "Offenbarungfahig" for Brunner's "Worterfahig." Cf. Emil Brunner, *Natur und Gnade: Gesprach mit Karl Barth* (Tübingen: n.p., 1934).

Muller, Brunner advocated that there can be no knowledge of a "transcendent" God apart from the revelation
of Jesus Christ. Ever cautious in his theological
expressions, Brunner avoided a Christomonism at this
point by indicating that the Father is revealed through
the Son and in the Holy Spirit. Put another way, the
name "Father" designates the origin and content of the
revelation, the "Son" refers to the historic Mediator,
and the "Holy Spirit," the present reality of this
revelation.[51] Here, then, is a real parting of the
ways between this Reformed theologian and some of his
critics. For Muller, as an instance of the latter, the
referent for the term "transcendent" is not the Word of
God, and all which is revealed through it, as it is for
Brunner, but the knowledge of God which lies *outside*
the revelation of Christ. Muller writes,

> The Kantian rift between noumenal and phenomenal
> is maintained [in Brunner's theology], for now the
> *terminus ad quem* of the entire historical self-
> manifestation of God is not a knowledge of tran-
> scendent God, as the orthodox theory of revelation
> based on the prophetic Word had indicated, but an
> acknowledgment of Jesus Christ as the fullness of
> God's revelation.[52]

For his part, Brunner repudiated the knowledge of the
transcendent God apart from the Word of God on two
grounds: first, it is beyond the purview of reason, a
faculty which when exercised beyond its proper limits
can only construct idols; second, it is not given in
revelation. The quest for such knowledge, therefore,
is vain and idle; it is an instance of speculation
which can only reveal the God of Wrath.

Yet another way in which Brunner indicated that
the Word of God is not without content is through his

---

[51]Brunner, *Doctrine of God*, 206-7.

[52]Muller, "Revelation or Revealer," 310.

understanding of the role of faith in the divine/human
encounter. Not surprisingly, his view is marked by
dialectical considerations. Thus, for instance, to the
question, "Is faith knowledge?" Brunner replied both No
and Yes. Faith is not knowledge in the sense of
knowing an object; faith knows quite literally nothing;
indeed, it arises, "where all knowledge is at an end,
both objective . . . and subjective."[53] Nevertheless,
there is a real sense in which faith is knowledge, not
theoretical knowledge, of course, but true self-
knowledge,[54] and knowledge of the Son of God as the
true reality.[55] In short, faith entails knowledge
which transcends reason, but it does not transcend the
Word.[56]

Though Brunner was unwilling to entertain the
philosophical question of the specific relation between
I-It truth and I-Thou truth when he wrote his early
work, *Truth as Encounter*, he did eventually consider it
in *Revelation and Reason*. However, a hint of lingering
reluctance on Brunner's part is revealed in his frank

---

[53]Brunner, *Church, Faith, Consummation*, 260.

[54]Ibid.

[55]Ibid., 261.

[56]When the personal knowledge received in the
divine/human encounter is expressed in language, it is
automatically transformed and one can even say "reduced," for it is then expressed in the currency of
I-It truth. Cf. Brunner, *Doctrine of God*, 25 and 41,
and note his distinction between direct and indirect
revelation. In addition, if this assessment is
correct, it means that one can move from the Word of
God to doctrine, but with reduction. One can also move
from the doctrine of the Bible to the Word of God but
only through the Holy Spirit who is the "point of
identity" (p. 29.), but one cannot move from doctrine,
considered by reason alone, to any significant knowledge of God. This is sheer speculation, unwarranted, and
could only be the task of a *Theologismus*.

acknowledgment at the outset of the discussion that such a question is foreign to the outlook of the Bible itself.[57] At any rate, one of the first items he stressed concerning these two truths is that they are not in opposition. Not surprisingly, given his apologetic concerns, Brunner unequivocally rejected the doctrine of a double truth in the sense that truth in one sphere, in science for example, could contradict truth in the other, in this case revelation--and vice versa.

Beyond these initial observations, Brunner posed the broader and much more difficult question of whether either of these truths, in terms of reason or revelation, could possibly become the basis for a synthesis which could incorporate the truth of the other. In other words, not only was he attempting to solve the problem of the relation between fact and value as the principal epistemological question of his age, but he was doing so, interestingly enough, against the backdrop of the larger question of the relation between the One and the many, unity and plurality--a question as old as the Pre-Socratics and as modern as Bradley. Simply put, the question is this: Is there really a unity behind the apparent diversity of truths?

Brunner first of all examined reason, as the epitome of I-It truth, as a possible candidate for this synthesis, but immediately rejected it because when this faculty is exalted, when humanity and its abilities are placed at the center of things, "everything," Brunner writes, "gets out of focus."[58] Reason, therefore, can neither be the basis for all truth, nor can revelation, I-Thou truth, be incorporated within its

---

[57]Brunner, *Revelation and Reason*, 309.

[58]Ibid., 374.

parameters. To the contrary, Brunner contended that it is within the truth of revelation that all which reason knows falls into place. "It is not God and His truth that must have room within the sphere of reason," he declares, "but reason and its truth must find its place in God."[59] The relation between the two kinds of truth, then, is such that the higher (I-Thou) includes the lower (I-It), but not the other way around.[60]

It might appear, in light of the preceding, that Brunner suggested a synthesis between the two kinds of truths that would make I-Thou truth the center with the result that the "doubleness" of truth would be overcome. However, such a conclusion, if drawn, would be erroneous. For although truth as encounter is considered a "higher" truth than brute fact, in the sense that Brunner affirmed the superordination of the personal over the impersonal,[61] truth as encounter--more specifically the Word of God--is unable to give an answer "to all questions."[62] In short, Brunner simply rejected the notion that the dualism of the concept of truth and of the criterion of truth could be eliminated by any monistic solution, "whether [it be] the monism of reason or that of the Word of revelation."[63] And so when a scholar like Schrotenboer claims that reality for Brunner is of two kinds, and when he notes, in addition, that the relation between these truths is one

---

[59]Ibid., 213.

[60]Ibid., 373.

[61]Ibid.

[62]Ibid., 381.

[63]Ibid., 379.

of incommensurability,[64] his analysis is not wide of
the mark.

Nevertheless, Brunner did suggest, paradoxically,
a unity between these two truths along Christological
lines in several places in his writings when he
concluded, for example, that "reason and the knowledge
which it acquires finds its ground and its purpose in
the Son."[65] And elsewhere he observed that "God's
Logos includes all the logos of reason within Himself,
but He Himself is Person, the eternal Son."[66] Is his
position, then, ultimately contradictory? Not really,
so long as it is remembered that Brunner wanted to
posit two things simultaneously: one, that duality
from the human perspective can never be overcome,
either through reason or the Word; second, that the
ultimate unity of these truths inheres in the Word of
God, though this unity has not been revealed.

Concerning this last point, Brunner taught that
there is more to the Word of God than can be known by
human beings--much more. And this means, of course,
that he employed the term "transcendent" in at least
two ways, not just one. His first use entailed the
revelation of the Person of Christ which is given in
faith (beyond human abilities, known in grace); the
other, the unity of the realms which is rooted in the
Word of God, but which is not given either to reason or
faith (beyond human ability, not known in grace). It
is a unity, then, not quite apparent though ultimately
real.

---

[64]P. G. Schrotenboer, *A New Apologetics: An
Analysis and Appraisal of The Eristic Theology of Emil
Brunner* (Kampen, Netherlands: J. H. Kok, 1955), 43.

[65]Brunner, *Doctrine of Creation*, 30.

[66]Brunner, *Revelation and Reason*, 373.

Moreover, perhaps it is precisely at this juncture, in terms of a quest for an ultimate unity beyond
duality, that the interpretation of Brunner's anthropology and his epistemology is most obvious. Because
human beings are creatures, not the Creator, they face
both God and the world. The two-fold understanding of
truth, therefore, can never be overcome from the human
perspective. Men and women are simply not absolute
subjects in the sense that God is, but are very much
concerned with a world of mundane fact, a world in
which they themselves are, at least in a certain sense,
objects. The unity which Brunner set forth, therefore,
Schrader's claim notwithstanding,[67] is perhaps more an
expression of faith than an epistemological judgment;
more a hope than a revealed truth; it is affirmed for
its organizing and integrating potential, though it is
virtually unknowable. Indeed, it most resembles--
rather than the experience of God in the event of
revelation--what Kant had in mind by the term
"noumenon."

---

[67]George Schrader maintains that the unity
beyond duality, the one truth, may be apprehended.
This view moves in the direction of a monism and of a
knowledge which Brunner thought impossible. See
Schrader, "Brunner's Conception of Philosophy," 191.

JAROSLAV PELIKAN AND THE TRADITION OF
CHRISTIAN HUMANISM

W. David Buschart

"The love of learning and the desire for God" is
not only the finest flower of the Benedictine
monasticism of the Latin Middle Ages; it is also,
in quite another dress, the leitmotiv of the
dedication to patient scholarship that I would
define as the genius of "Christian humanism."[1]

I

The work of Jaroslav Jan Pelikan, Jr., is beginning to be recognized as a significant contribution to
the historical and theological scholarship of our time.
By virtue of publications such as *The Riddle of Roman
Catholicism*, *Historical Theology*, and the five-volume
*The Christian Tradition: A History of the Development
of Doctrine*, Pelikan's work is often conceived of as
that of a historical theologian.[2] However, there is

---

[1]Jaroslav Pelikan, "Paul M. Bretscher, Christian Humanist," *The Cresset* 37 (1964): 4. Except where
otherwise indicated, sources cited in this essay are
authored by Jaroslav Pelikan.

[2]Reviewers of Pelikan's books often refer to
him in this way, and he has often referred to himself
as, among other things, "a historical theologian"
(e.g., *Bach Among the Theologians* [Philadelphia:
Fortress, 1986], ix; "Creation and Causality in the
History of Christian Thought," in *Issues in Evolution*,
ed. Sol Tax and Charles Callender [Chicago: University

more to Pelikan's work--more to his vocation--than that
of a historical theologian.

In 1983, Pelikan was recipient of the Jefferson
Award and chosen to deliver the Jefferson Lectures in
the Humanities.[3] This is the highest honor that the
United States bestows on humanist scholars. Several
years later, the Divinity School of the University of
Chicago honored him as Alumnus of the Year, citing,
among other contributions, "his leadership of Christian
humanism within the arts and sciences."[4] These two
awards are indicative of the fact that for a complete
and accurate understanding of Jaroslav Pelikan's
writings, the spirit which undergirds and informs his
work must be comprehended. That spirit is the spirit
of humanism, Christian humanism.[5]

Pelikan's affinity for the principles of Christian
humanism developed early. He describes his childhood
home as one where "both the theological tradition and
humanistic culture were so much [his] daily bread"
that he finds any "antithesis between them quite

---

of Chicago Press, 1960], 40; and "The Theological
Library and the Tradition of Christian Humanism,"
Concordia Theological Monthly 33 [1962]: 722).

[3]These lectures were published as *The Vindication of Tradition* (New Haven: Yale University Press,
1984).

[4]Donald P. Gilles, "Jaroslav Pelikan: Alumnus
of the Year," *Criterion* 26 (1987): 3.

[5]The spirit of Christian humanism is also that
which permeated the work of Bard Thompson. However,
the Christian humanism increasingly evident in Pelikan's work is, as will be seen, akin to that of
Erasmus, while that which informs Thompson's work is,
perhaps, more like that of Martin Luther. Cf. Yasuko
Grosjean's reflection on Thompson in the epilogue of
this volume.

incomprehensible."[6] Not only the Old Testament
prophets and the New Testament apostles, but Emerson,
Gibbon, Shakespeare, Mozart, and Bach were frequent
guests in the Pelikan home. For Pelikan, then, the
terms "Christian" and "humanist," or "Christian" and
"intellectual," are by no means mutually exclusive. On
the contrary, according to Pelikan no individual can
fulfill with integrity one of these callings without a
commitment to the other. Moreover, this truth has a
corollary at the institutional level: "The church and
the university need each other, for neither without the
other can fulfill its high vocation."[7]

Pelikan's life and works stand as a vindication of
such a position. While his sojourn is rooted in the
Church, he has always been more 'at home' in the
university than he has in either the Church or the
divinity school. He has observed that, "When I came to
university as a student . . . I knew I was in my
natural habitat."[8] In *Scholarship and Its Survival:
Questions on the Idea of Graduate Education*, he writes,
"Although in my own career I completed professional
school and graduate school in the same year, I had long
since decided without hesitation that scholarship, not
the practice of the [ministerial] profession, was my

---

[6]"Tradition, Reformation, and Development," in
Frontline Theology, ed. Dean Peerman (Richmond, VA:
John Knox, 1967), 107.

[7]"The Christian As an Intellectual," *The
Christian Scholar* 45 (1962): 6. Pelikan continues,
"Indeed, I suspect that neither without the other can
be trusted, therefore I pledge my allegiance to both."

[8]Pelikan also indicates that, by contrast, he
"found the seminary atmosphere confining." (Interview
by the author, March 10, 1987, Yale University, New
Haven, CT.)

vocation."[9]

In remarks made in 1971, at the public dedication
of *Historical Theology*, Pelikan concludes an autobio-
graphical reflection by saying, ". . . I have found
myself moving more and more toward the humanities as
the context of my research and teaching, identifying
myself with intellectual history rather than theology."[10] Grounding a 1981 "apologia for Christian
humanism" in his own "academic and intellectual
odyssey," he characterizes his odyssey as a movement
"From Reformation Theology to Christian Humanism."[11]

He sees no conflict between his scholarly work and
his commitment to the Christian tradition. Indeed, "My
primary ministry," he says, "is at my desk and through
my work as a scholar. I'm really not an activist,
. . . I'd rather know than do; I'd rather try to serve
the cause [of Christianity] by means of scholarship."[12]
His vocation is that of the scholar, and his scholarly
work embodies the principles of Christian humanism.

Pelikan's understanding of, and appreciation for,

---

[9]*Scholarship and Its Survival: Questions on the
Idea of Graduate Education* (Princeton: Carnegie
Foundation for the Advancement of Teaching, 1983), xviii.

[10]"Paul M. Bretscher, Christian Humanist," 4.
There are similarities between trends in Pelikan's
professional sojourn and that of Adolf von Harnack.
See Pelikan's description of Harnack's increasing self-
identification with historians rather than theologians
(*Historical Theology: Continuity and Change in Christian Doctrine* [New York: Corpus Instrumentorum, 1971],
141; cf. G. Wayne Glick, *The Reality of Christianity*
[New York: Harper and Row, 1967], 87-89).

[11]"From Reformation Theology to Christian
Humanism," *Lutheran Forum* 16 (1982): 11-15.

[12]Pelikan, quoted in Patrick Granfield, "An
Interview with Jaroslav Pelikan," *American Ecclesiastical Review* 155 (1966): 106; also 124.

the tradition of Christian humanism find expression
both in his early writings on "the Christian intellectual,"[13] and in his more recent writings on scholars
and scholarship. By turning to these works, one can
perceive Pelikan's portrait of the Christian humanist;
and that portrait is requisite for accurately comprehending Pelikan's perspectives on scholarship and
the university, two of the contexts in which the spirit
of Christian humanism finds expression.

II

The Christian humanist is characterized, Pelikan
suggests, by "a passion for being."[14] He concurs with
Augustine's statement that "*esse qua esse bonum est--*
'being is good simply because it is being'."[15] The
Christian humanist "believes that by the power of God,
who has created and goes on creating all things new
every day, all things have an essential goodness,
impervious to any destructive force."[16] Simply put,
this passion for being consists in the affirmation of
the goodness of God's creation. Indeed, "the created
universe" is "the bearer and arena of God's grace."[17]

-----

[13]The second half of the book bearing this
title, *The Christian Intellectual* (New York: Harper and
Row, 1965), is devoted to "Christian Thought and the
Humanities" and devotes a chapter to "The Theologian as
Humanistic Scholar." The terms "Christian intellectual" and "Christian humanist" are, in Pelikan's usage,
virtually synonymous. For example, see references to
his friend and colleague Paul M. Bretscher as a
"Christian intellectual" and as a "Christian humanist"
in *The Christian Intellectual* (dedication page) and
"Paul M. Bretscher, Christian Humanist."

[14]"Christian As an Intellectual," 7.

[15]Ibid., 7-8.

[16]Ibid., 7.

[17]Ibid., 8.

Pelikan emphatically and repeatedly asserts the
goodness, the integrity, and the inherent value of all
things created. And this includes, above all, human
beings.

Human being, as created being, possesses divinely-
given goodness, integrity, and value.[18] Pelikan stands
with Reformation theology, as he understands it, in its
"recognition of what the human mind and spirit had done
and could do, and a recognition of all such achievements on their own terms."[19] This "recognition" is
warranted by virtue of the fact that human beings are
beings created by God. The human being "is not
essentially a stranger to this world, since both man
and the world are creatures of God."[20] Particularly in
earlier writings, Pelikan acknowledges the seriousness
of the human predicament.[21] "Man is a stranger in this
world as it now is existentially," Pelikan writes,
"because both man and the world are alienated from

---

[18]See "Grundtvig's Influence," in *The Rescue of
the Danish Jews*, ed. Leo Goldberger (New York: New York
University Press, 1987), 174, 177, and 179.

[19]"From Reformation Theology to Christian
Humanism," 13.

[20]*The Shape of Death: Life, Death and Immortality in the Early Fathers* (Nashville: Abingdon,
1961), 62.

[21]E.g., "History As Law and Gospel, I," *The
Cresset* 12:4 (1949): 16; "History As Law and Gospel,
II," *The Cresset* 12:5 (1949): 19-20; "The Doctrine of
the Image of God," in *The Common Christian Roots of the
European Nations* (Florence: Le Monnier, 1982), 1:56;
"Imago Dei: An Explication of *Summa Theologiae*, Part 1,
Question 93," in *Calgary Aquinas Studies* (Toronto:
Pontifical Institute of Mediaeval Studies, 1978), 27-48.

their Creator."[22] Yet, the overriding emphasis in Pelikan's statements about human being is an affirmation that all persons, whether or not they claim Jesus Christ as Lord, are endowed by the Creator with inherent worth and talents which bring glory to God.[23]

This conviction precludes a false compartmentalization or hierarchy of value for human endeavor. Christ's work of redemption is a work to "redeem the total life of the total man."[24] Consequently, "there is no such thing as a 'religious' part of our lives, for our entire life has been redeemed."[25] He writes,

> There does not need to be a theological preamble to justify artistic creativity or scientific discovery or historical research--or any other human good. For such human goods belong to the order of creation, which is, within its limits, its own justification.[26]

In fact, according to Pelikan, ". . . a basic element in the life in God is the joyful sharing in the goodness of the world and the richness of what man has

---

[22]*Shape of Death*, 62-63; also see "Study of Christian Doctrine," unpublished paper, 1949, Archives, Moellering Library, Valparaiso University, Valparaiso, IN, 7; *The Cross for Everyday: Sermons and Meditations for Lent* (St. Louis: Concordia, 1952), 48-49; "The Marxist Heresy: A Theological Evaluation," *Religion in Life* 19 (1950): 361; "Totalitarianism and Democracy: A Religious Analysis," in *God and Caesar*, ed. Warren A. Quanbeck (Minneapolis: Augsburg, 1959), 104-5; and "The Liberation Arts," *Liberal Education* 59 (1973): 293.

[23]See "Practical Politics," in *The Christian in Politics*, ed. Alfred Looman and Albert Wehling (Valparaiso: Valparaiso University Press, 1950), 12; cf. *Spirit Versus Structure: Luther and the Institutions of the Church* (New York: Harper and Row, 1968), 87.

[24]*Cross for Every Day*, 107.

[25]Ibid., 108.

[26]"From Reformation Theology to Christian Humanism," 13.

been able to discover and to dream."[27]   He warns that
". . . in trying to be more than a natural human being
a Christian (and therefore a theologian) must be
careful not to be less than a natural human being."[28]
Theologians must recognize that they belong "not only
to the communion of saints but also to the communion of
the created."[29]   And, as already noted, to be counted
among "the created" is to be counted as good, for God
is the Creator.

In addition to a belief in the goodness of
creation and the dignity of human being, the passion
for being entails an affirmation of the "continuity of
nature and grace."[30]   Finding this notion in both
Augustine and Luther, one of Pelikan's favorite bons
mots is, ". . . grace does not abolish nature but
sustains and perfects it."[31]   In a 1966 address,

---

[27]*Christian Intellectual*, 125-26.

[28]*Obedient Rebels: Catholic Substance and
Protestant Principle in Luther's Reformation* (New York:
Harper and Row, 1965), 191.

[29]Ibid.

[30]"Angel and Evangel," *Concordia Theological
Monthly* 45 (1974): 7; also see *Human Culture and the
Holy: Essays on the True, the Good, and the Beautiful*
(London: S. C. M., 1959), 86; "We Hold These Truths to
Be Self Evident: Reformation, Revolution, and Reason,"
in *The Historical Context and Dynamic Future of
Lutheran Higher Education*, ed. J. Victor Hahn (Washing-
ton, DC: Lutheran Educational Conference of North
America, 1976), 17; and "From Reformation Theology to
Christian Humanism," 12.

[31]"Angel and Evangel," 7; cf. *Christian
Intellectual*, 102. Also see "We Hold These Truths to
Be Self Evident," 17; "Imago Dei: An Explication of
Summa Theologiae, Part I, Question 93," 48; "From
Reformation Theology to Christian Humanism," 12; *The
Riddle of Roman Catholicism: Its History, Its Beliefs,
Its Future* (Nashville: Abingdon, 1959), 147; *Human*

Pelikan criticizes "the defenders of the sacred" who
are "manning the ramparts, hopeful that they can exalt
the sacred by denigrating the secular, and glorifying
grace by insulting nature."[32] He says that to set the
sacred against the secular or grace against nature is
to posit "a false antithesis." Rather,

> Work and worship, learning and devotion are
> fundamentally inseparable. The secular does not
> derive its validity from the sacred, for it is the
> good creation of the very God whom the sacred
> professes to celebrate. Nor dare the sacred be
> collapsed into the secular, for thereby the
> secular would be deprived of the revelation and
> grace by which its true secularity is fulfilled.
> Grace does not abolish nature, nor is it identical
> with nature, but by it nature is sustained and
> fulfilled to be itself.[33]

Pelikan believes that "The Holy whom the Christian
faith worships in the beauty of holiness is not limited
to any single 'sacred' area of life, but is the all-
pervading and all-ruling Holy One, the Maker of heaven
and earth, the Saviour of all men, the Spirit who makes
us completely His own."[34]

Human creatures, in particular, possess a dignity

Culture, 86; *Medieval Theology*, 285, and 290; and
Reformation of Church and Dogma (1300-1700) (Chicago:
University of Chicago Press, 1984), 384.

[32]"Sacred and Secular," *Catholic Digest* 31
(November 1966), 8. Pelikan in no way desires to
denigrate the secular; indeed, he affirms both its
validity and its value. At the same time, he is
critical of those who place matters which are not
strictly theological "beyond the purview of the
Christian faith" (*Riddle*, 57). Also see "Atheism," in
Encyclopaedia Britannica, 14th ed., 1967, 667-68; and
"Christianity in Western Europe," in *The Encyclopedia
of Religion*, ed. Mircea Eliade (New York: Macmillan,
1987), 385.

[33]"Sacred and Secular," 8.

[34]*Human Culture*, 157.

associated with living in the context of a transcendent
relationship and enjoying the life of the mind. Human
beings exist, and exist only, in relation to Someone
greater than themselves.[35] Pelikan says,

> Our common human experience, while valid, is not
> altogether sufficient; for a human being, whether
> male or female, is not only a remembering,
> reflecting and resolving species. A human being
> is one who prays . . . .[36]

Pelikan is of the conviction that ". . . a man's life
does not consist in the abundance of the things which
he possesses, nor yet in the techniques he has learned
for acquiring them, but in the qualities of mind and
spirit that enable him to survive both adversity and
prosperity . . . ."[37] He says that ". . . the mind of
man was made for more than the here and now."[38] The
human mind was made by God, and thus is to be highly
valued.

The "cultivation of the mind" is therefore of
great importance to Pelikan. It is of importance not
merely for "the earning of a living," but ". . . the
primary concern of the cultivation of the mind is the
quality of life."[39] He finds the deprecation of human
intelligence "especially offensive when it is done in
the name of faith in God, since it is the common
consent of Jewish and Christian traditions that intel-

---

[35]"Totalitarianism and Democracy," 111-12.

[36]"Liberation Arts," 297.

[37]*Christian Intellectual*, 125.

[38]"Theological Library and the Tradition of
Christian Humanism," 720.

[39]*Christian Intellectual*, 124.

ligence is itself the image of God."[40] He commends the
Reformers and early fathers for knowing "what later
theology has often forgotten, that the human possibilities of the reason and of the natural man do not have
to be denigrated to let the grace of God shine."[41] And
with Edward Gibbon he shares "the conviction that it is
our reason that separates us from the brute and that
defends us from the brute within."[42] Thus, Pelikan
affirms that "We can think to the glory of God."[43]

   With this commitment to the cultivation of the
mind, the Christian humanist is necessarily characterized by a reverence for language.[44] For Pelikan,
human language is a "divine gift."[45] "The Christian

---

[40]"Darwin's Legacy: Emanation, Evolution, and
Development," part of "Darwin's Legacy," sound record-
ing of the 18th Nobel Conference, Gustavus Adolphus
College, 5-6 October 1982, cassettes nos. 7 and 8,
Archives, Gustavus Adolphus College, St. Peter, MN.

   [41]*Obedient Rebels*, 191; also see "Natural
Theology in David Hollaz," *Concordia Theological
Monthly* 18 (1947): 253-63, and "Fathers, Brethren, and
Distant Relatives: The Family of Theological Dis-
course," *Concordia Theological Monthly* 33 (1962): 716.

   [42]"What Gibbon Knew: Lessons in Imperialism,"
Harper's Magazine 253:1514 (1976): 13.

   [43]T. H. Hartman, "You Can Think to the Glory of
God," *Correspondent* (Autumn 1960): 3.

   [44]Here, as elsewhere, Pelikan draws upon the
example of the Protestant Reformers of the sixteenth
century, particularly their dependence upon the
philological studies of the Renaissance. See *Spirit
Versus Structure*, 71; "From Reformation Theology to
Christian Humanism," 11-12; "The Wisdom of Prospero,"
in *Minutes of the Ninety-fourth Meeting of the Association of Research Libraries* (Washington, DC: Association
of Research Libraries, 1979), 71; and *Jesus Through the
Centuries: His Place in the History of Culture* (New
Haven: Yale University Press, 1985), 152-60, and 166-67.

   [45]"The Christian As an Intellectual," 10.

intellectual knows," writes Pelikan,". . . that man's capacity for speech lies somewhere near the center of his uniqueness. Both the misery and the grandeur of humanity are bound up with the gift of language." One of the implications of this is that ". . . a reverence for what language can do if it is used properly, and a horror of what language can do if it is misused, belong to the equipment of the educated man."[46]

There are at least two linguistic tools to which Pelikan gives special emphasis. The first of these is clarity of expression in one's "mother tongue." As far as Pelikan is concerned, anyone who would presume to be a "scholar" must be "one who is at work in original research and who can interpret this research with the power and clarity of the mother tongue to students and readers alike."[47] If language is a gift of God, the Christian humanist is to use it responsibly. Yet, mastering the language with which one is raised is not enough.

"I do not at all agree with those who cling to one language and despise all others." So writes Martin Luther[48]--and so says Jaroslav Pelikan. The second linguistic tool to which Pelikan gives emphasis is facility in classical and foreign languages.[49] "In our

---

[46]Ibid., 9.

[47]"A Scholar Strikes Back," *The Catholic World* 200:1197 (1964): 150.

[48]Martin Luther, "The German Mass and Order of Service, 1526," in *Luther's Works*, 55 vols. (Philadel-phia: Fortress, 1955-72), 53:63; also see *Bach*, 118.

[49]Pelikan praises his Doktorvater, Wilhelm Pauck, for being "in complete control of the nuances of a language that is not his mother tongue." ("Wilhelm Pauck: A Tribute," in *Interpreters of Luther: Essays in Honor of Wilhelm Pauck*, ed. Jaroslav Pelikan [Philadel-

own time," he says, ". . . the capacity of the research
library to be a powerful dukedom is threatened not only
by the loss of the Greek and the Italian Renaissance
imported from Constantinople, but of the Latin that it
continued to cultivate."[50] He decries the "monolingual
illiteracy of the educated classes" of the United
States.[51]

Anyone who would be genuinely "educated" must make
use of "the corrective lenses of an additional language."[52] These "lenses" help to transcend the
cultural boundaries which are a function of time and/or
place. Pelikan has recently observed that, "The older
I get the more I find my affinities with Erasmus." He
identifies these "affinities with Erasmus" with his own
"essentially Renaissance humanistic understanding of
what scholarly study is," such as an interest in
language and languages, particularly Latin and Greek,
and a preoccupation with the great literature of those
languages.[53] Facility in languages other than one's

---

phia: Fortress, 1968], 5.) However, while he regards
Augustine as "Perhaps the greatest Christian intellectual of them all" ("The Christian As an Intellectual,"
7-8), with Peter Brown and other scholars, Pelikan
perceives the detrimental consequences which Augustine's virtual ignorance of Greek language and culture
had upon his thought (see *The Mystery of Continuity:
Time and History, Memory and Eternity in the Thought of
Saint Augustine* [Charlottesville: University Press of
Virginia, 1986], 7-8).

[50]"Wisdom of Prospero," 71.

[51]"'A Decent Respect to the Opinions of
Mankind,'" *Scholarly Publishing* 8 (1976): 13. Also see
"Special Collections: 'A Key to the Language of
America,'" *Books at Brown* 29/30 (1982-83): 8.

[52]"Book: Remedy for the Soul," *Publishers'
Weekly* 193 (10 June 1968): 42.

[53]Interview by the author, March 10, 1987.

own gives access to information and insight from persons of the past, as well as from contemporaries in other societies.

The pursuit of such insight is implicit in a genuine respect for and affirmation of human existence. Thus, in addition to a passion for being and a reverence for language, the Christian humanist is characterized by a deep appreciation for the heritage of the past, manifested in "an enthusiasm for history."[54] This enthusiasm for history is "reverent in its regard for tradition, classical as well as Christian."[55]   As has already been noted, the mind of the Christian humanist acknowledges the continuity of nature and grace, and recognizes the sacredness of the secular. The sacred is not ignored, and the secular is not belittled. There is reverence for all that the past has bequeathed to us.

For the Christian humanist, history provides more than a record of human civilization, significant though that is. Pelikan suggests that a true enthusiasm for history involves an openness to "the activity of the Spirit, unpredictable though it is," an appreciation for "the variety of the Spirit, distressing though this often is to our preconceived notions," and an attentiveness to "the leading of the Spirit in the church, novel though this continues to be." It is an enthusiasm for God's activity in the world, "in its infinite variety and underlying unity."[56]

Pelikan's own career and thought are marked by a pervasive and sustained preoccupation with historical

---

[54]"The Christian As an Intellectual," 10.

[55]"Paul M. Bretscher, Christian Humanist," 4.

[56]"The Christian As an Intellectual," 11.

studies. Indeed, Pelikan's pursuit of the past began
in his boyhood: ". . . it was with the reading of
Emerson in my childhood that most of my own intellectual interest began; and it was through [Emerson's]
Representative Men, in unlikely combination with
Gibbon's *Decline and Fall*, that I then resolved to
become a historian."[57] The determination to recognize
both the sacred and the secular has enhanced his study
of history and theology.

There are yet other characteristics of "a mind
imbued with Christian humanism."[58] This mind is
"basically literary in its intellectual style" and
"aesthetic in its fundamental modes of perception."[59]
Thus, in addition to "information" and "intelligence,"
the humanist scholar engages disciplined "imagination."[60] "Always somehow preferring both/and to
either/or,"[61] the mind of the Christian humanist is one

---

[57]Preface to *Nature: A Facsimile of the First
Edition*, by Ralph Waldo Emerson (Boston: Beacon, 1985),
vii; cf. *The Excellent Empire: The Fall of Rome and the
Triumph of the Church* (New York: Harper and Row, 1987),
xii.

[58]"Paul M. Bretscher, Christian Humanist," 4.

[59]Ibid.

[60]"A Gentleman and a Scholar," 3.

[61]"Paul M. Bretscher, Christian Humanist," 4.
There are other formulas in Pelikan's writings which
are virtually synonymous with that of "both/and." For
example, he often employs the formula of "identity plus
universality" when discussing the Catholicity of
Christianity (see *The Finality of Jesus Christ in an
Age of Universal History: A Dilemma of the Third
Century* [London: Lutterworth, 1965], and *Riddle*, 21-
33.) More recently, in the final pages of *Jesus* (pp.
228-33; also 19 and 20), Pelikan celebrates the spirit
of "universality-with-particularity" which he perceives
in contemporary perspectives, both sacred and secular,
on Jesus Christ.

of breadth and catholicity. The agenda of the Christian humanist entails "mediation" between alternative perspectives,[62] a "refusal to choose from among alternatives that [have] equally legitimate authority."[63] The Christian humanist seeks to include the broadest possible range of perspectives, theological and non-theological, in research and reflection.

Pelikan's concept of the Christian humanist is perhaps best summarized in the following words:

> "The love of learning and the desire for God" is not only the finest flower of the Benedictine monasticism of the Latin Middle Ages; it is also, in quite another dress, the leitmotiv of the dedication to patient scholarship that I would define as the genius of "Christian humanism."[64]

III

The values and characteristics of the Christian humanist delineated above inform Pelikan's vision of the university. He believes it is impossible to overestimate the importance of "general" or "liberal" undergraduate education,[65] of which the humanities[66]

---

[62]*Christian Intellectual*, 28.

[63]*Bach*, 115. The words quoted here are employed to describe Bach, yet they provide, in Pelikan's own words, an apt expression of the spirit of both/and which marks Christian humanism.

[64]"Paul M. Bretscher, Christian Humanist," 4.

[65]Pelikan uses these two terms, "general education" and "liberal education," interchangeably (e.g., "A Gentleman and a Scholar," 3).

[66]Throughout the publications in which Pelikan discusses university education, "the humanities" and "the liberal arts" for the most part are used interchangeably. It appears that Pelikan envisions three major divisions of study within the university: humanities, social sciences, and natural sciences (e.g., *Scholarship*, 28; "'A Decent Respect to the Opinions of Mankind,'" 14; "The Research Library, An

are a necessary and central part. Graduate education,
including professional education such as that carried
out in schools of law and medicine, must be built on
this foundation. Pelikan also calls upon the university to include the study of Christian doctrine within
its universe of scholarly inquiry. The inclusion of
such study is not only possible; it is necessary if the
university is to fulfill its mission.[67]

Pelikan believes that there is great need "in our
undergraduate responsibilities, to deepen still further
our commitment to liberal learning."[68] He is of the
conviction that "A liberal education is fundamentally
an end in itself, worth pursuing for its own sake."[69]
Ours is an age in which "the very heritage of the
liberal arts is under attack."[70] He suggests that
within the American educational system there is "a
preference for vocational training over liberal

Outpost of Cultural Continuity," *Imprint of the
Stanford Library Associates* 6:2 [1980]: 7; also see
Ronald S. Crane, *The Idea of the Humanities and Other
Essays, Critical and Historical* [Chicago: University of
Chicago Press, 1967], 1:3-4). In this schema, the
humanities encompass "literature, language, and
history" ("Escape to Esthetics," *The Center Magazine*
20:1 [1987]: 57; cf. a reference to history claiming
"membership in the social sciences as well as the
humanities" ["Special Collections," 7]).

[67]See "In Defense of Research in Religious
Studies at the Secular University," in Jaroslav Pelikan
et al., *Religion and the University* (Toronto: University of Toronto Press), 1-19; and *Christian Intellectual*, Ch. 8, "The Theologian as Humanistic Scholar."

[68]"A Gentleman and a Scholar," 4.

[69]Ibid.; also see "Dukedom Large Enough:
Reflections on Academic Administration," *Concordia
Theological Monthly* 43 (1972): 297-98.

[70]"Theological Library and the Tradition of
Christian Humanism," 719.

education and for the sciences over the humanities, but
for engineering over both the sciences and the
humanities."[71]

In an apologetic for the liberal arts, Pelikan
identifies four qualities, four "liberation arts,"
cultivated by an education rooted in the humanities.
"The first such art is historical remembrance."[72]
Pelikan says,

> . . . the liberal arts provide a way of seeing
> that history and tradition, so often interpreted
> as the dead hand of the past, can instead become a
> way--indeed, I am convinced, the only way--to
> deliver us from what Lord Acton once called "the
> tyranny of environment and the pressure of the air
> we breathe."[73]

Another liberation art is that of "critical reflection." Critical reflection is the way by which we make
the substance of historical remembrance our own:
". . . tradition cannot be a vital force in our life
and thought unless we have learned to apply to it the
ruthless and unrelenting discipline of critical
reflection."[74]

A third liberating art is "moral resolve." Among
the fruits of education in the liberal arts are the
abilities to look beyond one's own situation and
viewpoint, and to strike a balance between pragmatism
and cynicism. These capacities provide part of the
foundation for "a workable ethic for our daily life."[75]

The last of the liberation arts which Pelikan
describes is "thoughtful reverence." Thoughtful

---

[71]Ibid., 720.

[72]"Liberation Arts," 293.

[73]Ibid.; cf. "Dukedom Large Enough," 298.

[74]"Liberation Arts," 294.

[75]Ibid., 295; cf. "Escape to Esthetics," 57.

reverence is indispensable. It is indispensable because, as he has declared elsewhere, ". . . a human being, whether male or female, is not only a remembering, reflecting and resolving species. A human being is one who prays."[76] And such reverence, and the prayer which accompanies it, is, in Pelikan's estimation, "not only compatible with, but supportive of, the total life of the mind."[77]

Liberal education offers many further benefits, not the least of which is its capacity to provide the only wholly adequate foundation for mature research and scholarship: ". . . the appropriate context of specialized scholarly research is nothing less than the full range of the arts and sciences, as represented by the undergraduate enterprise of [the] university."[78]

Pelikan laments the fact that undergraduate education has fallen prey to the influences of an age of specialization. Any genuinely liberal education must be broad enough to incorporate "the best in the tradition of humanistic thought--Greek, Hebrew, and Christian."[79] However, rather than offering "liberal education in the arts and sciences," far too many colleges and universities have structured "overspecialized" courses of undergraduate study.[80] This preference for early--in his opinion, premature--specialization unfortunately results in an under-

---

[76]"Liberation Arts," 297.

[77]Ibid.

[78]*The Aesthetics of Scholarly Research* (New Orleans: Tulane University, 1984), 2; also see "Defense of Research in Religious Studies," 12.

[79]"Liberation Arts," 292.

[80]"A Gentleman and a Scholar," 3-4.

graduate major taking the form of "a miniature graduate
program."[81] In contrast, Pelikan suggests that
undergraduate majors are best conceived "as a summation
and a climax for undergraduate study," rather than as a
"foundation . . . for graduate study."[82] He therefore
recommends movement toward divisional majors rather
than departmental majors.[83]

Pelikan is nothing less than a crusader for the
integrity of and an ambassador on behalf of the value
of graduate education. Yet, his commitment to graduate
education is inextricably related to his equally
intense commitment to undergraduate liberal education.
The quality of graduate education and the scholarly
enterprises associated with it are "bound up with the
state and the fate of general education."[84] Pelikan is
of the opinion that graduate and professional education
"can be futile unless they are based upon that fullness
of mind and wholeness of vision that results from truly
humane learning."[85] Moreover, ". . . in any graduate
program the student's lack of preparation in the
graduate discipline is easier to repair than is a
neglect of general education."[86]

The spirit of Christian humanism, so evident in
Pelikan's convictions about education, leads him to
insist that the university is where Christianity, its
history and doctrine, ought to be studied, by both

---

[81]*Scholarship*, 32-33.

[82]Ibid., 33-34.

[83]Ibid., 38.

[84]Ibid., 25-26; also 42.

[85]*Christian Intellectual*, 125.

[86]*Scholarship*, 38.

Christians and non-Christians. Indeed, the university
curriculum is incomplete without such study.

Citing his own professional sojourn as "a not
atypical case," Pelikan asserts that choosing to study
Christian doctrine in a university, rather than, for
example, a church-related college or a divinity school,
is not necessarily "the result or even the cause of a
crise de foi."[87] And even though it is also possible
that a student may experience a *crise de foi*,
". . . any religious faith ought to be able and willing
to take its chances on this process, or it will not be
worthy either of our scholarly research or of our
personal commitment."[88]

In a 1962 address entitled "Fathers, Brethren, and
Distant Relatives," Pelikan describes "the family of
theological discourse." This "family" consists of
"fathers," referring to "a deep regard for the theological tradition," "brethren," who represent "a fraternal
consideration of our theological contemporaries," and,
of particular interest here, "distant relatives,"
denoting "an appreciative attention to non-theological
thought."[89] In a variety of ways, Pelikan repeatedly

---

[87]"The Research University and the Healing
Professions," *Criterion* 15 (Autumn 1976): 27; cf.
Pelikan's defense of Adolf von Harnack against charges
that he contributed to "widespread apostasy" (*Historical Theology*, 82).

[88]"Defense of Research in Religious Studies,"
19; also see "Voices of the Church," in *Proceedings of
the Thirty-Third Annual Convention of the Catholic
Theological Society of America*, ed. Luke Salm (The
Bronx, NY: Catholic Theological Society of America,
1979), 12.

[89]"Fathers, Brethren, and Distant Relatives,"
711. Two years later, in *Obedient Rebels* (Ch. 13, "The
Catholic Context of Protestant Theology"), Pelikan
articulates much the same thought under the categories

argues that the study of theology[90] must include within its scope "non-theological thought."

A number of benefits accrue from studying doctrine in conjunction with non-theological disciplines. Not least among these benefits is the assistance afforded to the historical theologian in the attempt to unravel the development of Christian doctrine.[91] Pelikan posits that ". . . intellectual history grounded in the history of literature has proven to be an extremely fruitful context for the understanding of certain doctrines at certain times."[92] Thus, "The investigation of the development of Christian doctrine in the history of theology is too important to be left to the theologians."[93]

---

of "tradition," "contemporary theology," and "pagan thought."

[90]In most instances when Pelikan uses the term "theology," he refers not to "systematic theology or dogmatic theology alone, but [to] the entire range of research and dialogue about the meaning of the Christian faith." ("The Functions of Theology," in *Theology in the Life of the Church*, ed. Robert Betram [Philadelphia: Fortress, 1963], 4.)

[91]Pelikan also considers the assistance afforded to biblical studies (e.g., *Obedient Rebels*, 192, and "Fathers, Brethren, and Distant Relatives," 716).

[92]*Historical Theology*, 114-15. Two examples to which Pelikan points are Perry Miller's work on New England Puritanism (see *Historical Theology*, 115-117), and the contribution of cultural anthropology to discerning the phenomenon of *lex orandi lex credendi* (see "Research University and Healing Professions," 30; and "A Gentleman and a Scholar," 2).

[93]*Development of Christian Doctrine: Some Historical Prolegomena* (New Haven: Yale University Press, 1969), 43. Paraphrasing and repeating this notion in a variety of forms throughout his writings, Pelikan adopts a remark by the French statesman Georges

The benefits of including non-theological voices within the framework of theological discourse also extend to ecumenical dialogue. By providing a context for "joint study and mutual confrontation under friendly but neutral auspices" and by illuminating "the non-theological factors" among various religious traditions, the 'secular' university can have a "ministry of reconciliation" between these traditions.[94]

Finally, the most fundamental benefit of engagement with non-theological thought is "the humanizing influence that only [this] thought can bring into theological discourse."[95] Pelikan warns, as noted earlier, that ". . . in trying to be more than a natural human being, a Christian (and therefore a theologian) must be careful not to be less than a natural human being." This warning is rooted in the passion for being, with its attendant respect for human being and human achievements. Again, Pelikan urges that ". . . the theologian learns through the study of non-theological and even non-Christian thought that he belongs not only to the communion of saints, but also to the communion of the created."[96] The theologian must be a "humanistic scholar,"[97] and the most natural

---

Clemenceau about war being too important to be left to the generals.

[94]*Riddle*, 200-201; also see 219.

[95]*Obedient Rebels*, 191; also see "Fathers, Brethren, and Distant Relatives," 716.

[96]*Obedient Rebels*, 191.

[97]*Christian Intellectual*, Ch. 8, "The Theologian as Humanistic Scholar."

habitat for the work of the humanistic scholar is the university.[98]

Pelikan acknowledges and responds to some objections to the inclusion of religious studies, including the study of Christianity, as a "humanistic discipline" in the university. A major objection is the criticism that such study de facto lacks objectivity, and therefore lacks scholarly integrity.[99] However, Pelikan contends that research in religion, including Christian doctrine, "forms an essential part of the work of the humanities in a secular university."[100] He writes,

> The case for religious studies within the humanities is part of the case for general education and for its bearing upon all forms of scholarship. Many a humanistic scholar has discovered that the decisive component in truly significant research is frequently the factor that could not have been supplied by any number of hours of further investigation but only by a close and continuing acquaintance with the best in the entire heritage of humanistic thought.[101]

By excluding or ignoring religious studies, any university which claims to offer an education which is broadening, which is genuinely "liberal," is "cutting itself off from one of the richest sources available"

---

[98]One interviewer observes that Pelikan "chose the academy as his setting because he thought the church a difficult place to retain 'one's scholarly integrity' and because he wanted to work where the history he studied for its own sake would be valued on those terms." ("The Christian Tradition," *The New Yorker* 61 [February 2, 1981]: 30.)

[99]See *Christian Intellectual*, 103-111; *Historical Theology*, xxii, and 129; and *Vindication of Tradition*, 67-68.

[100]*Christian Intellectual*, 103; also see "Defense of Research in Religious Studies," 3.

[101]*Christian Intellectual*, 111.

for this endeavor.[102] The university must recognize
that there are contributions to be made "in both
directions" between theological studies and "secular
thought."[103] It is Pelikan's commitment to the
humanities and his concern for the availability of all
the resources necessary for competent scholarship that
leads him to conclude,

> As a result of the dichotomy between the study of
> theology and the study of arts and sciences . . .
> humanistic scholarship is often unable to probe
> the origin and development of fundamental concepts
> in the history of ideas. The literature of the
> Bible, the forms of the liturgy, and the vocabu-
> lary of dogma have been a part of the equipment of
> the literate man in the West for so long that
> their atrophy threatens to make history unintel-
> ligible to the historian.[104]

The mission of the university and the work of its
scholars requires the resources which only the scholarly study of Christianity, its history and doctrine, can
provide.

In light of Pelikan's beliefs that the study of
Christianity can and ought to be carried out in the
university, and that the university can and ought to
include within its purview the study of Christianity,
it is not surprising that Pelikan suggests that
seminary-based study for Christian ministry is best
conducted in the context of the university.[105]
Carrying out its mission in close relationship to the
university is in the best interests both of the

---

[102]Ibid., 112.

[103]*Historical Theology*, 79.

[104]Ibid.

[105]For those who anticipate attending a non-
university-related seminary, Pelikan recommends a year
or more of study at a secular university. (Hartman,
"Think to the Glory of God," 5.)

seminary and of the Church.

This understanding of seminary education reflects Pelikan's self-identified indebtedness to "the inspiration of German *Universitatstheologie*,"[106] the pattern for which is "based on the twin principles of an intellectual foundation and a bias toward the humanities."[107] For Pelikan the church, including the seminary, and the university are "inextricably intertwined in their commitment and in their fate. Neither can survive as we have known it without the other."[108]

IV

The principles and values of the tradition of Christian humanism, thoughtfully incorporated into Pelikan's vision for the university as an institution, have equally important implications for scholars and scholarship.[109] Most of the characteristics requisite for the scholar's vocation are the fruits of a liberal education,[110] and all reflect the principles to which Pelikan has been dedicated in his own work.

As noted earlier, part of the humanistic tradition is a reverence for language; and for Pelikan this reverence 'begins at home', with one's native tongue. Facility in the mother tongue, manifest especially in clarity of expression, must be developed in under-

---

[106]"Defense of Research in Religious Studies," 16-17.

[107]Karl H. Lutcke, "Principles of Theological Education in Germany," trans. M. Bourke, *Scottish Journal of Theology* 36 (1983): 434.

[108]"Dukedom Large Enough," 300.

[109]For a general discussion, see "Scholarship" in *The Melody of Theology: A Philosophical Dictionary* (Cambridge, MA: Harvard University Press, 1988).

[110]*Scholarship*, 25.

graduate education. Otherwise the doctoral disserta-
tion "seems to be asking students to learn how to build
a wall when they have not yet learned to lay brick and
spread mortar."[111] And, in turn, the remedial work
which needs to be done during graduate training
subtracts from time and energy that should be devoted
to the cultivation of scholarly skills.[112]

Further, the scholar must possess the use of
languages other than the mother tongue.[113] Graduate
education and a career in scholarship have traditionally presupposed such competence. Yet, Pelikan
perceives a trend toward "reduction or total elimina-
tion" of foreign language requirements from many Ph.D.
programs.[114] Consequently, it is

> all the more urgent to enforce explicitly the
> intellectual and cultural assumptions that in fact
> were presupposed by that system. Part of the
> general education of the "gentleman" in the final
> decades of the twentieth century, and above all of
> the general education of the scholar, must be a
> responsible acquaintance with some other culture,
> past or present. Ordinarily, though not neces-
> sarily, this acquaintance should include the use
> of its language.[115]

Yet, there is more to being a scholar than possessing

---

[111]Ibid., 28.

[112]Ibid.

[113]Ibid., 29.

[114]Ibid.

[115]Ibid., 31; cf. "Book: Remedy for the Soul,"
42; "Research Library," 8; and "Special Collections,"
8. Taking his cue from Robert Burns and John Henry
Newman, Pelikan occasionally depicts the genuinely
educated person as "a gentleman and a scholar" (e.g.,
"A Gentleman and a Scholar," 2, and Scholarship, Ch. 3,
"A Gentleman--and A Scholar?"). He qualifies the
gender reference of this term, indicating that he
includes within its meaning both men and women (see "A
Gentleman and a Scholar," 2, and Scholarship, 27).

facility with language and languages. There can be "no
ducking the issue of integrity in scholarly and
scientific research."[116]

"The structure of the university is a very fragile
thing. It depends upon trust--trust in one another,
trust in learning, trust in reason."[117] One must "go
beyond competence . . . to those qualities of mind and
spirit that form character and conscience and that
shape integrity."[118] Drawing upon John Henry Newman's
thought, Pelikan says, ". . . the mores and traditions
of scholarship have been based on a definition of
integrity and character of which the 'gentleman' . . .
has been the epitome." "It was," he continues, "quite
simply, unacceptable morally to cheat or to exploit or
to take unfair advantage" of other scholars and the
fruits of their labors.[119] Thus, Pelikan observes,

> There is a fundamental moral difference between
> the legitimate expression of the ambition to
> succeed in scholarly research, . . . and the
> exploitation, without due credit, of an assis-
> tant's research, or the appropriation of a con-
> clusion originally articulated, but not yet
> published, by a colleague or a student.[120]

The Chrsitian humanist affirms the inherent dignity of
human being and human endeavor. In keeping with this,
Pelikan believes that scholarship is a high calling and

[116]*Scholarship*, 59.

[117]"Faculties Must Reassert Powers They
Defaulted," *Los Angeles Times*, 16 June 1968, sec. G,
p. 3.

[118]*Scholarship*, 55.

[119]Ibid., 55-56; cf. John Henry Newman, *The
Idea of a University*, ed. I. T. Ker (Oxford: Oxford
University Press, 1976), 165, and 172-73.

[120]*Scholarship*, 59.

that the scholar is to pursue scholarly research with integrity.

The importance of scholarly research becomes even more apparent in the first chapter of *Scholarship*, where Pelikan defends the proposition that "scholarly research defines the nature of the university."[121] Advancing his proposition, he approvingly quotes Harnack's declaration that "The distinctiveness of German universities is expressed in the combination of research and teaching."[122] Pelikan self-consciously stands within the heritage of this nineteenth-century German tradition of intense commitment to the combination of both teaching and research, of which tradition Harnack was one of the most illustrious practitioners.[123] For Pelikan, Harnack "embodied" the

[121]Ibid., 5; also see "After the Campus Turmoil: A Plea for Reform," *Panorama--Chicago Daily News*, June 15, 1968, p. 9; "Faculties Must Reassert Powers They Defaulted," 3; and "Research University and Healing Professions," 26-30.

[122]Adolf von Harnack, "Ansprachen bei der Einweihung des Neubaues des Kaiser Wilhelm-Instituts fur Arbeitsphysiologie," in *Aus der Werkstaat des Vollendeten* (Giessen: Alfred Topelmann, 1930), 251; quoted in *Scholarship*, 8.

[123]*Scholarship*, 7-8, 10; cf. 53-54, and "'A Decent Respect to the Opinions of Mankind,'" 14. Also see "Dukedom Large Enough," 297-99; "Research Library," 7; and Zoe Ingalls, "Yale's Jaroslav Pelikan: 'Bilingual' Scholar of Christian Tradition," *Chronicle of Higher Education* 26 (May 4, 1983): 4.
In an essay on American Methodism, Pelikan suggests that there is a harmful "theological attitude" among Americans wherein they "are simply not willing to assign as much importance to . . . scholarship as European, and especially German, Protestants do." ("Methodism's Contribution to America," in *History of American Methodism*, ed. Emory Stevens Bucke [Nashville: Abingdon, 1964], 3:605.) Cf. John M. Stroup, "The Idea of Theological Education at the University of Berlin: From Schleiermacher to Harnack," in *Schools of Thought*

"scholarly ideal" of research.[124]

Teaching is "dependent on learning," and learning is "dependent on the art of scholarly research."[125] Yet, teaching and research, information and intelligence--in a word, competence--is not enough. If they are to be of the highest calibre, scholars and their scholarship must be marked by imagination.[126] "[The] ingredients of research are," Pelikan writes, "in whatever may be the right proportions, information, intelligence, and imagination."[127]

Scholarly research is an "art." It entails the exercise of imagination "in a style that can only be identified as *aesthetic*."[128] Pelikan considers Harnack and Etienne Gilson to be "masters" in whom he sees "the combination of technical information and critical intelligence made luminous, perhaps incandescent, by the power of disciplined imagination."[129] And the foundation for a "disciplined" or "aesthetic" imagination is nothing less than a catholicity of intellect

---

in the Christian Tradition, ed. Patrick Henry (Philadelphia: Fortress, 1984), 157, and 162-63.

[124]*Scholarship*, 53. According to Pelikan, "Harnack is still spoken of with awe as the high priest of objective historical research, who could assert the right of research in religion to be taken seriously simply by pointing to his own achievements as a scholar, author, and editor" (*Christian Intellectual*, 104-5).

[125]*Aesthetics of Scholarly Research*, 10.

[126]"A Gentleman and a Scholar," 3.

[127]Ibid.

[128]*Aesthetics of Scholarly Research*, 3, emphasis his.

[129]"A Gentleman and a Scholar," 3.

which is rooted in cultivation of the mind through
liberal education.

He concludes that "aesthetic and critical
imagination derived from the total context of the arts
and sciences, is what sets significant research apart
from research that is merely competent."[130] Reflecting
upon his own work in 1964, Pelikan observes:

> . . . the secret component or x-factor in truly
> significant research, at least in my field, is
> frequently the factor that could not have been
> supplied by any number of hours of further digging
> in the sources, but only by a close and continuing
> acquaintance with the best in our entire range of
> thought and literature.[131]

The perimeters of the best scholarship are constituted
by nothing less than "the best in our entire range of
thought and literature."

V

The characteristics and values of the Christian
humanist which Jaroslav Pelikan describes and defends
are mirrored in his own career and thought. His
writings manifest the breadth of inquiry and universality of interest which is the embodiment of the
humanist's spirit of "both/and." In his work one finds
a scholar characterized by a respect for the life of
the mind and the dignity of human being, a reverence
for language, an appreciation for the heritage of the
past, and an awareness of the illuminating role of
imagination in scholarship. Christian humanism is not
only a subject about which Pelikan writes. It constitutes one of the guiding leitmotivs, perhaps even
the guiding leitmotiv, of career and thought. And this
leitmotiv manifests itself in both the changes and the

---

[130]*Aesthetics of Scholarly Research*, 3.

[131]"Defense of Research in Religious Studies,"
12; also see note 101 above.

continuities of Pelikan's career and thought.

The locus of Pelikan's career has moved from Church to academy. His sojourn is one which he describes as progressing "from a seminary of the Church to university divinity schools to a faculty of arts and sciences and a history department in that faculty."[132] An examination of the chronological development of his corpus of writings reveals an increasing manifestation of his affinities with Erasmus and the emergence of an increasingly explicit apologetic for the spirit of Christian humanism.[133] Thus, the overall course of changes in Pelikan's thought and career may be conceived of as one which moves "from Reformation theology to Christian humanism."[134]

At the same time, Pelikan's career and thought can be properly understood only when also seen in terms of the continuities within. His career is one of abiding commitment to the vocation of the scholar. His writings manifest from the earliest days a respect for the discipline of history. And underlying and inform-

---

[132]"From Reformation Theology to Christian Humanism," 11.

[133]For example, while he has written on Martin Luther as recently as 1983, the large majority of his writings on Luther and Lutheranism appeared in the earlier portion of his career, prior to 1968. By contrast, his more recent works include *Jesus Through the Centuries: His Place in the History of Culture,* and *Bach Among the Theologians.* Perhaps the most suggestive illustration of his increased affinity with Erasmus is the fact that, although in the 1950's Pelikan served as one of two general editors for the standard English-language edition of *Luther's Works,* he currently serves as one of the advisors for a critical English-language edition of the collected works of Erasmus (*The Collected Works of Erasmus* [Toronto: University of Toronto Press, 1975-]).

[134]See p. 252 above.

ing both of these is a lifelong embracing of the
tradition of Christian humanism. Consequently, some of
the changes are perhaps not so much manifestations of a
change of mind or heart as they are an exploration and
articulation of values and understandings which have
matured over the years. As has been said of Newman so
too it can be said of Pelikan that his is

> a mind of unity; growing, articulating, arranging,
> acquiring new truth from meditating on old truth
> . . . but a man with the same mind all his life
> . . . a mind with principles formed early, and
> then expanded, adapted, recast, and yet recog-
> nizably the same principles . . . .[135]

Not least among these principles is the spirit of
Christian humanism.

During a recent interview, in response to being
asked to comment on his present "self-understanding,"
Pelikan said,

> How would I describe myself? I guess I would
> describe myself as a Christian humanist. I have
> been doing so. . . . Yes, I think that has been a
> constant, I mean it has developed and changed, but
> I think it has been there . . . from the begin-
> ning.[136]

The spirit of Christian humanism, with its joyful
affirmation of the goodness of the world and the
inherent value of what human beings have been able to
discover and to dream, permeates Pelikan's professional
life and work. There is harmony rather than conflict
between the sacred and the secular. Grace does not
abolish nature, but sustains and perfects it. Human

---

[135]These are words used by Owen Chadwick to
describe one of the major influences upon Pelikan's
work, John Henry Newman. See Owen Chadwick, *Newman*
(Oxford: Oxford University Press, 1983), 5.

[136]Interview by the author, March 10, 1987. In
discussing this point, Pelikan made reference to his
address entitled "From Reformation Theology to Christian Humanism."

282

being, language and the life of the mind are gifts
bestowed by the Creator, and for Pelikan, therefore,
". . . the life of scholarship and the untrammeled
exercise of the critical intelligence applied to
significant issues cannot be surpassed as a form of
human fulfillment."[137]

---

[137]"Research University and Healing Professions," 30.

EPILOGUE

BARD THOMPSON
AND THE DREW UNIVERSITY GRADUATE SCHOOL

Yasuko Morihara Grosjean

Introduction[1]

I had the privilege of serving as Bard Thompson's Administrative Assistant for the last eight years of his deanship. However, my first contact with Dean Thompson goes back to the late sixties when I was working in Central Stenography in Mead Hall at Drew University as a graduate student wife. I was often assigned the task of typing his office-work, academic manuscripts, and other work from the Graduate School Office. Later, I became a Ph.D. candidate at Drew and took his seminars on the Reformation Era. Soon after finishing my doctorate, I became his Administrative Assistant.

For many people, there was an equation which can be stated two ways: Bard Thompson was the Graduate

---

[1]Dean Thompson's accomplishments at Drew have been reported in various Drew publications. I will here repeat portions of these accounts only as necessary. For further detail, see Kenneth Cole, "The Man Who Nourished the Graduate School," *Drew* (June 1984): 14-16; Gordon Harland, "The Best Years of Our Lives," and John W. Bicknell, "Light the Candles," in *Silver Anniversary Addresses*, The Drew Graduate School Occasional Papers No. 1, 1980. Dean Thompson summarized a decade of progress in the 1983-84 *Report on Annual Giving*, The Graduate School, Drew University, 36-37.

School, and the Graduate School was Bard Thompson. How
did this come to be? How did people come to see Dean
Thompson as the personification of the Graduate School?
How did the Graduate School come to make us think of
Dean Thompson? The answer to these questions requires
us to look at this man as a person, as a teacher and
scholar, and as a dean.

The Person

Dean Thompson was formal in his style. He was the
image of the gentleman. During the summer, students
would come in to the office wearing shorts and sneak-
ers. In the early years the offices were not air
conditioned, and even though he would be working in
shirt sleeves, when it was time for the student
appointment, he would retreat to his office and put on
his jacket regardless of the temperature. For him,
there was a form to things, a formality to be maintained, a public presence to be established. But this
was not a formality for the sake of show. Rather, it
was an expression of the man, and he projected an image
of dignity which set a tone for the Graduate School.
And while "image" now often suggests an appearance
without reality, in him the image and the man were one.

While many people saw the formal side of the Dean,
fewer people were aware of his keen sense of humor.
This was the humor of the scholar whose immense
vocabulary and profound knowledge opened the contradic-
tions of life that are the basis of the deepest humor.
Not infrequently, gales of laughter could be heard in
his office. He often would make a comment with a
little chuckle or a sly look on his face, waiting for
me to react. Sometimes it was necessary to ask him
what he meant because I did not have the full context.
I think he relished those explanations. For me it was
an enriching of my education. While scholarship and

administration were serious business for him, he
nevertheless found humor to be a means to help keep
perspective.

The Teacher

To appreciate Bard Thompson in his role as a dean,
one must know him as teacher, for he was a teaching
dean. When I first registered for his seminar on
Martin Luther, I was quite nervous. He did not assign
papers or exams. Our class work consisted of in-depth
discussion of assigned materials. Though I had become
acquainted with this style of American education, I did
not care for it. I was anxious because the entire
grade depended upon class discussion, and as a non-
native speaker of English I sensed myself to be at a
serious disadvantage in such oral discussions. The
reading assignments for the Dean's seminars were quite
demanding, and his questions, which were distributed
only at the beginning of each seminar session, were
pointed yet comprehensive. The student who did not do
the assigned reading with the fullest attention could
not respond. I vividly remember one occasion when a
student asked him a seemingly legitimate question. He
answered, "If you had done your assigned reading for
today, you wouldn't ask that kind of question. What do
you think?" After that, everyone read the assignment
for each class very seriously and carefully. Since he
often asked us to quote the specific passages from the
primary sources, reading of secondary sources alone
simply would not suffice. He wanted his students to
wrestle with the original texts themselves, not someone
else's interpretation. It was in these seminars that I
learned what scholarly reading and analysis, questioning and argument are about.

As a teacher he demanded a high standard of
excellence in academic performance from his students,

but he required no less of himself. As his Administrative Assistant, I learned how jealously he guarded his time for class preparation. This was frustrating when a problem that required his attention arose, and I would want him to take time then-and-there to deal with it. I would think to myself, "He has been teaching these subjects for years. He could teach off-the-cuff." But he did not compromise. He could often be found in his study in the University library with Calvin's *Institutes* or Zwingli's *Commentary on True and False Religion* open on his desk. As a result, his classes were among the most challenging and thought provoking I have ever had.

The Dean

Bard Thompson accepted the deanship at the most critical time in the life of the Drew Graduate School. The school had been organized in 1955. A University controversy in the late 1960's had deeply affected the Graduate School. As a result, about a dozen Graduate Faculty from the Theological School resigned, and many doctoral students left the school. Graduate admissions were halted. Enrollment dropped to one-fifth of its previous level. He assumed the deanship in March 1969, entrusted by the University trustees with the responsibility of rebuilding the Graduate School.

As Dean he followed the same course that he followed in teaching. He focused first on the programs in the biblical and theological areas, which had been the mainstay of the Graduate School from its beginning. Admissions were resumed in these areas as faculty were appointed. However, the restoration of these programs did not complete the job he had been given by the trustees. It was now time to move forward and realize more fully the potential of the Graduate School based on and growing out of the strengths of the Theological

School and College of Liberal Arts of the University.
This led to some reorganization in the traditional
areas. He added more Graduate Faculty from the College
of Liberal Arts in order to strengthen the English
Literature program and to increase the interdisciplinary thrust of the Graduate School. Most significantly, four new programs were developed.

In 1974, the Ninetenth-Century Studies program was
added as an interdisciplinary Ph.D. program to take
advantage of Drew's library resources and professional
strengths in nineteenth-century literature, religion,
and social and intellectual history. The program
brought together faculty from the theological areas of
the Graduate School, and from art, philosophy, English,
history, and political science in the College. A
faculty post in the history of science was created in
order to round out the program.

Another innovative program was established in
1977, the Ph.D. in Liturgical Studies. This program is
based on a consortium arrangement with New York and New
Jersey institutions and professors. There are only two
or three such programs in the United States. The
vision for this program emerged from his own sense of
the importance of liturgy for Protestantism, a sense
which resulted from his Reformation studies. He had
served as an official Protestant observer at Vatican
II, and thus had witnessed firsthand the beginnings of
monumental changes in the Roman Catholic liturgy. His
Liturgies of the Western Church, now in its twelfth
printing, is a standard work for teachers and students
alike in the field of liturgics.

In 1975 the Graduate School developed a Master of
Arts in Liberal Studies, primarily for teachers and
those who wanted a challenging form of continuing
education. It was designed as a Summer program.

primarily to accommodate teachers, who could more
readily attend during this time. Courses centered on
Western ideas and institutions. When other schools
began imitating the program, he reorganized it and
renamed it the Master of Letters program. He conceived
and implemented the entire program, from curriculum
design to the appointment of professors. Due to
sustained interest, courses in this program are now
offered throughout the year.

Capitalizing on Drew's rich library holdings and
faculty strengths in Methodist studies, a Ph.D. program
in Methodist Studies was added as a sub-area of
Theological and Religious Studies in 1979. Subsequently, the Methodist Archives were relocated to the
Drew campus. As a result of these developments, Drew
has become a national center for research in Methodism.
In 1984 a Master of Arts program in International
Affairs replaced the Master of Arts in Political
Science. The United Nations semester program and
Drew's proximity to New York City reinforce a global
awareness on campus and have drawn students to campus
for the study of international affairs.

In addition to some of its distinctive areas of
study, the Graduate School has two other strengths,
prized by students and faculty alike, cultivated by
Dean Thompson: small classes and individualized
programs of study. Small classes encourage dialogue
and personal contact between faculty and students, and
Graduate school policies allow students to have an
active part in shaping their programs to meet chosen
goals. Both of these dimensions of the Graduate School
were cultivated by Dean Thompson's constant concern
that the school be a community of scholars working
together for common aims--not a collection of teachers
and students following their own paths without regard

for the others. Dean Thompson undertook and encouraged
a number of activities which supported the goal of
being a Graduate School with a community identity.

Among these was initiatives was the strengthening
of the Graduate Students Association (GSA), which had
been formed in 1968 in response to the crisis which had
so deeply impacted graduate students. It became one
important way for students from the various areas and
at widely differing points in their programs to come
together, to get to know each other, to share common
student concerns, to engage in dialogue across all
lines, and to become a student body rather than a
collection of individuals. As the Dean worked on
problems the Graduate School faced, he drew upon the
GSA. Representatives from the GSA were added to the
standing faculty committees on Policy and Planning,
Academic Standing, Language, and Colloquium. Students
gained direct participation with voice and vote on
almost all matters relating to the Graduate School.

First and foremost was a constant emphasis on
maintaining an interdisciplinary, environment for
graduate study at Drew. At the faculty level, the
monthly Aquinas Seminar was established to provide a
structured program of presentations and discussion on
topics embracing the entire range of disciplines of the
Graduate School. The Aquinas Seminar provides an on-
going opportunity for the faculty to engage in interdisciplinary dialogue. In addition, the annual
Colloquium brings faculty and students together with
outside speakers to reflect upon a wide range of
interdisciplinary topics. These colloquia brings to
campus leading scholars from both here and abroad.

Graduate School regulations provide that the
student's program is under the supervision of the Dean
and an adviser appointed by the Dean. As a means of

supervising and maintaining contact between the
students and the Graduate School Office, Dean Thompson
instituted the "annual check-up." All students were
expected to meet with him to discuss their program.
Consequently, even students who did not take courses
from Dean Thompson were able to have personal contact
with him.

Just as locating the Graduate School in S. W.
Bowne Hall had been an important step in developing the
Graduate School's own identity, so too, the establishment of the Commons Room in Bowne Hall was vital in
providing graduate students with a place that was
theirs alone. Dean Thompson rigorously guarded the
room as a place set aside especially for graduate
students. Appropriately, it was named the "Thompson
Graduate Commons" upon his retirement as Dean.

As the size and diversity of the student body
increased, the GSA and the Graduate School Office
together provided for a more formal orientation
program. Students and faculty were invited to the
Dean's Hospitality, generally held once a month, for
conversation and sherry. A high point of the annual
social calendar of all members of the Graduate School
community was the Dean's Annual Reception held at his
home, in early May. Since May showers had rained more
than once on the Dean's reception, he often anxiously
watched the weather reports as the time approached.

The Legacy

I would like to suggest several legacies of Bard
Thompson's tenure at Drew. His first and most important legacy is the existence of the Graduate School
itself. He fulfilled the task set for him by the
trustees. Going beyond simply restoring the school, he
established a tradition of integrity. The defense of
the Graduate School from attack within and without was

always at the top of his agenda. He vigorously
defended the integrity of the Graduate School in its
own right. He insisted without compromise that the
office in Bowne Hall was the Graduate School Office,
not the Graduate Office. The Graduate School is not an
extension of the College or Seminary. Rather, it is
related to them as a full constituent school within the
University structure. This, as much as anything else,
helped formulate the equation which identified Bard
Thompson with the Drew Graduate School. When he spoke,
it was for graduate education in a Graduate School in a
University.

The second legacy is the shape of the Graduate
School. Graduate education at Drew has been organized
into a number of areas. In the early part of his
deanship, the areas were Biblical Studies, Theological
and Religious Studies, Religion and Society, English
Literature, and Political Science. He insisted on the
integrity of each area and supported each in its work.
Later, the Nineteenth-Century Studies program was added
as a separate area, and Political Science was reorganized and renamed International Affairs. Throughout he
aimed to maintain the interdisciplinary character of
graduate education.

The third legacy is an understanding of graduate
education carried away by the students who were here
while he was dean. Four elements mark this understanding. First is an image of what a scholar should be.
By his own example more than anything else, he embodied
for the Graduate School community the image of what
graduate education meant. The term "Renaissance man"
appropriately expresses the ideal, though I do not
recall that he ever identified himself as such. His
own research into Renaissance art exemplified the
constant desire to gain knowledge and understanding in

fields beyond one's initial area of specialization.
The theologian's knowledge must include fields such as
literature, history, and art. Since knowledge must be
both intensive and comprehensive, graduate education
must involve the mastery of a discipline, but it must
also be interdisciplinary.

Second, there is a standard for the use of
language. When we think of Dean Thompson, we think of
a master of the written word. This characteristic
stands out in the memory of both students and faculty.
He consistently modeled the ideal that graduate
education must involve mastery in the use of language.
The student should know his or her own language and the
languages of scholarship, especially Latin, which he
freely used.

Third, graduate education is to be pursued for its
own sake. There has been a long period during which
the tight job market discouraged people from undertaking graduate education. Nevertheless, as the students
who received his annual August letters know, he
constantly urged students to pursue graduate studies
for their own satisfaction, knowledge and stature. The
love of knowledge and intellectual adventure are reason
enough to enter the race and finish the course.

Finally, scholarly work undertaken is to be
carried-out in accord with the highest standards of
excellence. The Dean was a perfectionist. While he
realized that perfection was not attainable, it
remained a goal, both for his personal scholarship and
for the Graduate School. He expected the best from
himself and he expected all members of a graduate
school community to strive for it as well.

The dynamics articulated in the Reformation slogan
Ecclesia reformata et semper reformanda also well
applies to Bard Thompson and the Graduate School. His

task was to re-form it, but that task is never done. It is always to be re-formed, and he was continually engaged in that ongoing task. The success of his work is reflected in the concluding thought of Gordon Harland's address at the Silver Anniversary celebration in 1980. Harland correctly observes that the Graduate School created under Dean Thompson's leadership "prompts many of us to remember Drew as the place where we spent 'the best years of our lives.'"[2]

---

[2] *Silver Anniversary Addresses*, 7.

BARD THOMPSON: A BIOGRAPHICAL SKETCH

Born on June 18, 1925, Bard Thompson grew up and
began his formal education in Pennsylvania. He
graduated from Mercersburg Academy in 1944 and from
Haverford College in 1946, being elected to Phi Beta
Kappa. Having enrolled in Union Theological Seminary,
New York, he was selected as a student delegate to the
First Assembly of the World Council of Churches,
Amsterdam, in 1948. He received his Bachelor of
Divinity degree from Union in 1949, and his Doctor of
Philosophy, specializing in Church History, from
Columbia University in 1953.

He began his teaching career at Candler School of
Theology, Emory University. He was on the faculty of
Vanderbilt University from 1955 to 1961, serving as
Buffington Professor of Church History and Director of
Graduate Studies in the Historical Field his final
years there. From 1961 through 1965 he was Professor
of Church History at Lancaster Theological Seminary,
Lancaster, Pennsylvania, and in 1964 served as observer
of the International Congregational Council at the
third session of the Vatican Council.

In 1965, he left Lancaster to come to Drew
University, where he served until his death in 1987.
Coming to Drew as Professor of Church History in the
Theological and Graduate Schools, he became Dean of the
Graduate School in 1969. Upon his retirement as Dean

in 1986, he continued on the faculty at Drew and was a member of the Center of Theological Inquiry, Princeton, New Jersey.

His *Liturgies of the Western Church*, first published in 1961, is currently in its twelfth printing. *A Bibliography of Christian Worship*, published by the American Theological Library Association, was released in 1989, and a major work virtually completed at the time of his death, *Renaissance and Reformation*, is forthcoming.

TEXTS AND STUDIES IN RELIGION